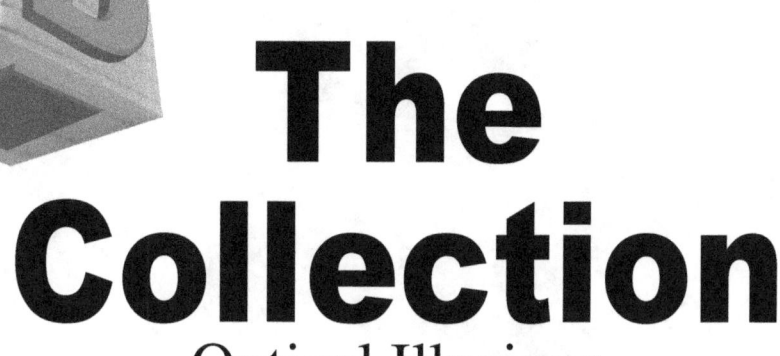

The Collection

Optical Illusions

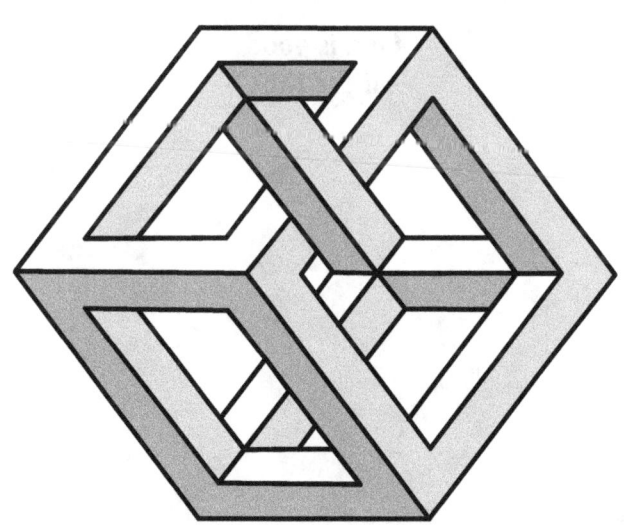

Robert John Morrissette

**God is good,
All the time!**

3D Optical Illusions
The Collection
Author: Robert John Morrissette
ISBN: 9780998941707

Publisher
Big Blue Skies of Idaho LLC
Coeur d'Alene, Idaho, 83815
United States of America

Printed by: CreateSpace, Charleston, SC, USA
Cover Design by: Robert John Morrissette

Other Books Also by Robert John Morrissette

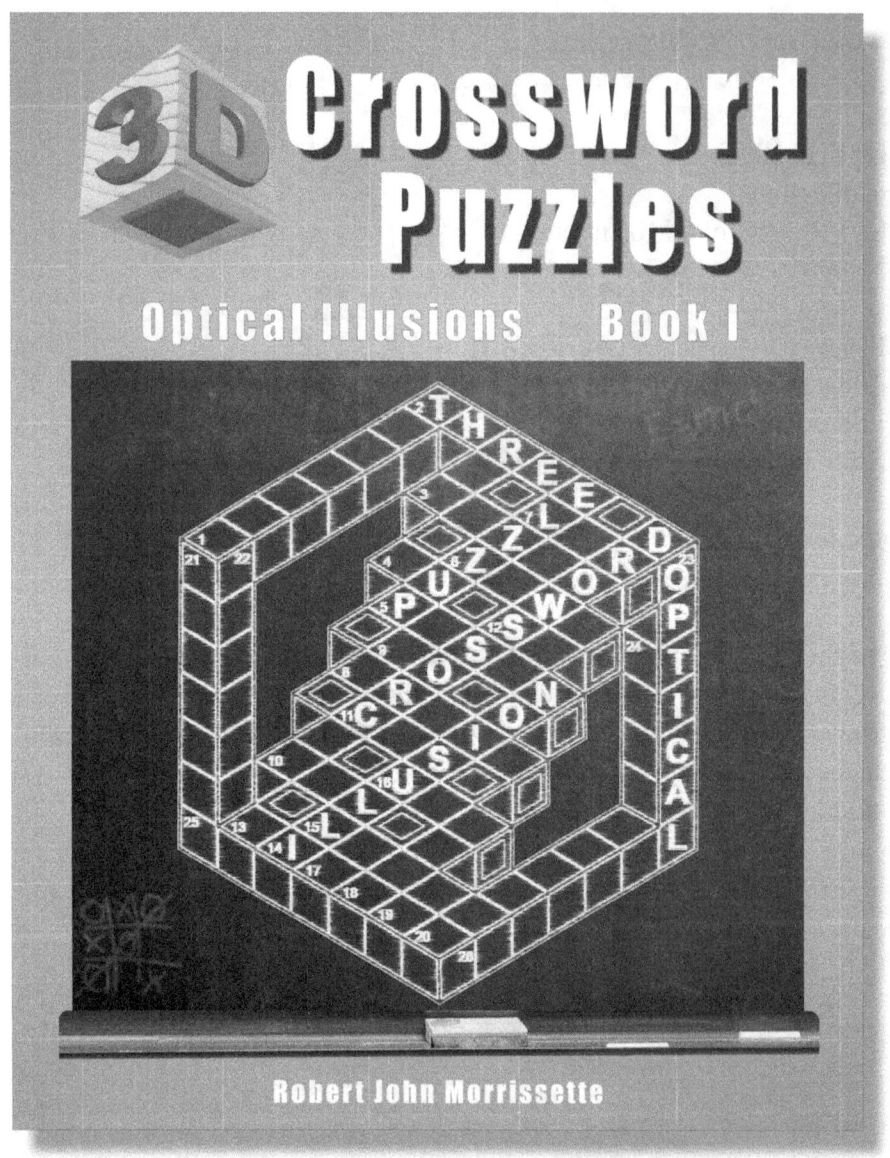

Combining:
• The challenge of crossword puzzles,
• The look of 3-dimensional rendering,
• And the fascination of optical illusions!
This book is sure to be a crossword experience you have never had before!
ISBN: 9780976354987

Sample Crossword Puzzles from Book I

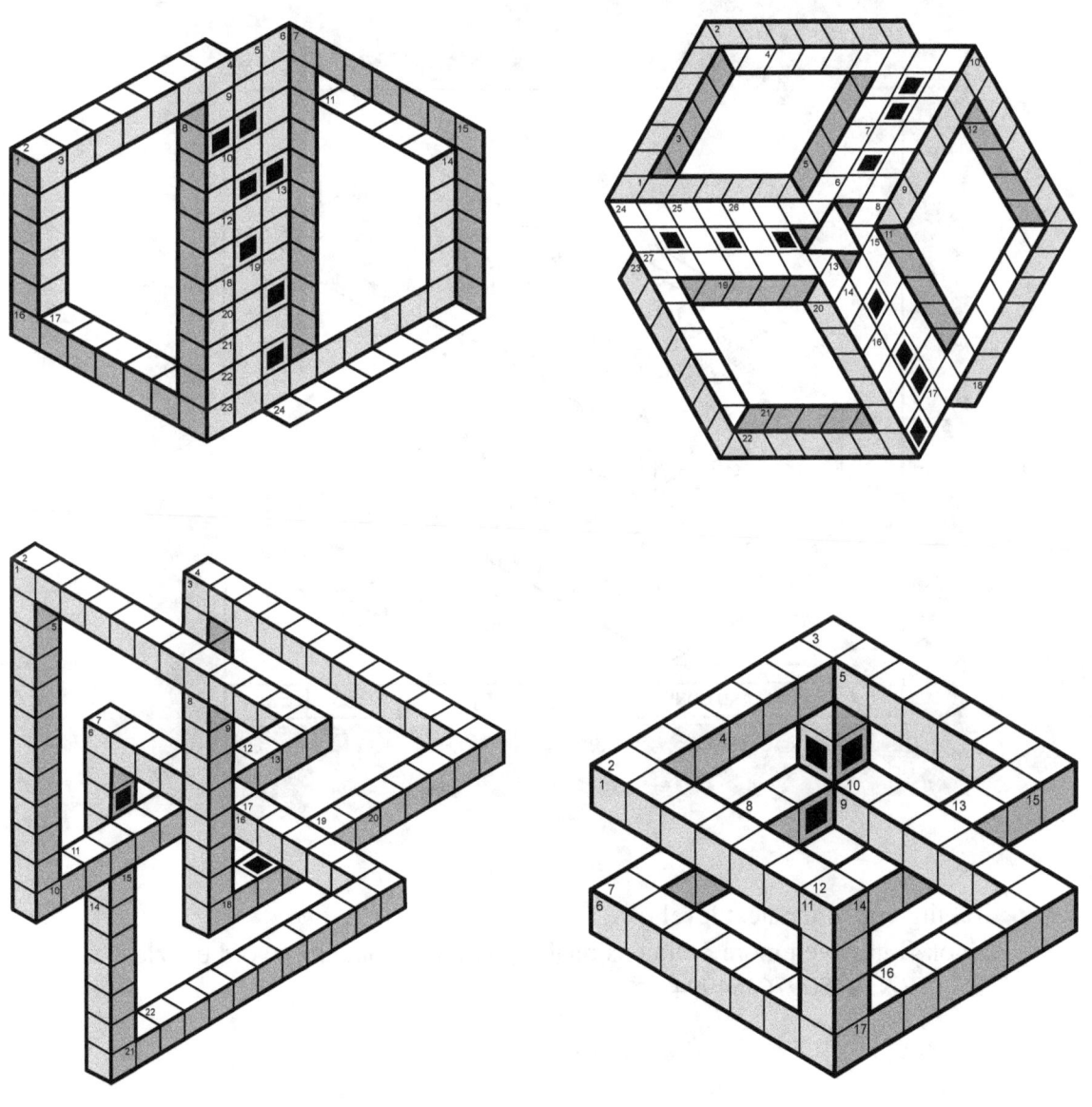

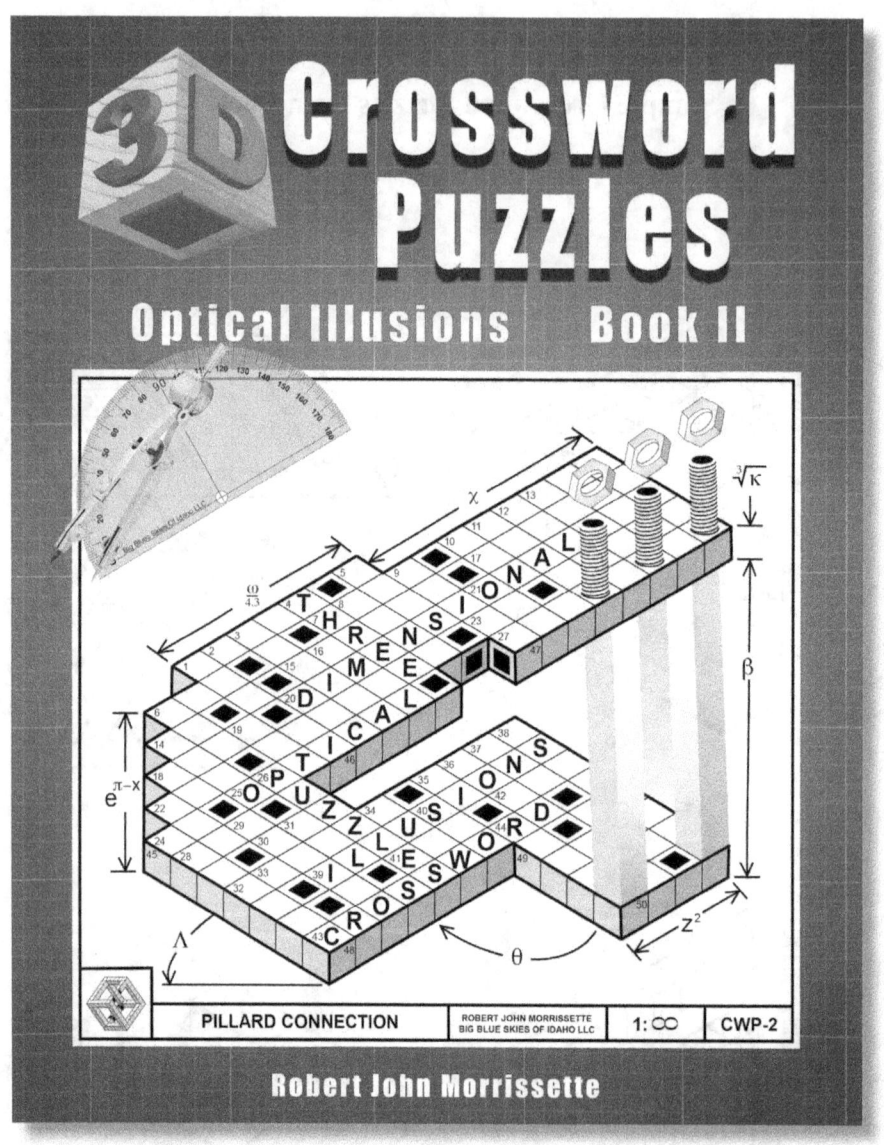

Taking you to the next level...
Book II has even more 3-dimensional, optical illusion, crossword puzzles!

ISBN: 9780976354994

Sample Crossword Puzzles from Book II

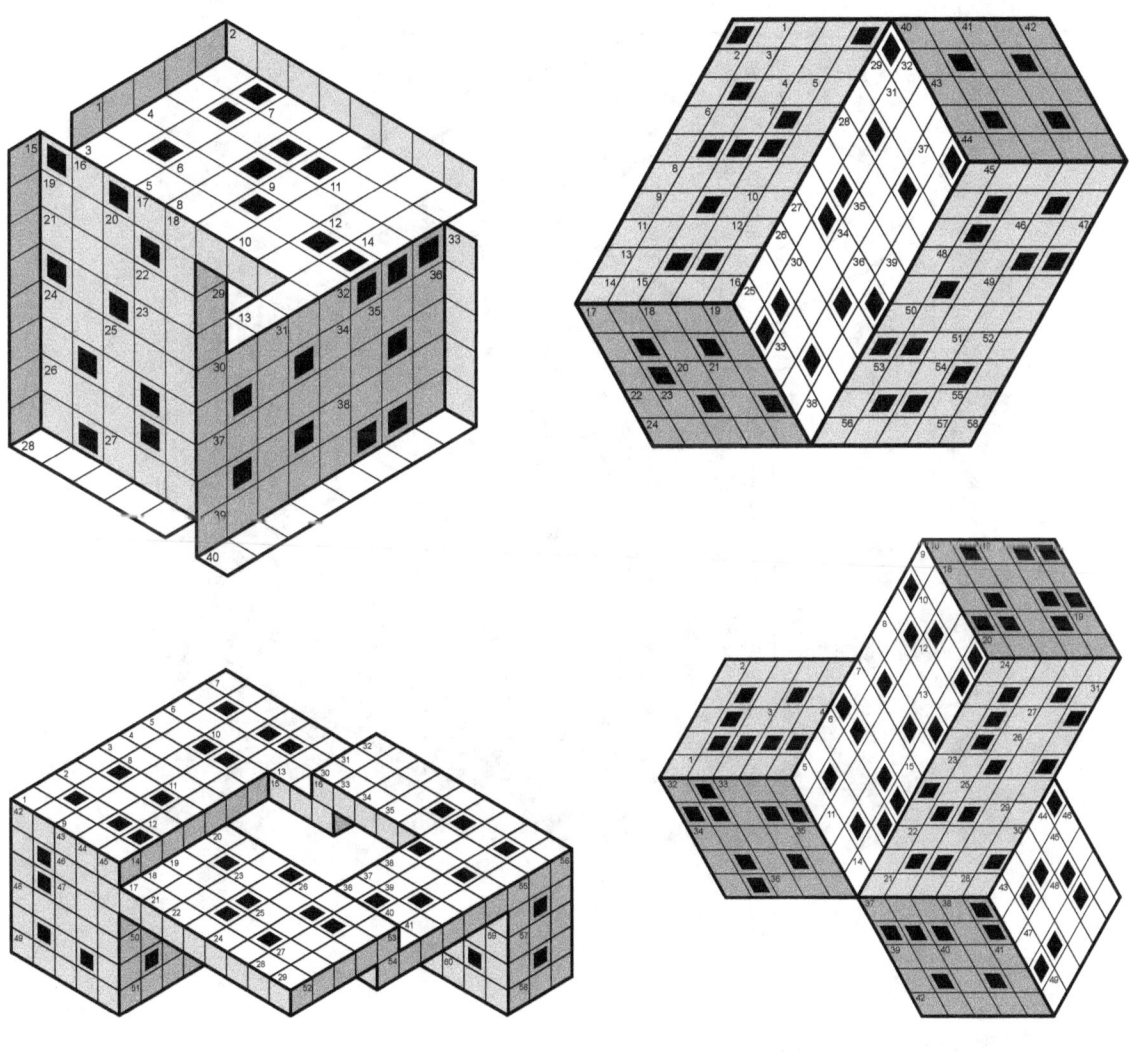

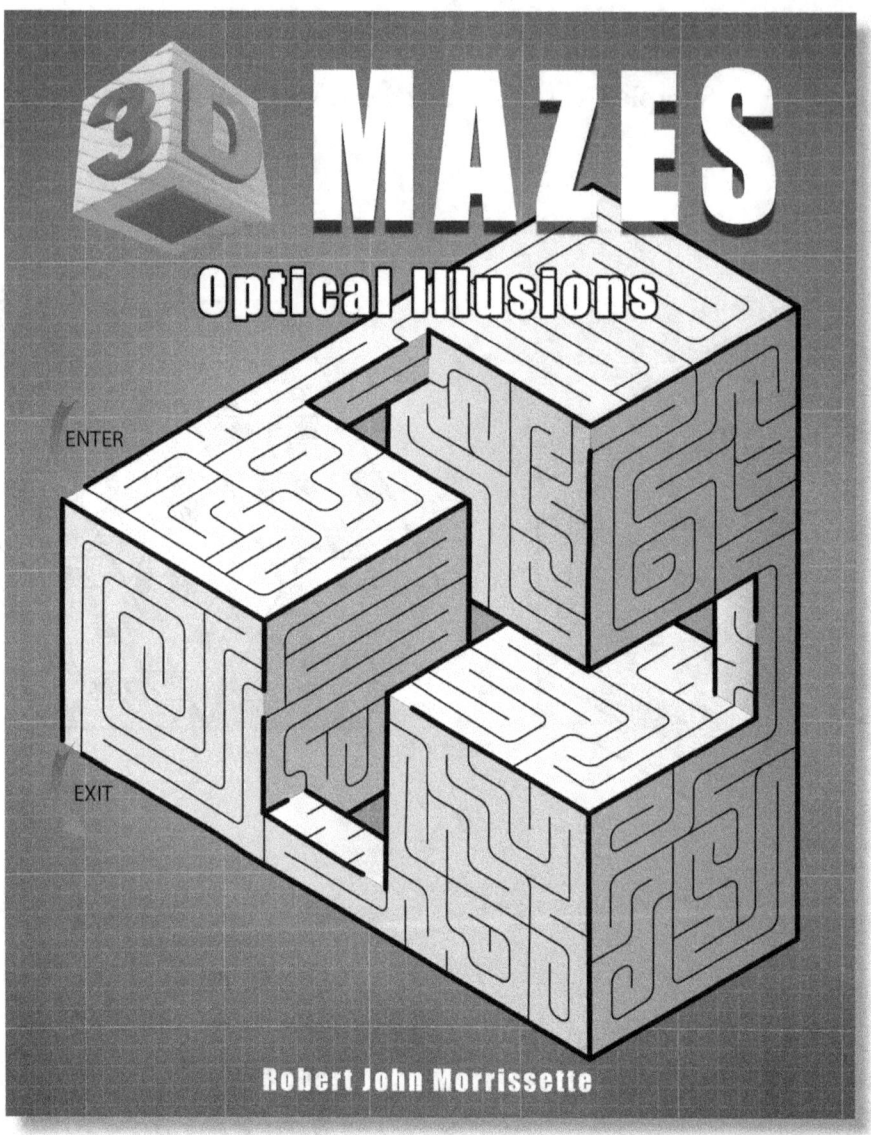

Combining:
• The challenge of maze-solving
• The look of 3-dimensional rendering,
• And the fascination of optical illusions!
This book is sure to be a maze-solving experience you have never had before!
    ISBN: 9780976354925

Sample Mazes

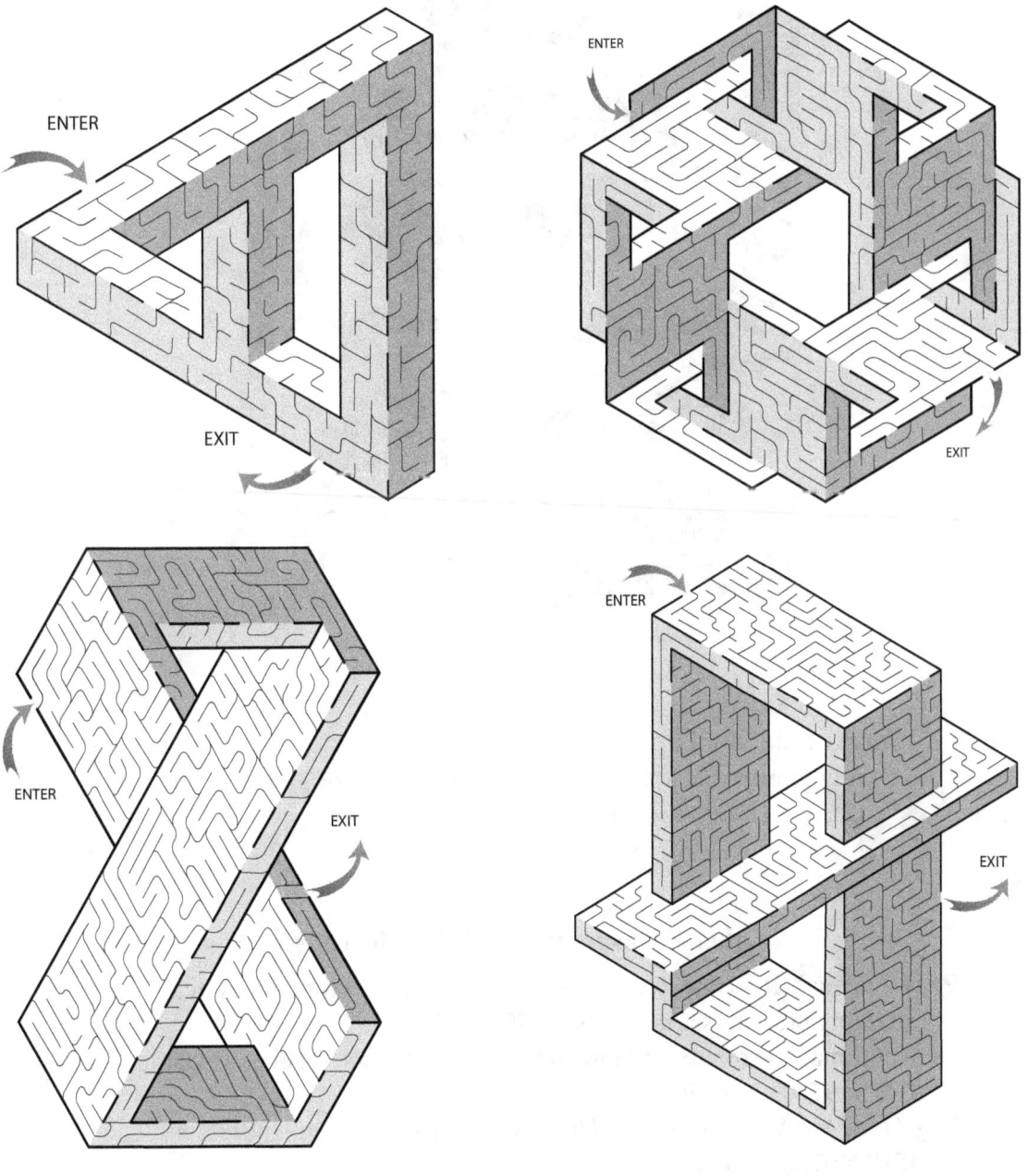

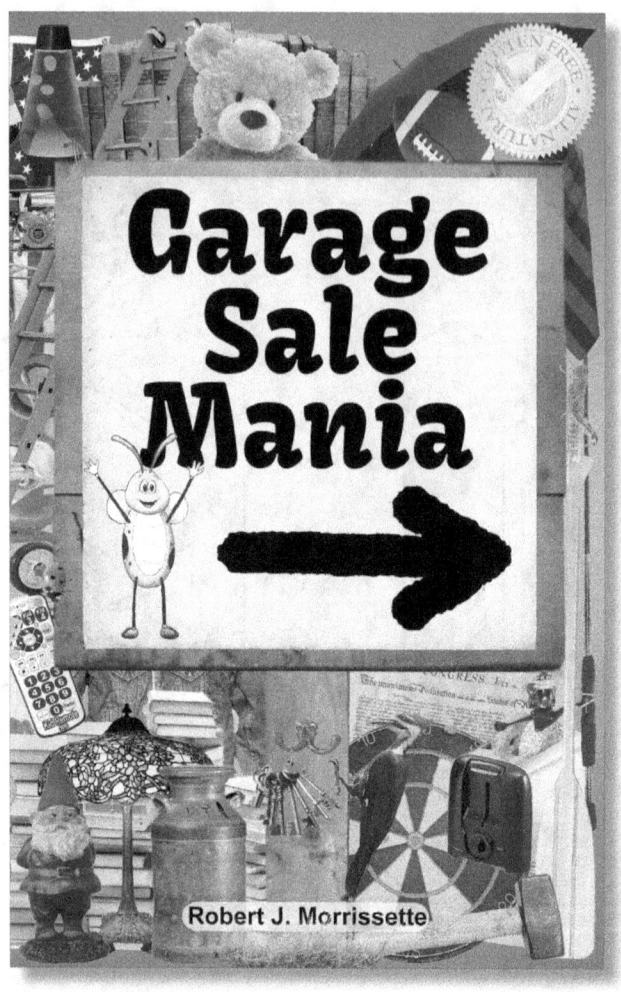

Garage Sale Mania
  A humorous book about the wonderful world of garage saling!
  ISBN: 9780976354956

Other Books by Robert John Morrissette

Pray Through It - How to identify and resolve past experiences that are
  affecting present issues. ISBN: 9780976354963
Generational Restoration: How to identify and resolve generational issues.
  ISBN: 9780976354970
Hey God, Are We There Yet? The rewards of waiting on God!
  ISBN: 9780976354949

Garage Sale Mania

If you love garage sales, or know someone who does, then this is the book for you!

Through the use of humor and creative illustrations, this book explores one of the greatest past-times, enjoyed worldwide!

Here are but a few of the fascinating topics addressed in the book:

- A Brief History of Garage Sales
- Testimonials
- Garage Sale Facts and Stats
- The "Garage-ological" System
- Garage Sale Addicts
- Garage Sale Mania Research
- Deals, Deals and More Deals
- Shopping Garage Sales
- Bargain Strategies
- Did Someone Say, "Fruitcake!"?
- A Garage Sale Essential
- Having a Garage Sale
- Selling Strategies
- Great Quotations in the History of Garage Sales
- Garage Sale Games
- And more!

3D

adjective | *THrē dē* |
1. having the quality of being three-dimensional.
2. having the appearance of length, breadth and depth.

Table of Contents

optical illusion

noun | ˈäptəkəl iˈlo͞oZHən |

1. something that deceives the eye by appearing to be other than it is.

2. an image that looks possible on paper but is impossible in reality.

Dice

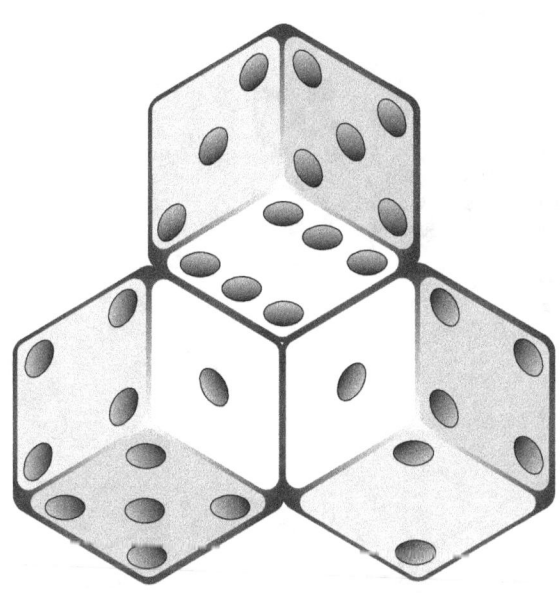

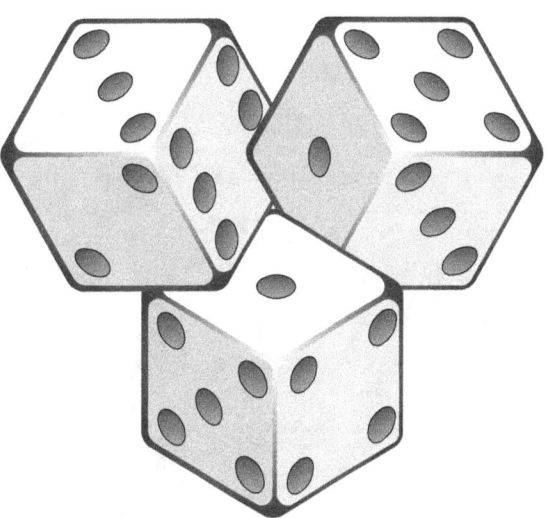

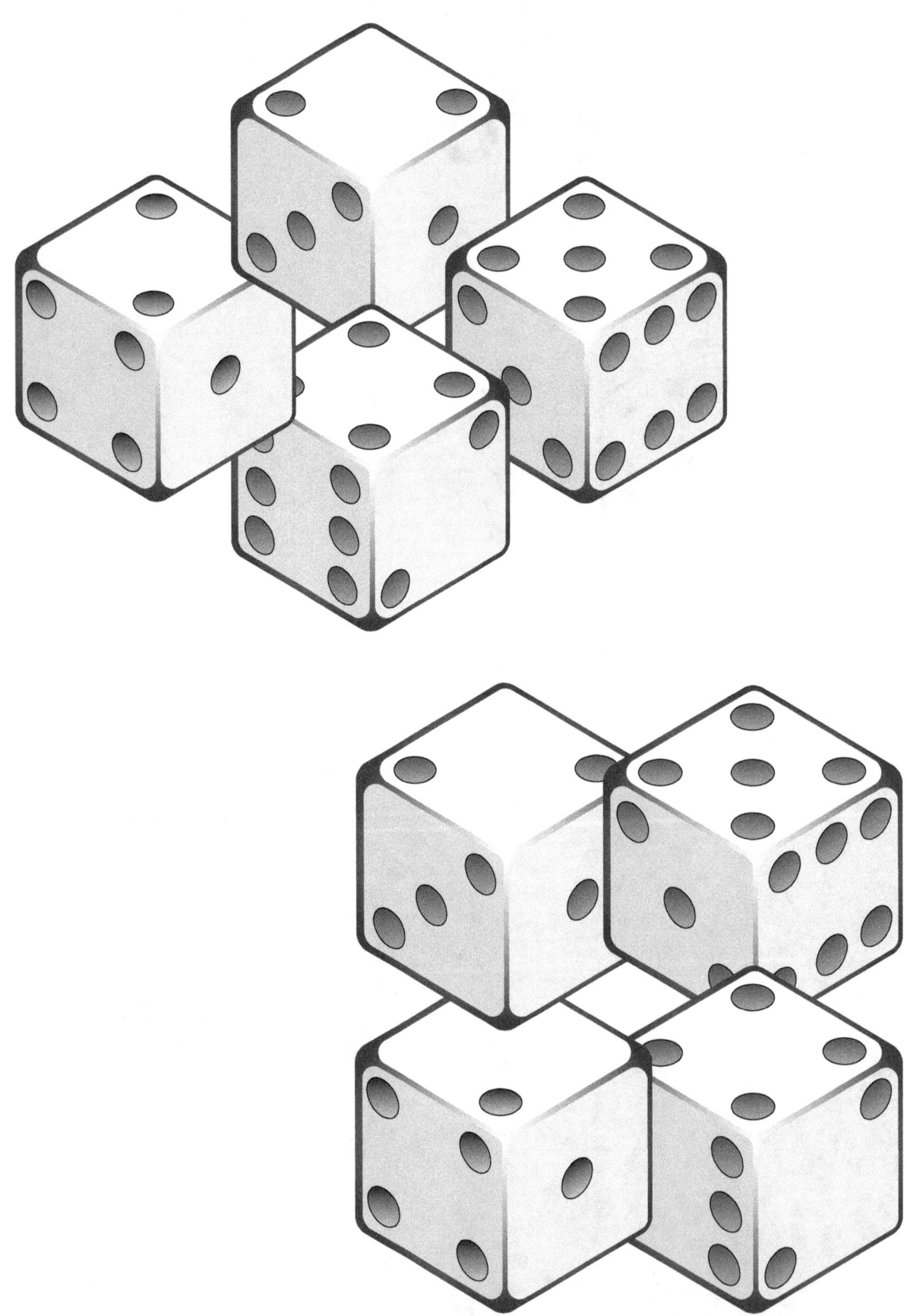

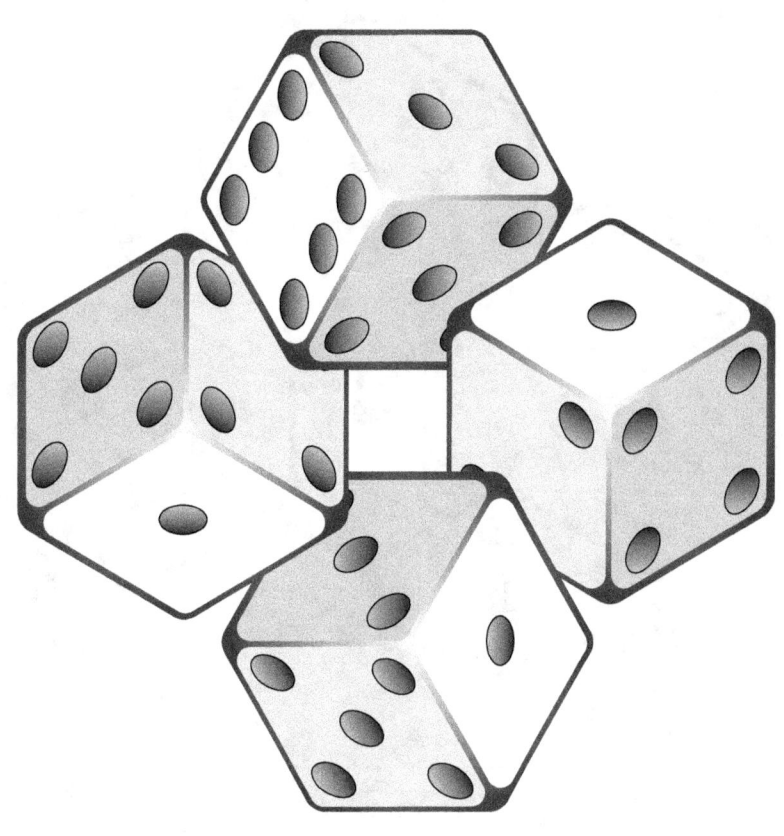

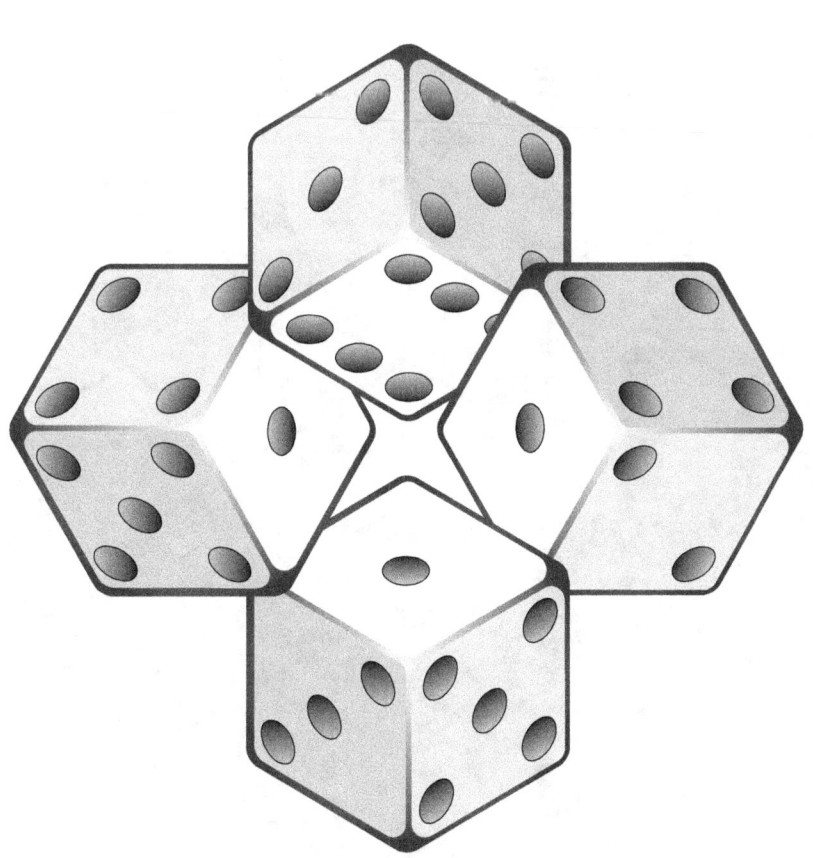

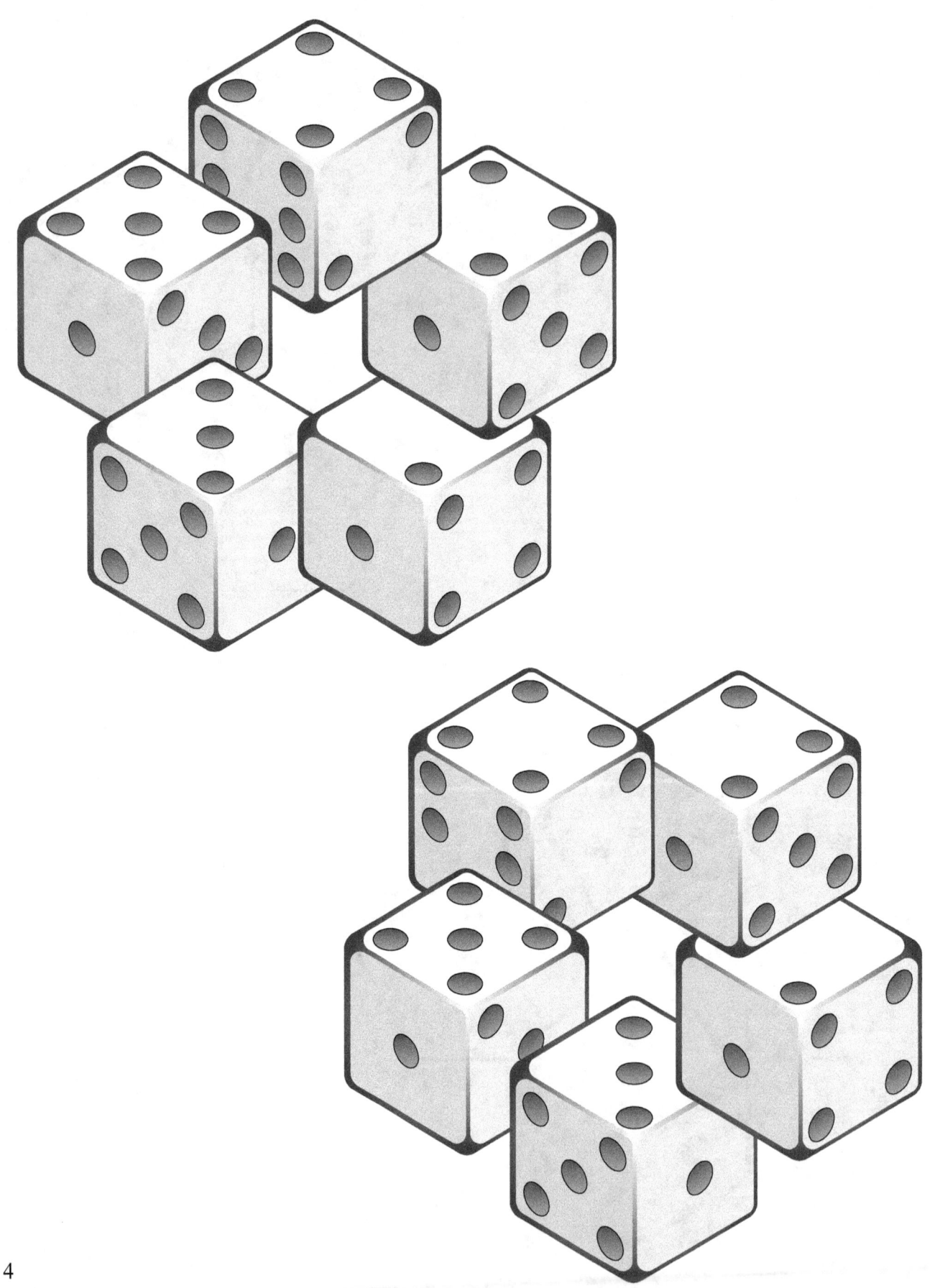

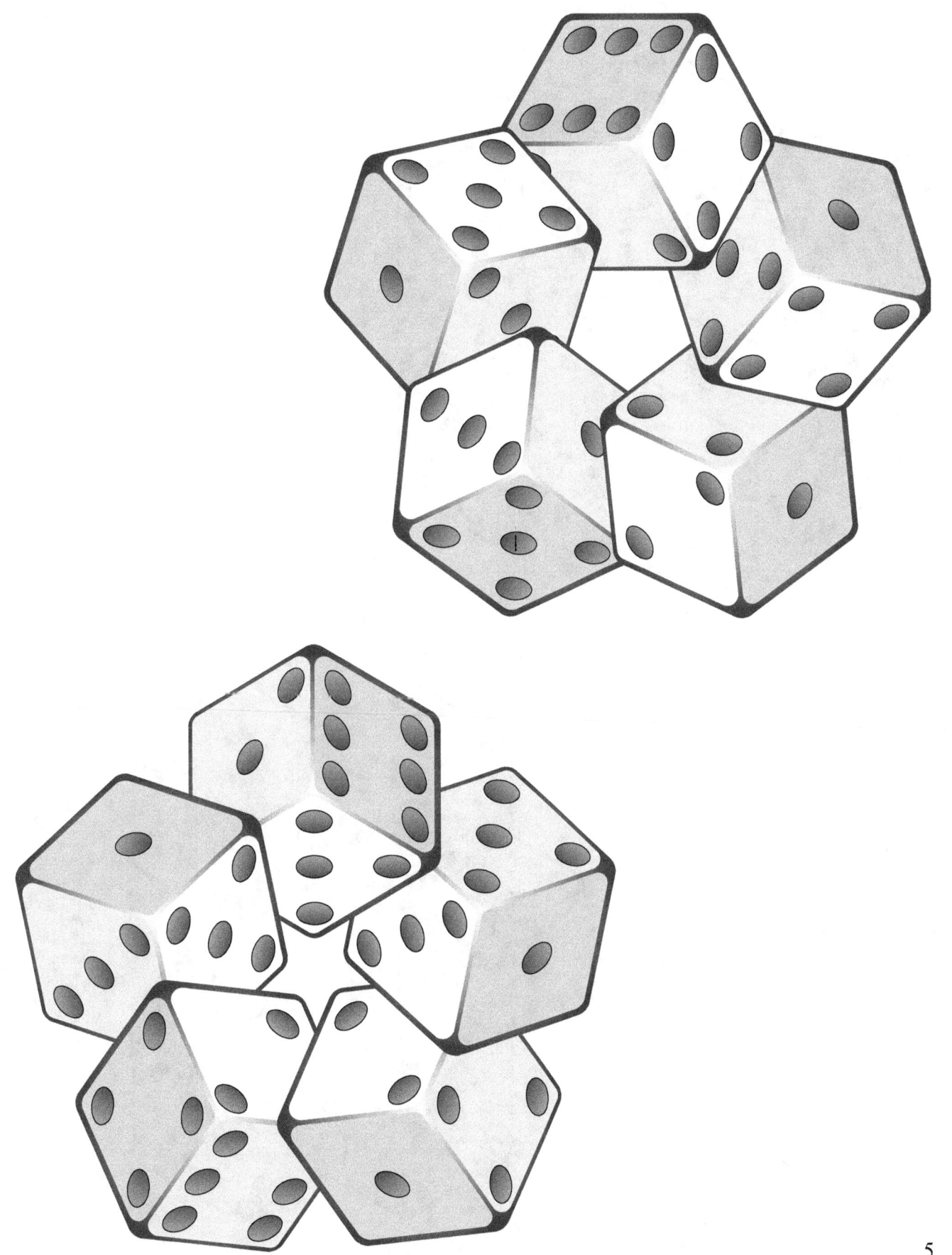

5

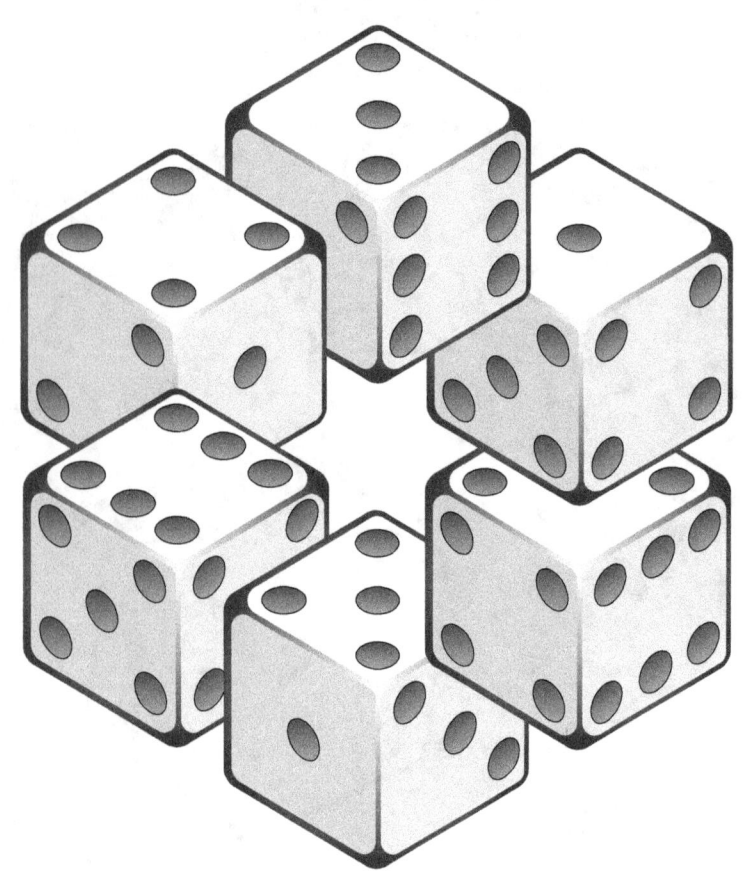

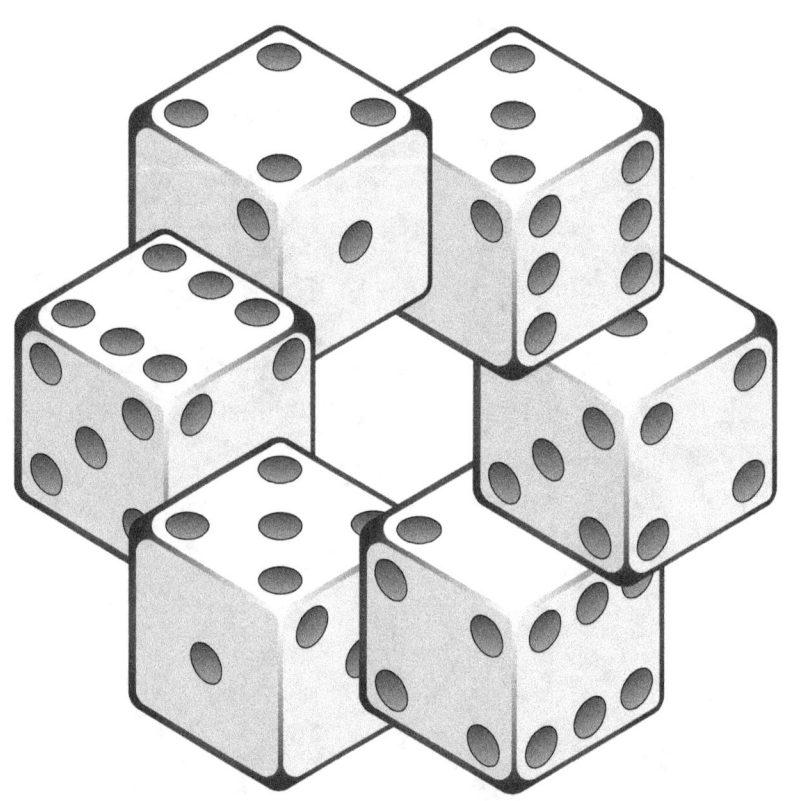

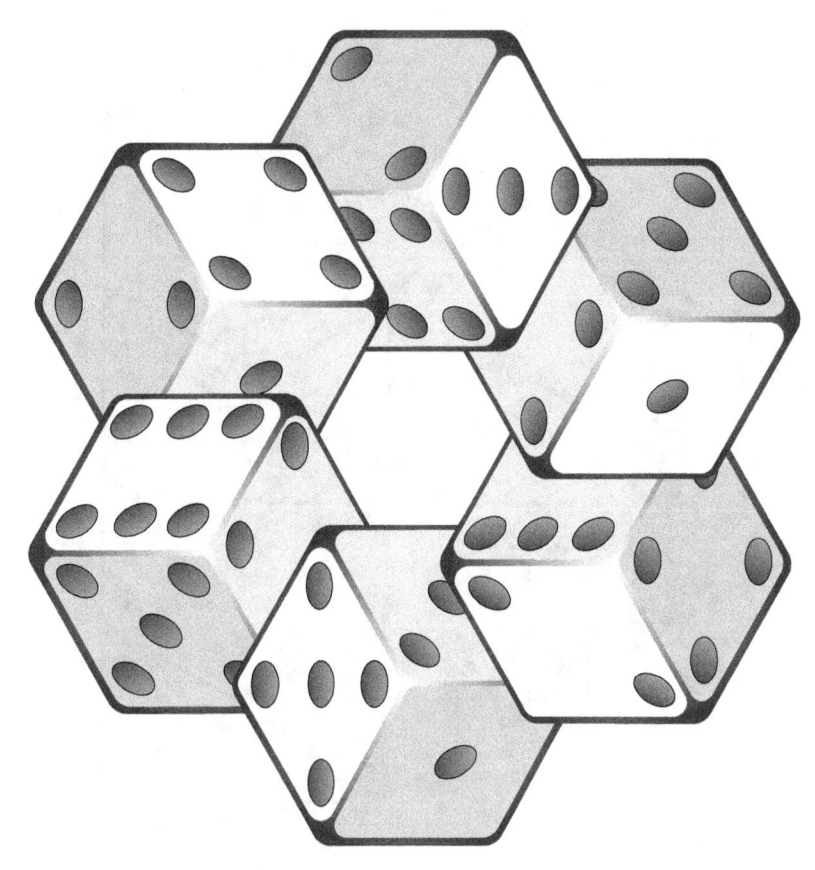

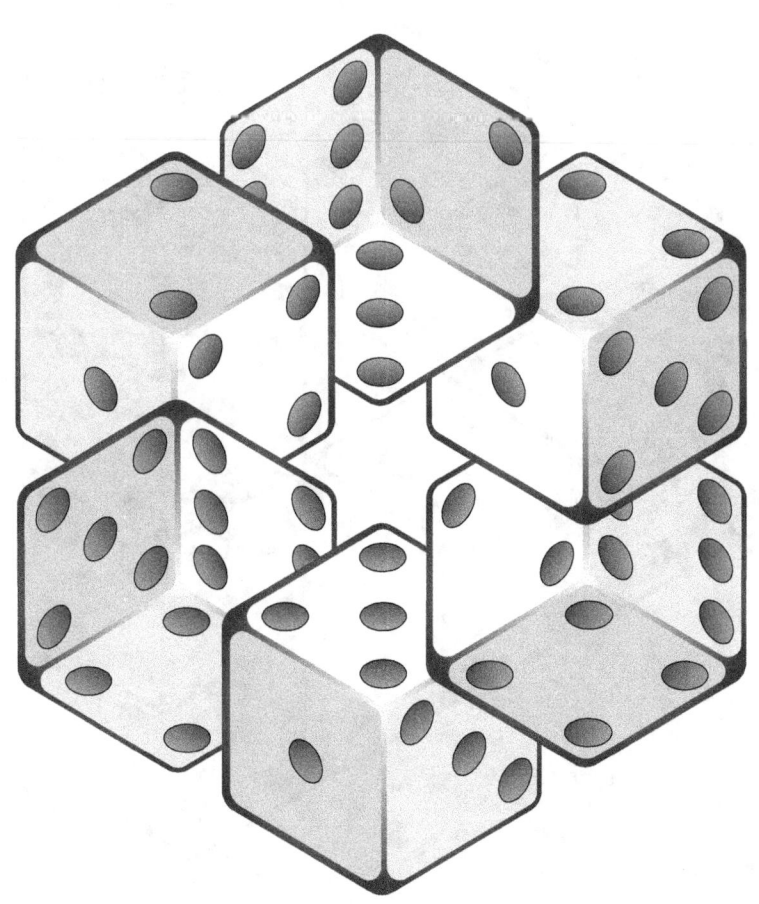

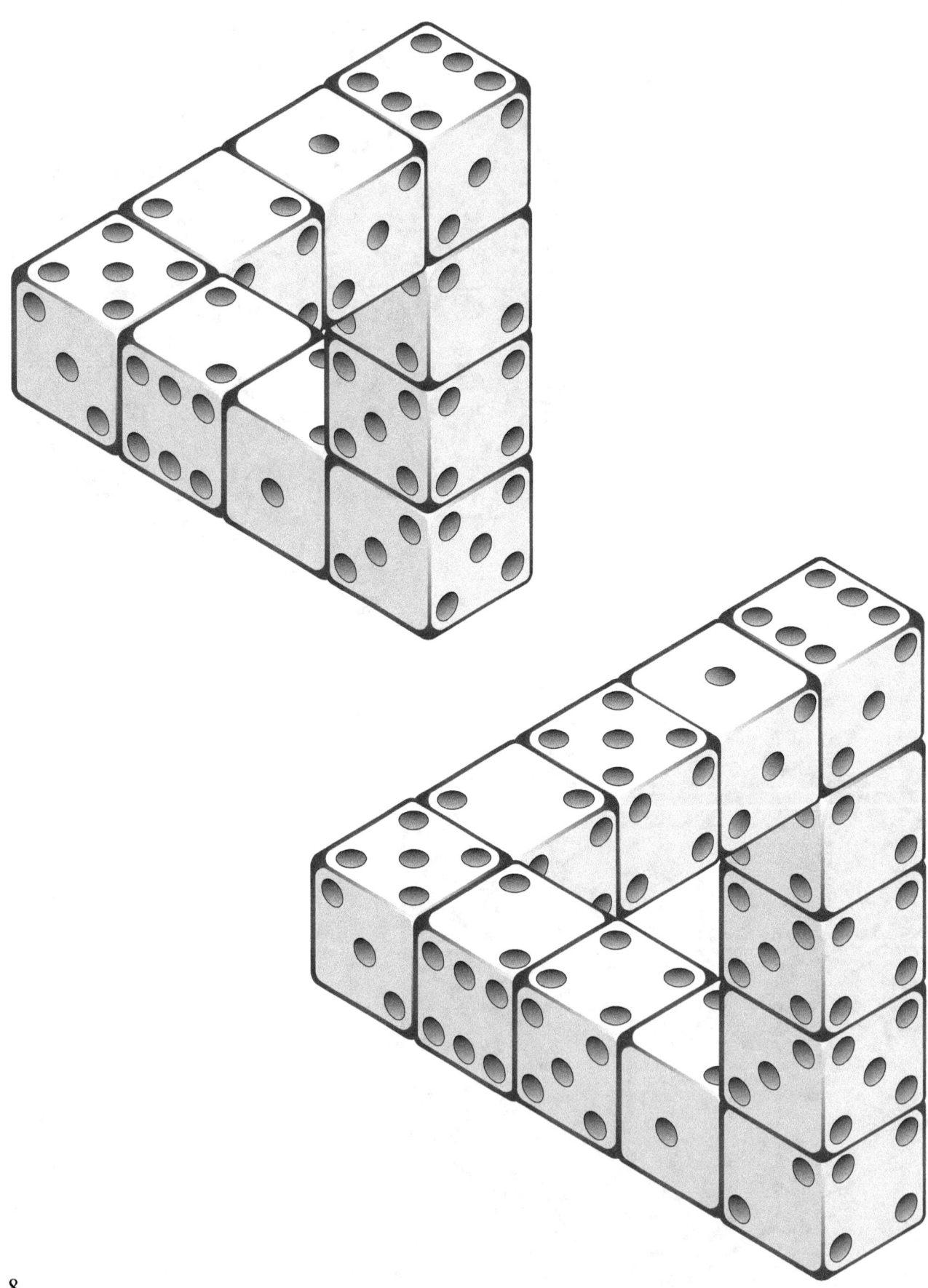

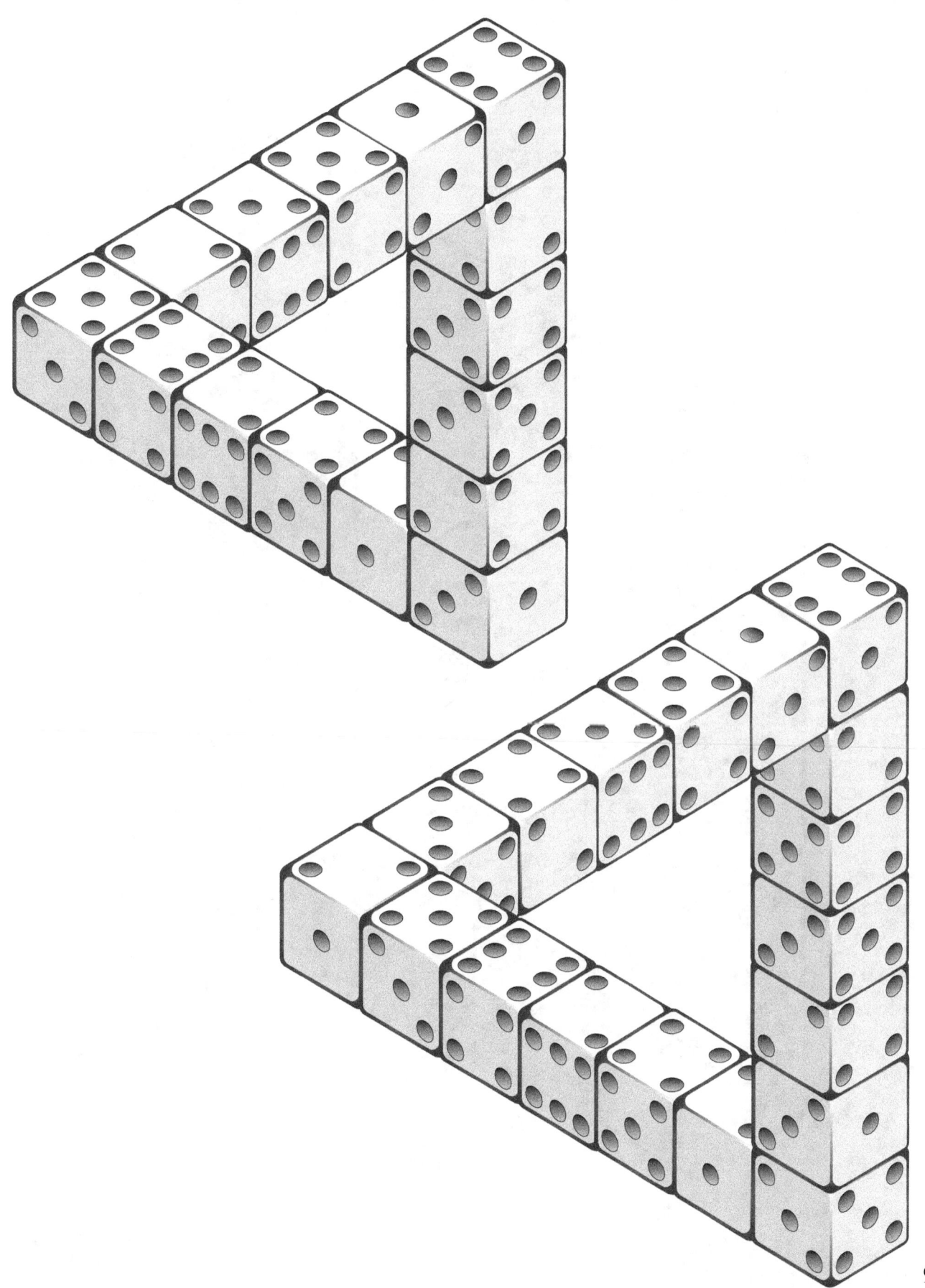

9

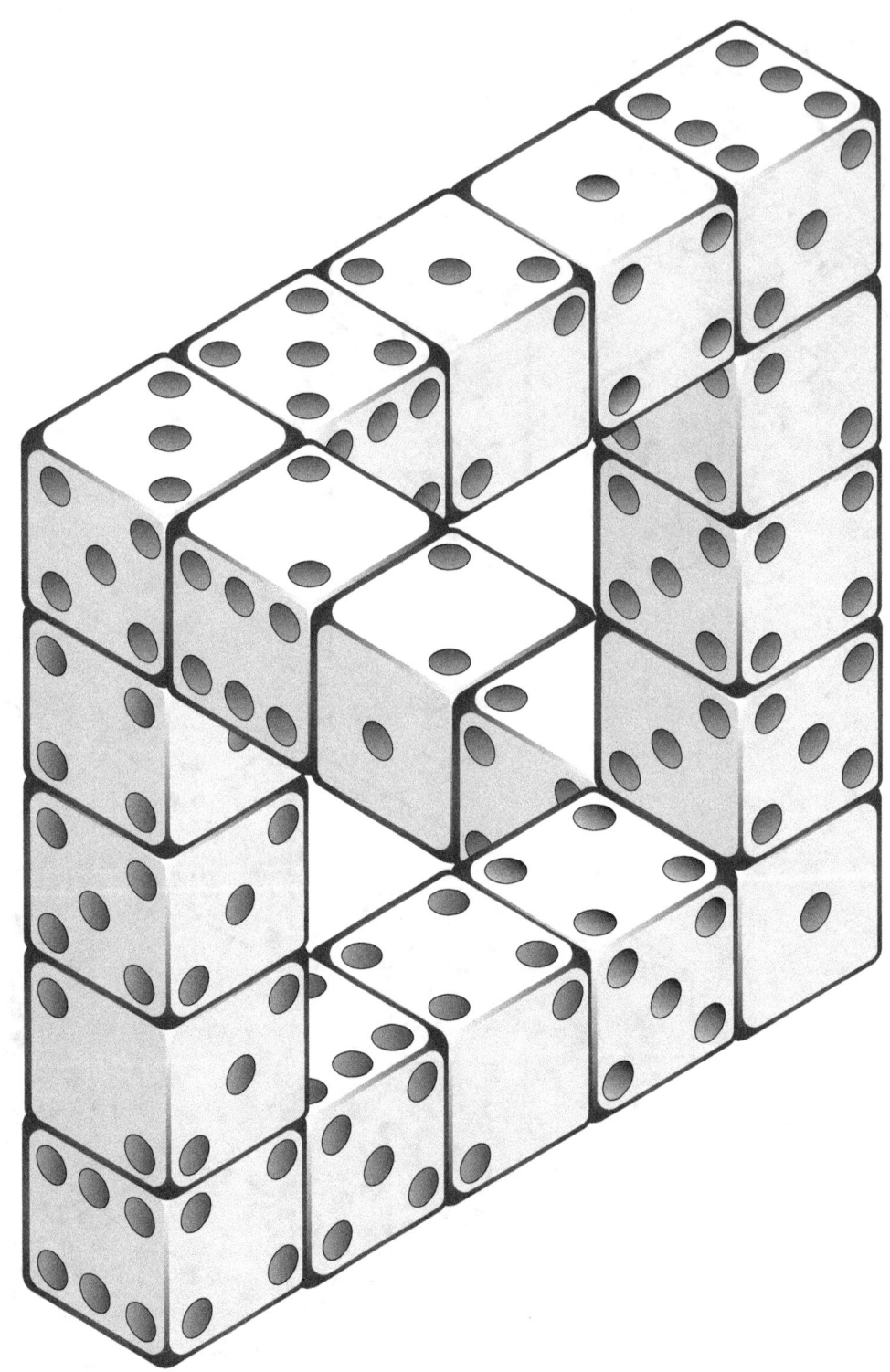

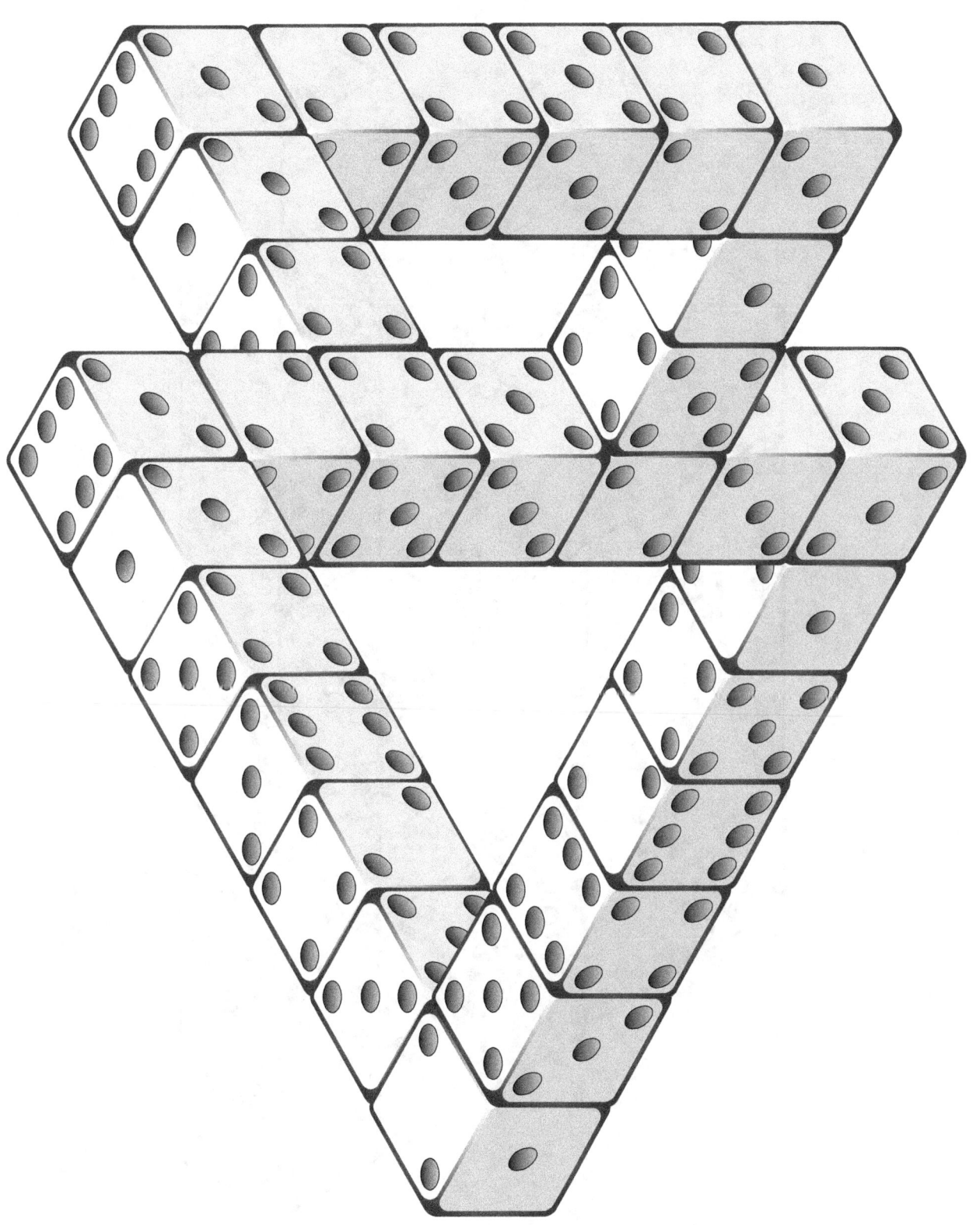

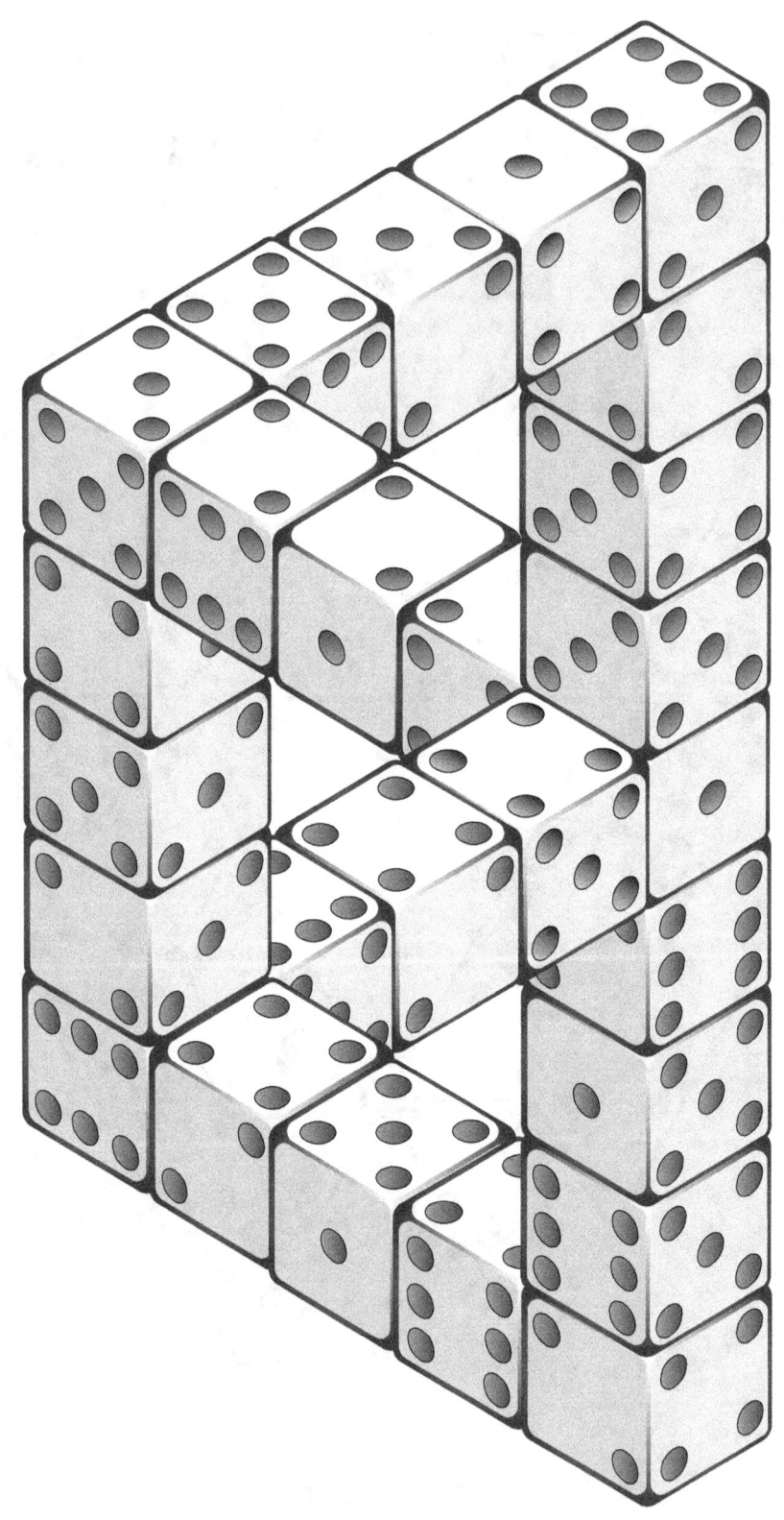

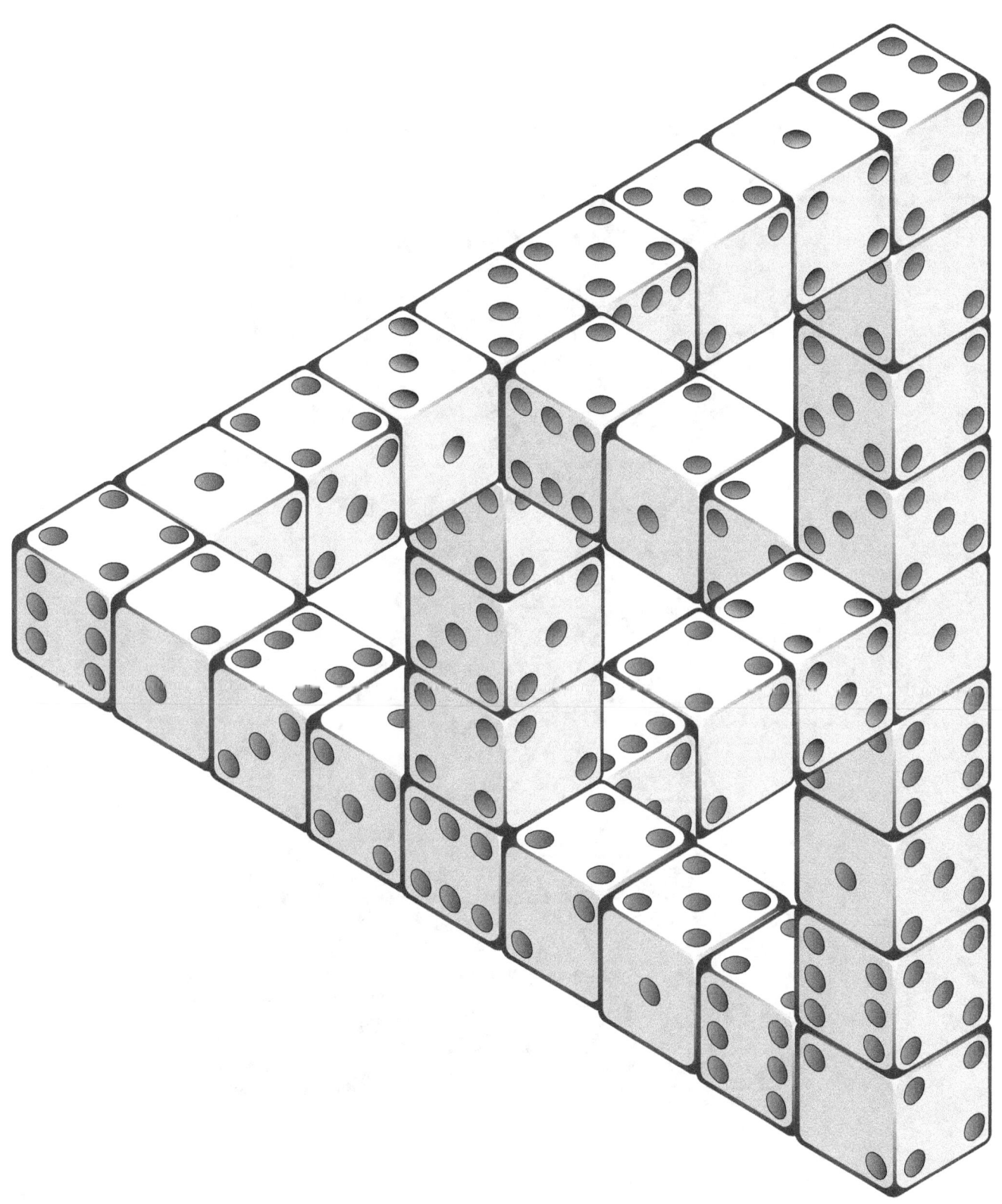

13

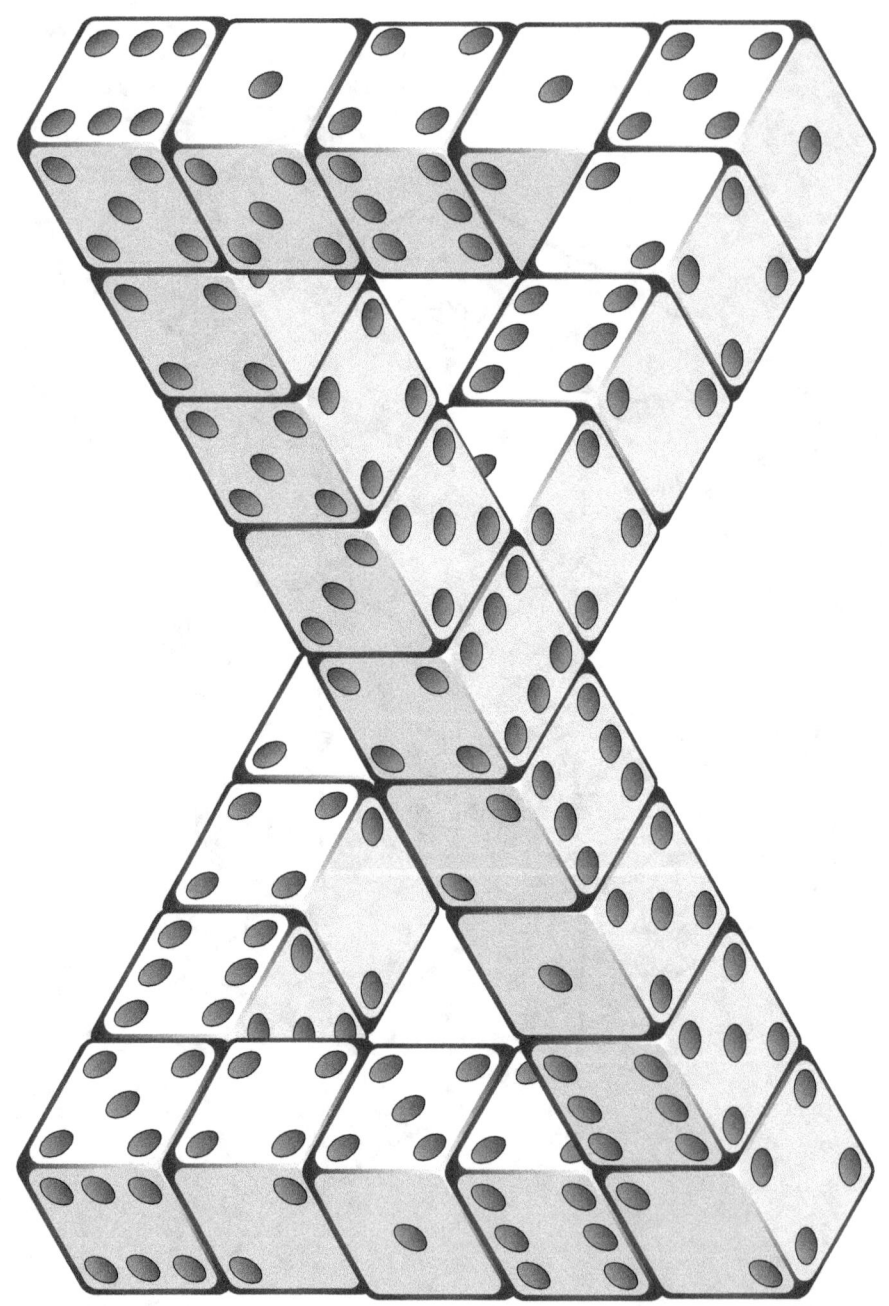

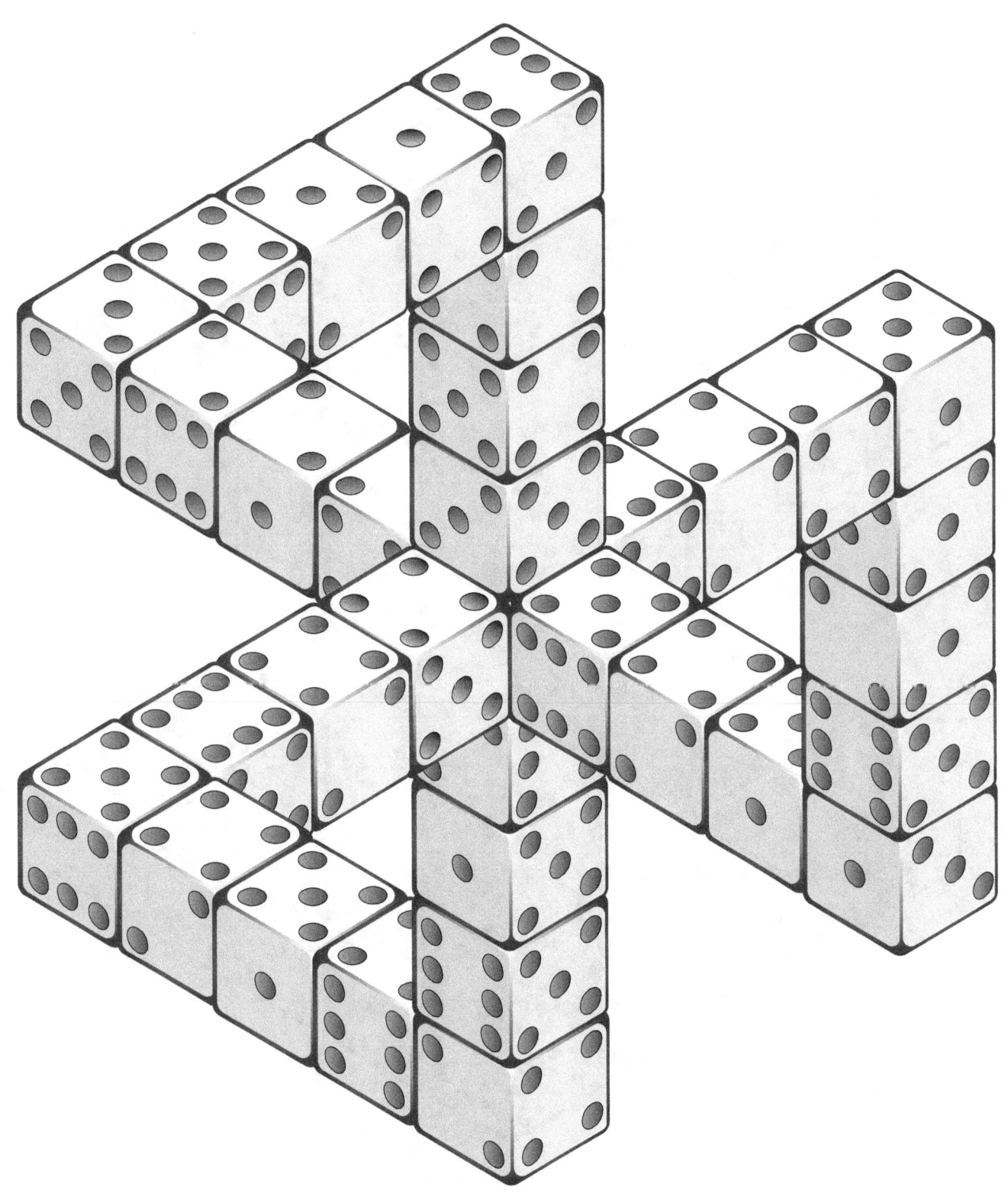

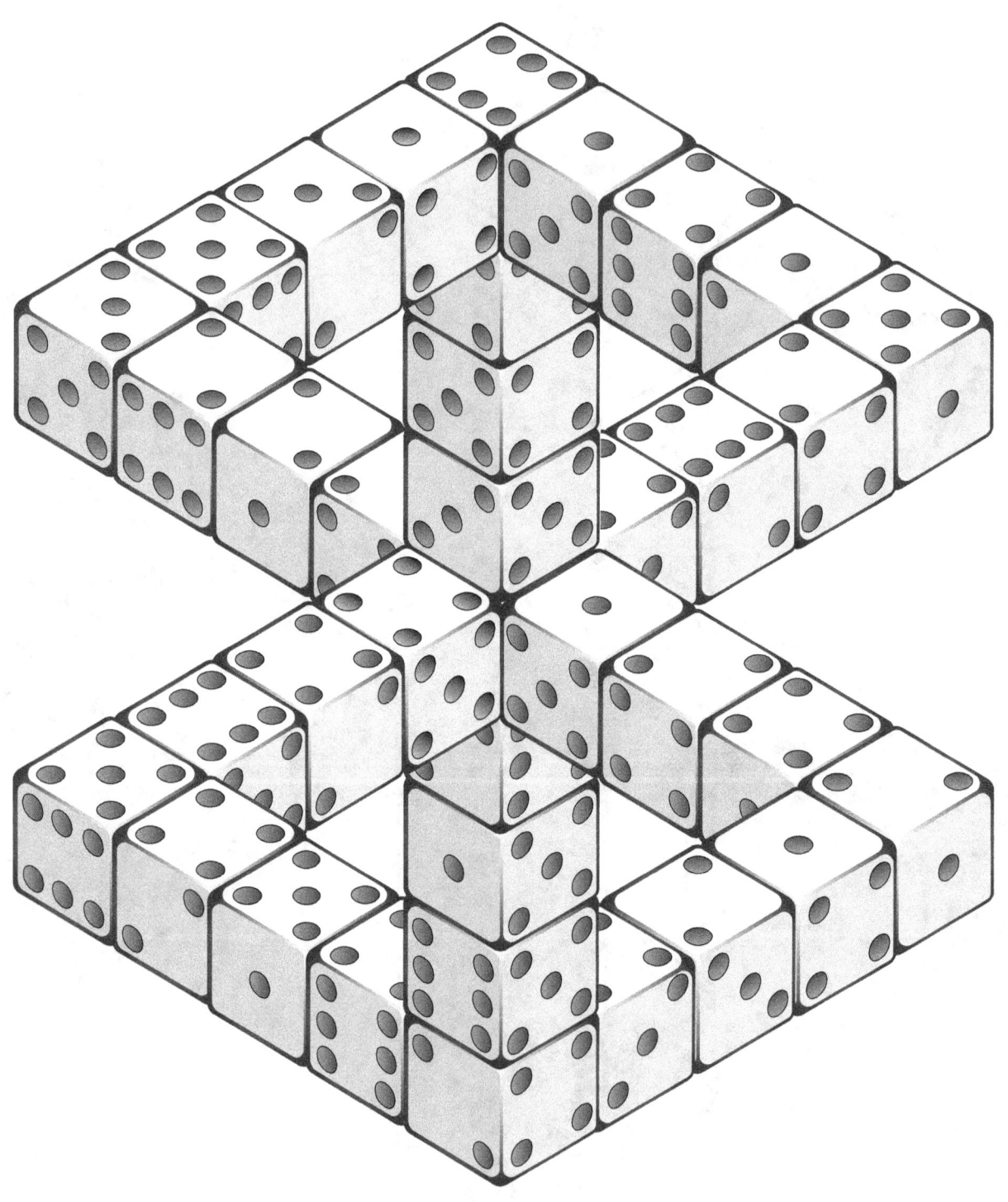

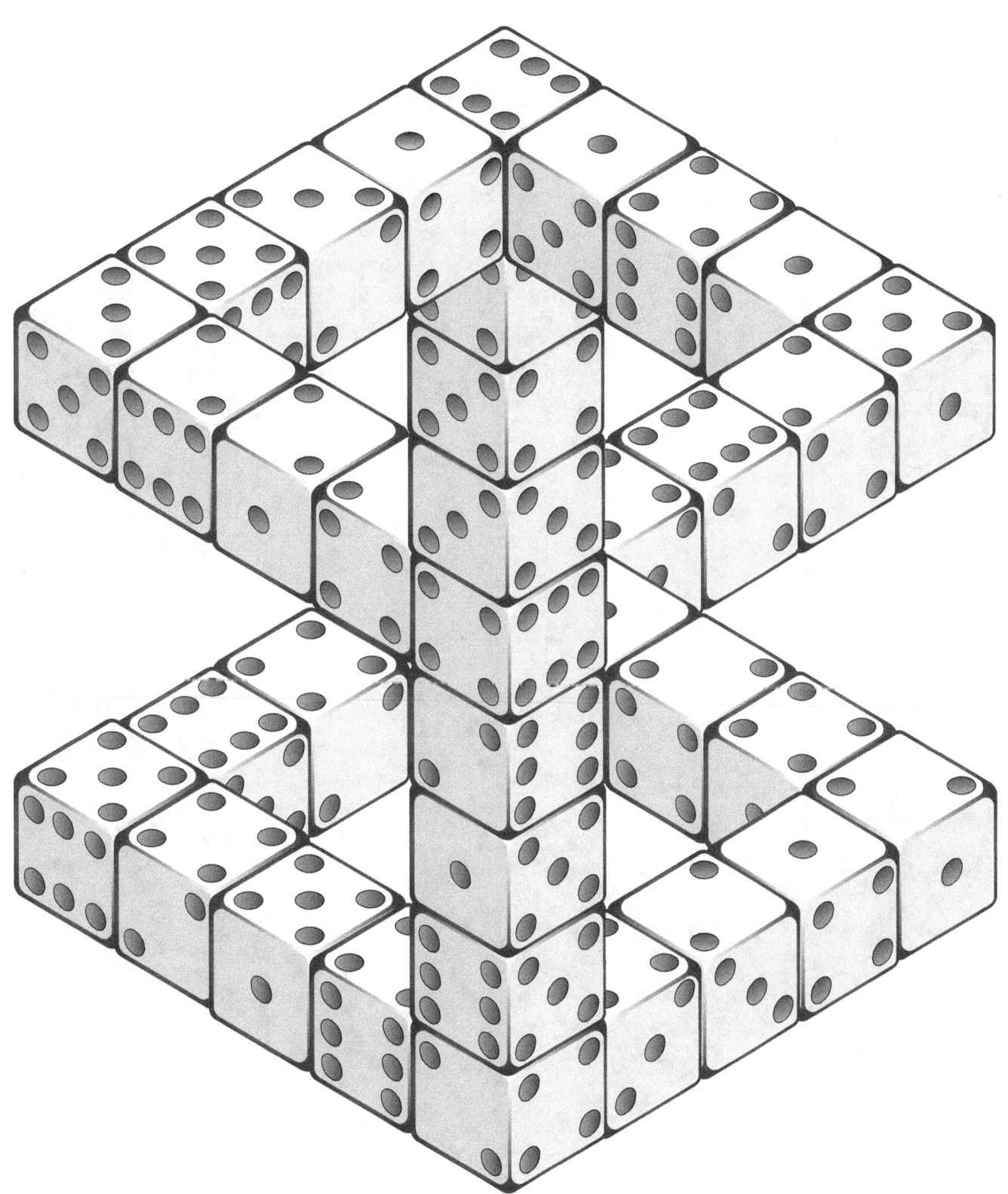

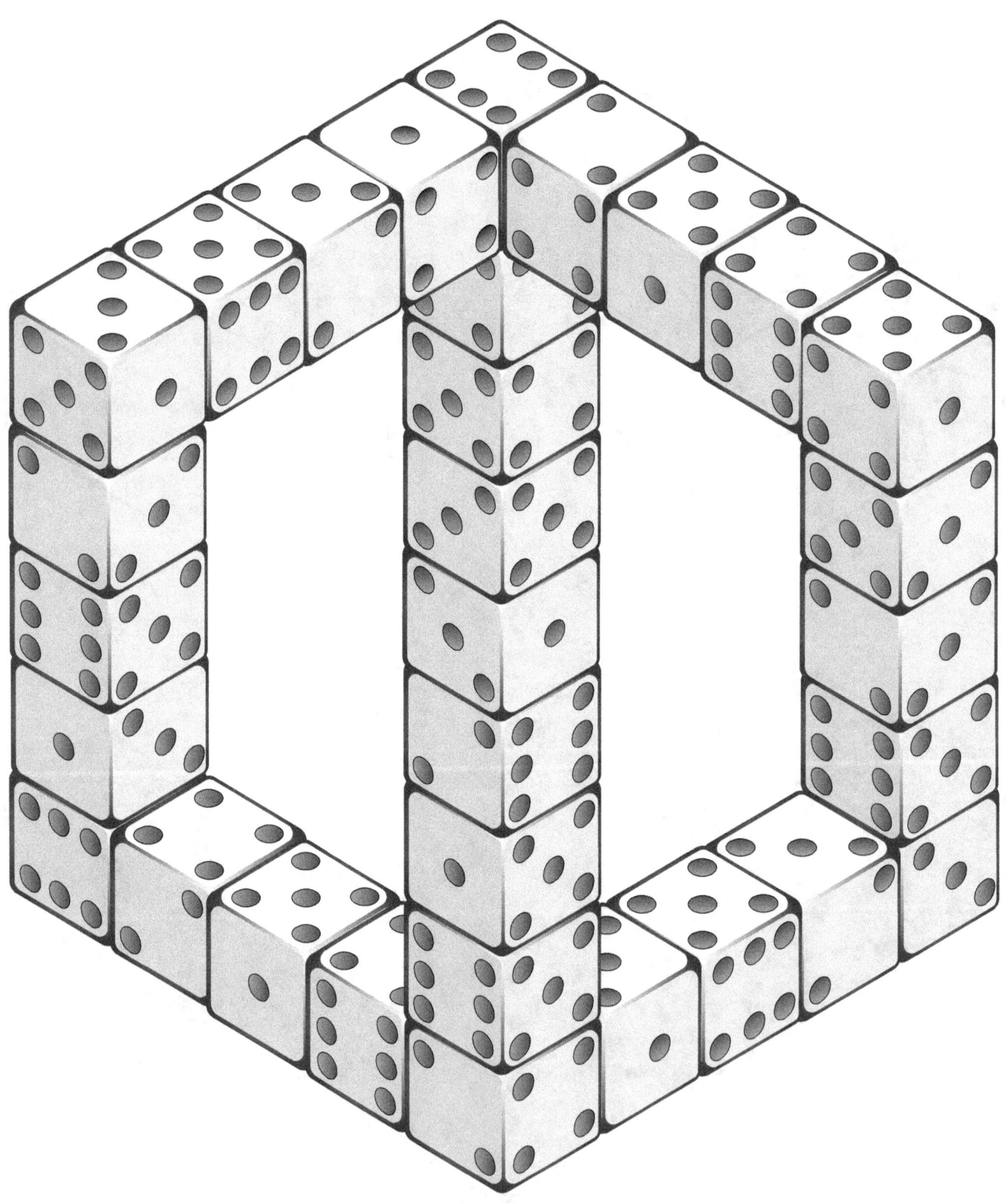

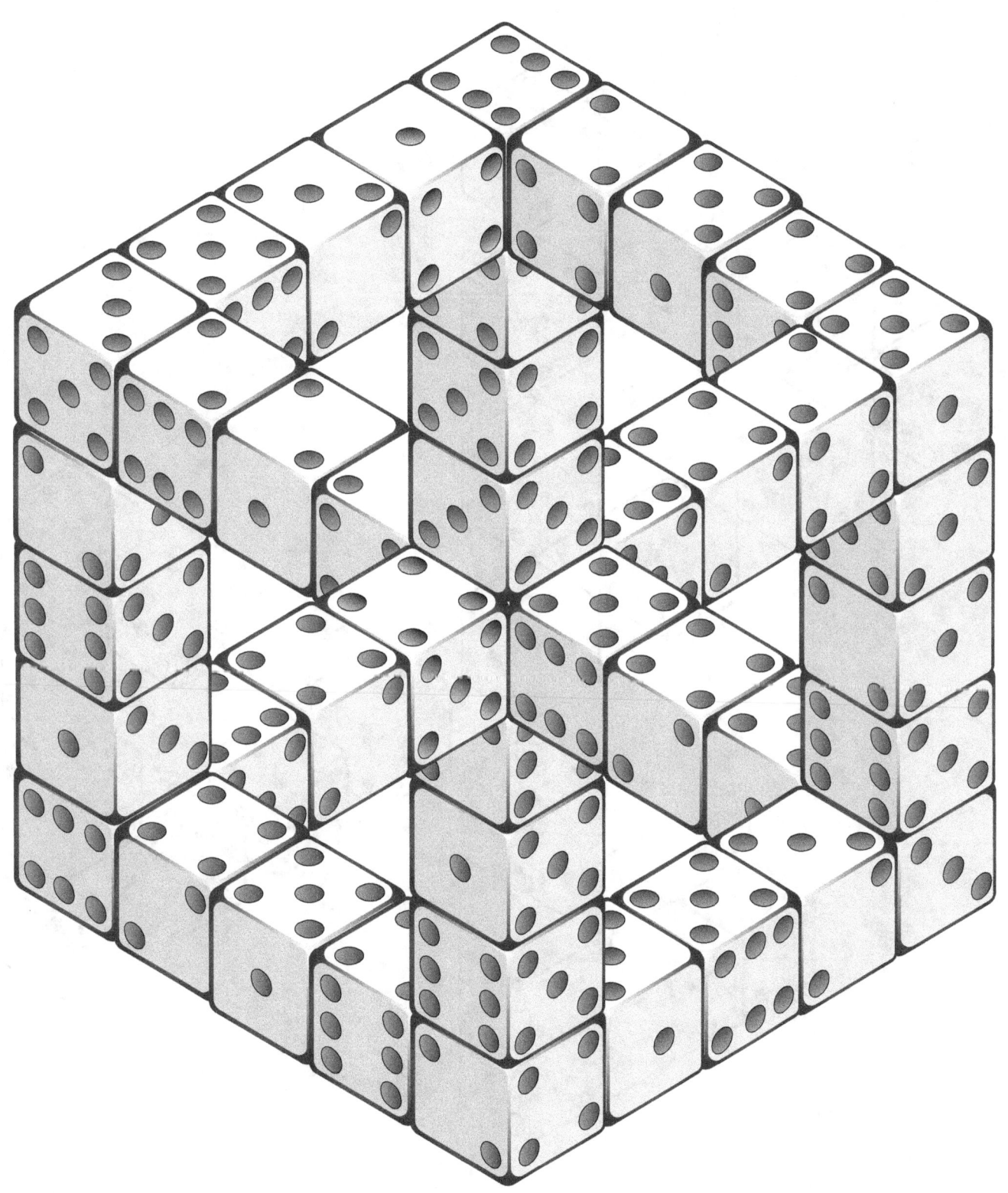

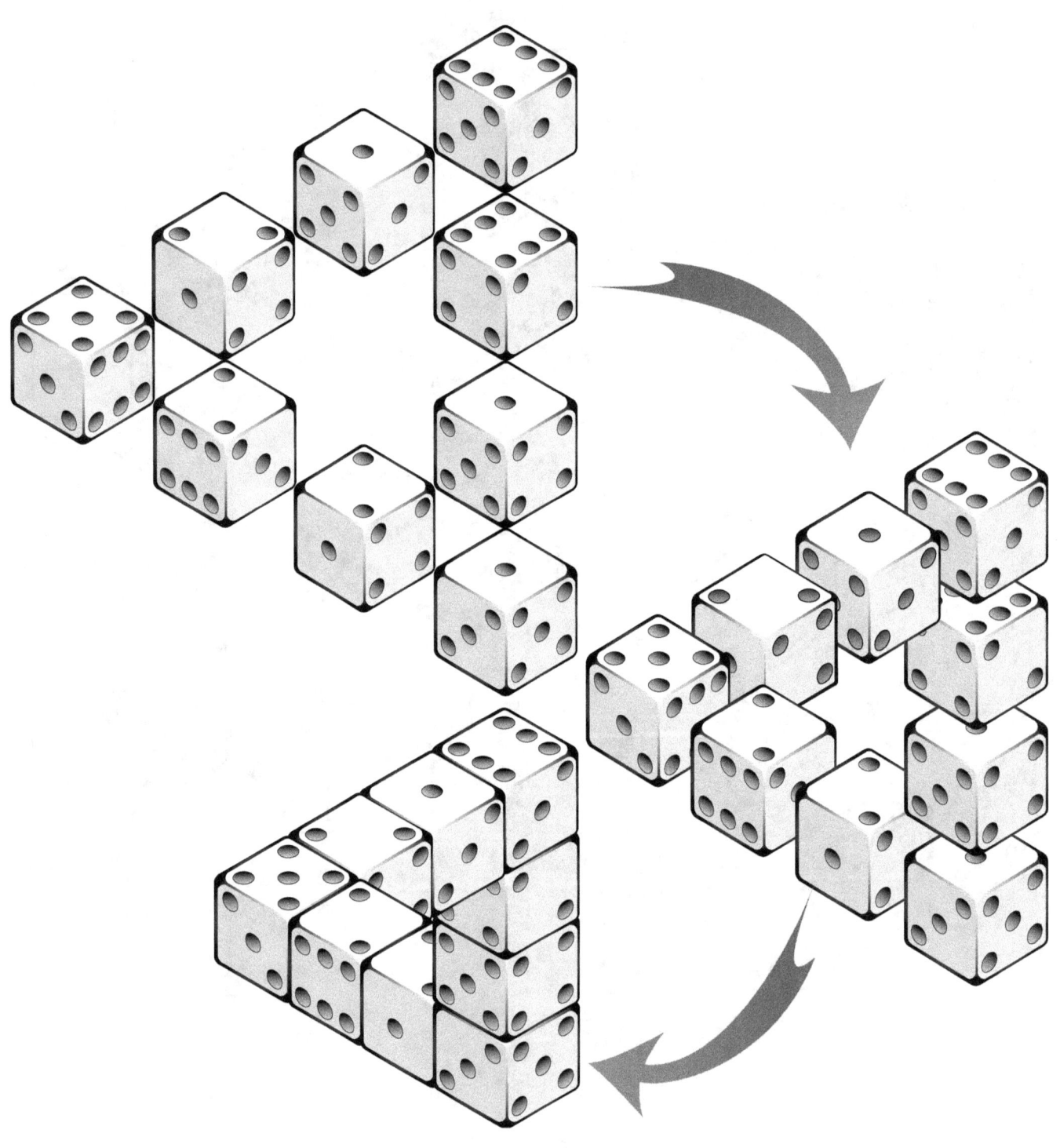

Cubes

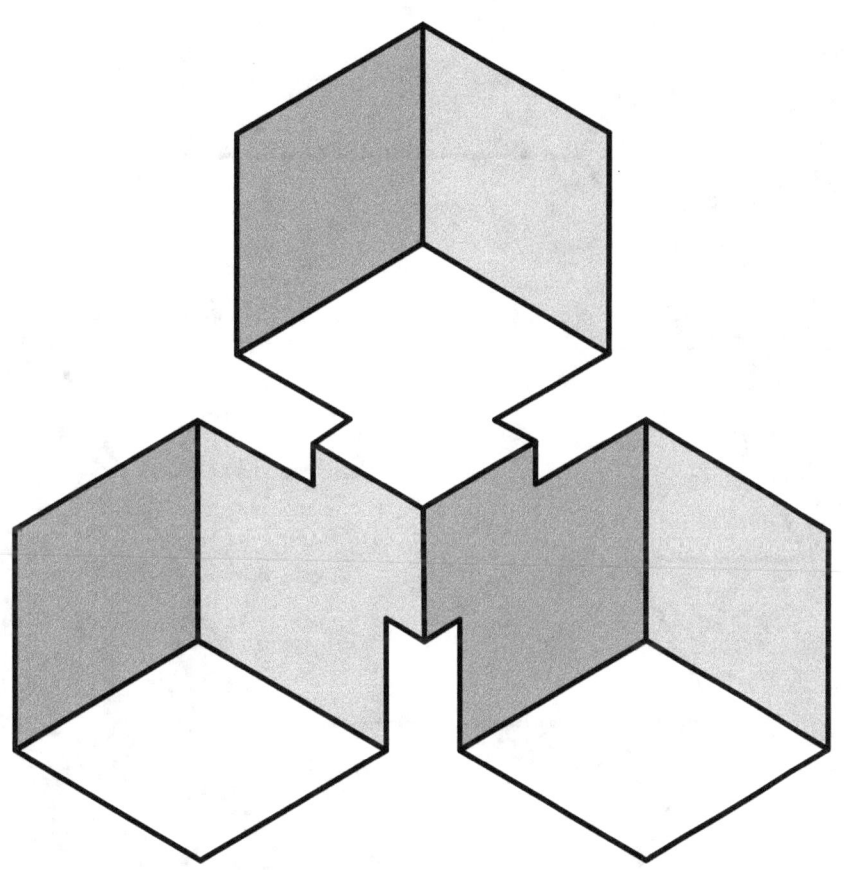

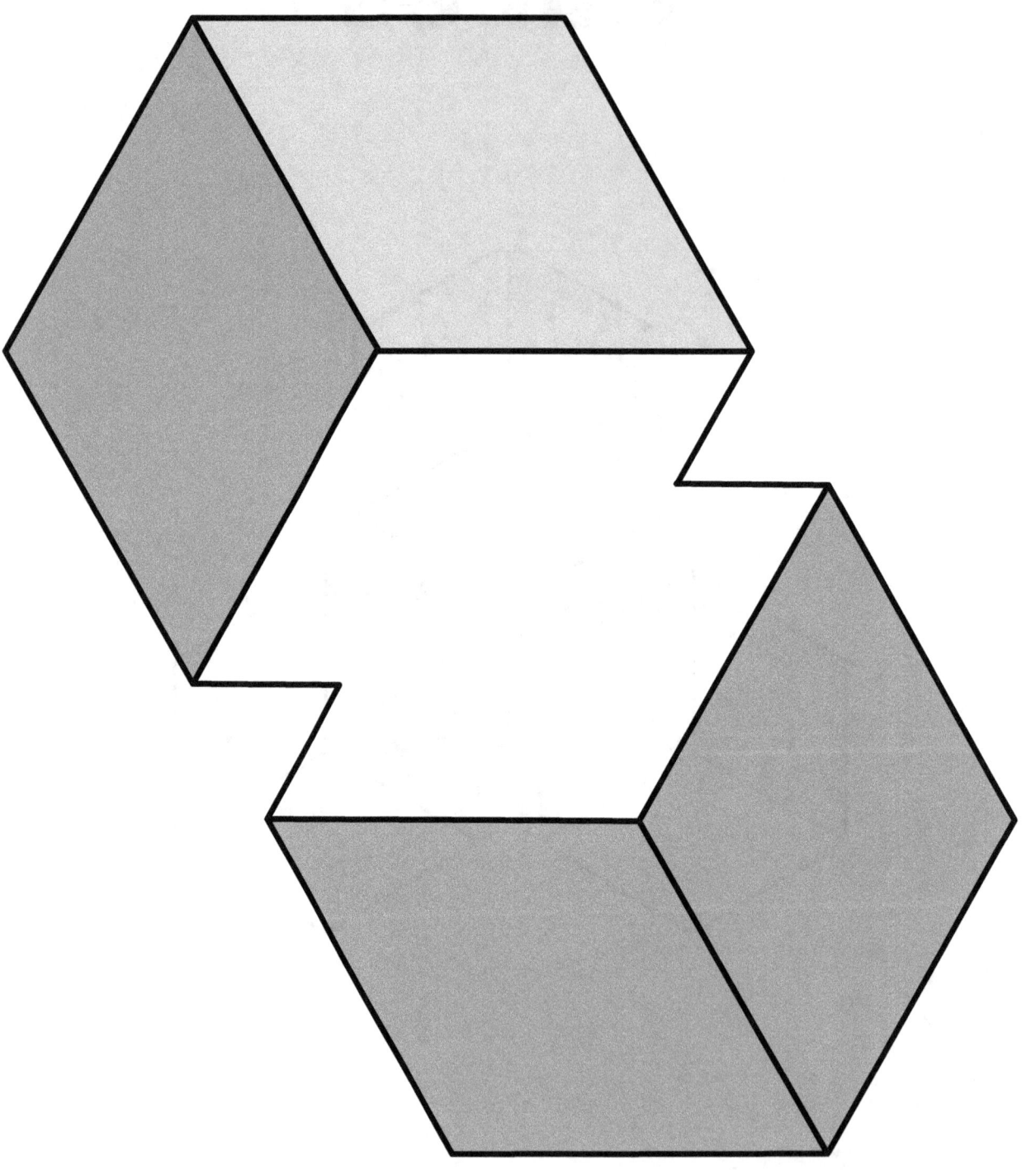

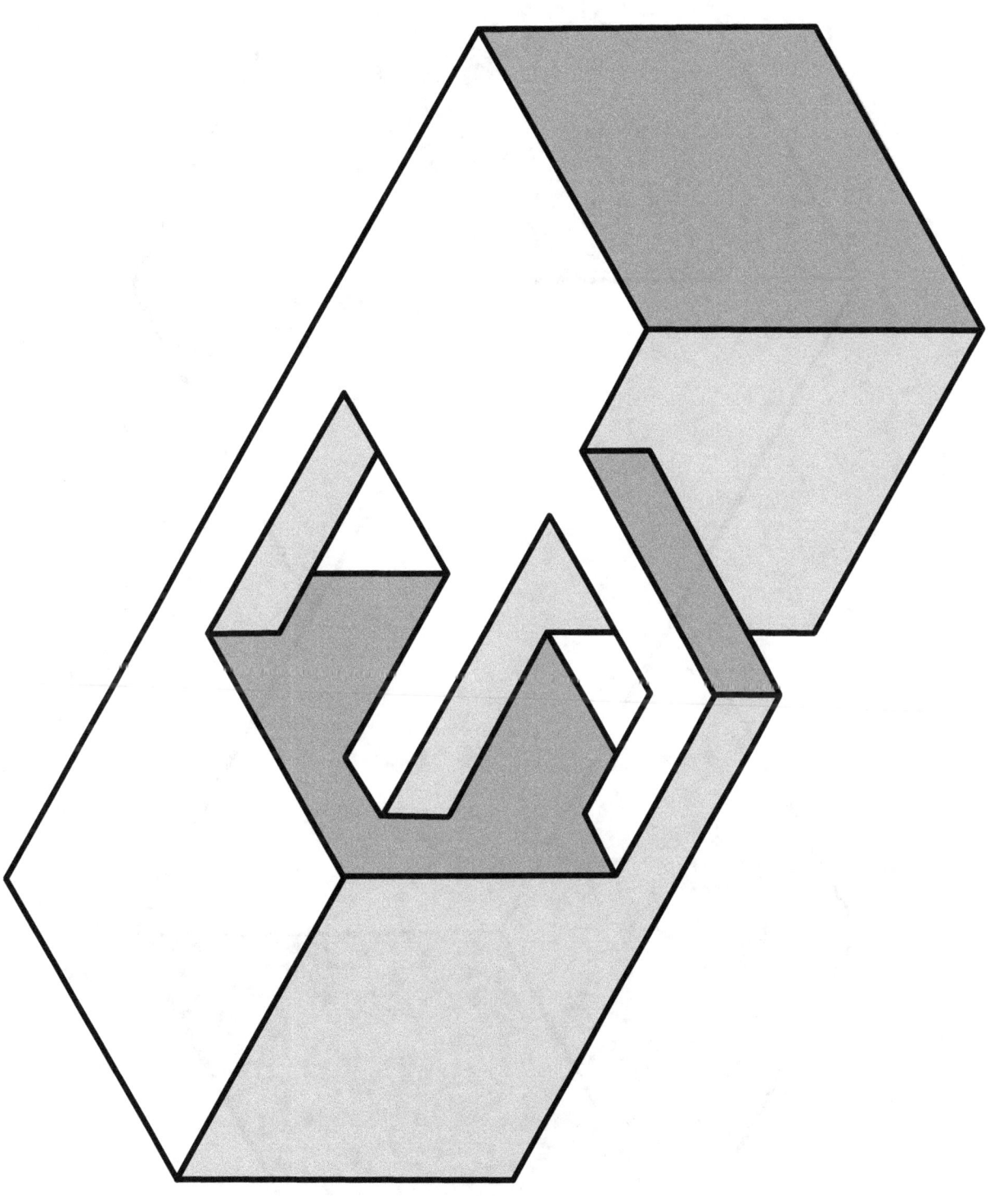

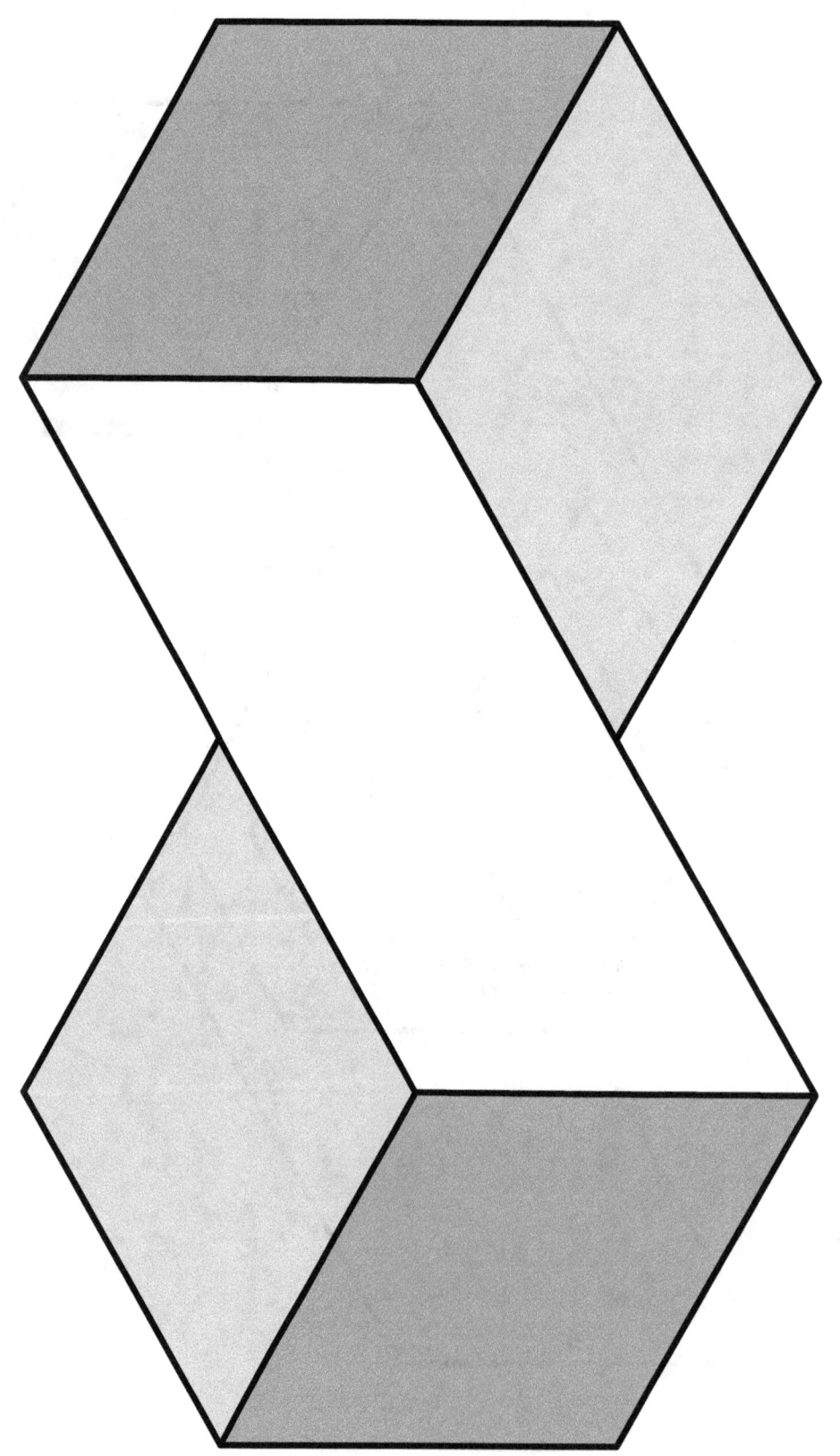

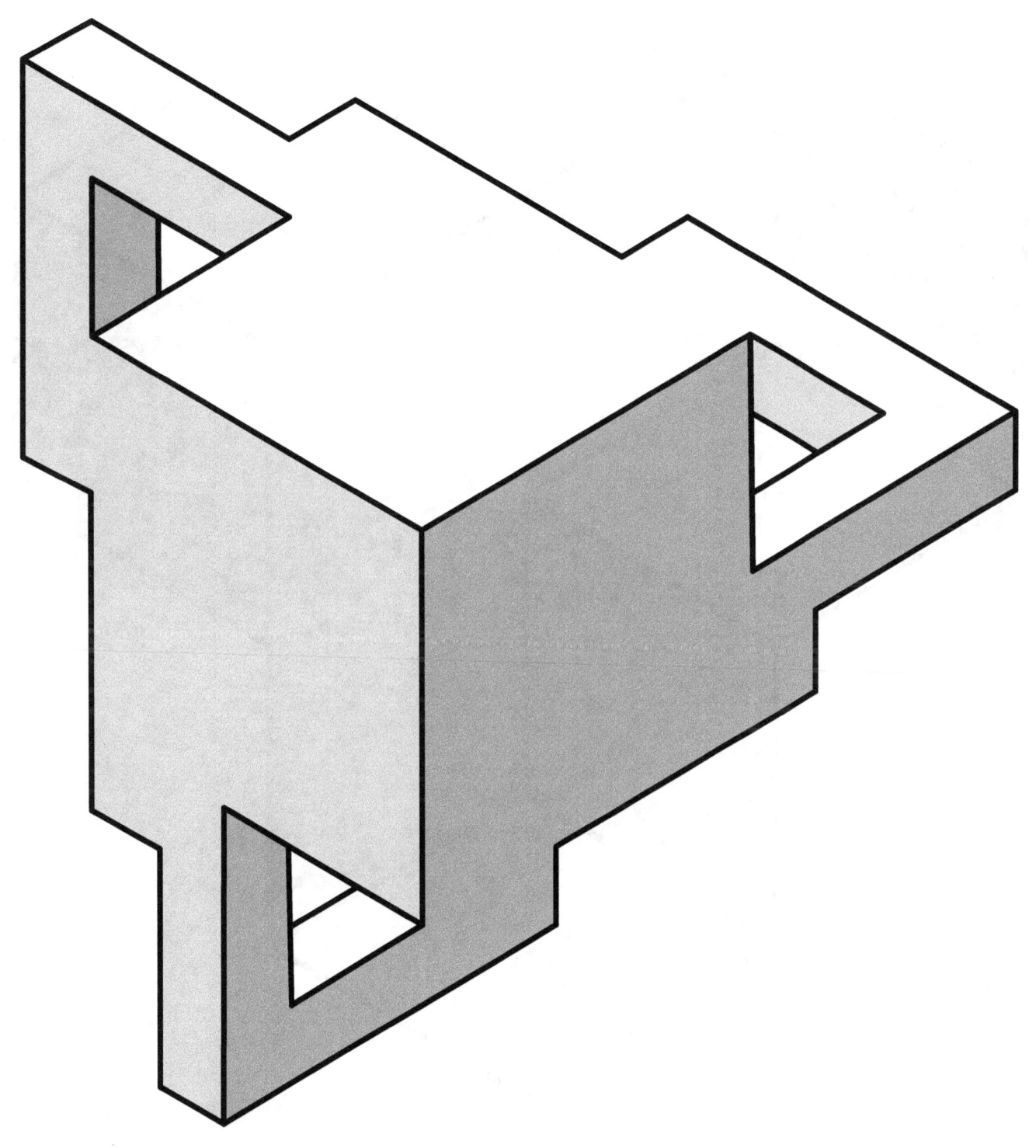

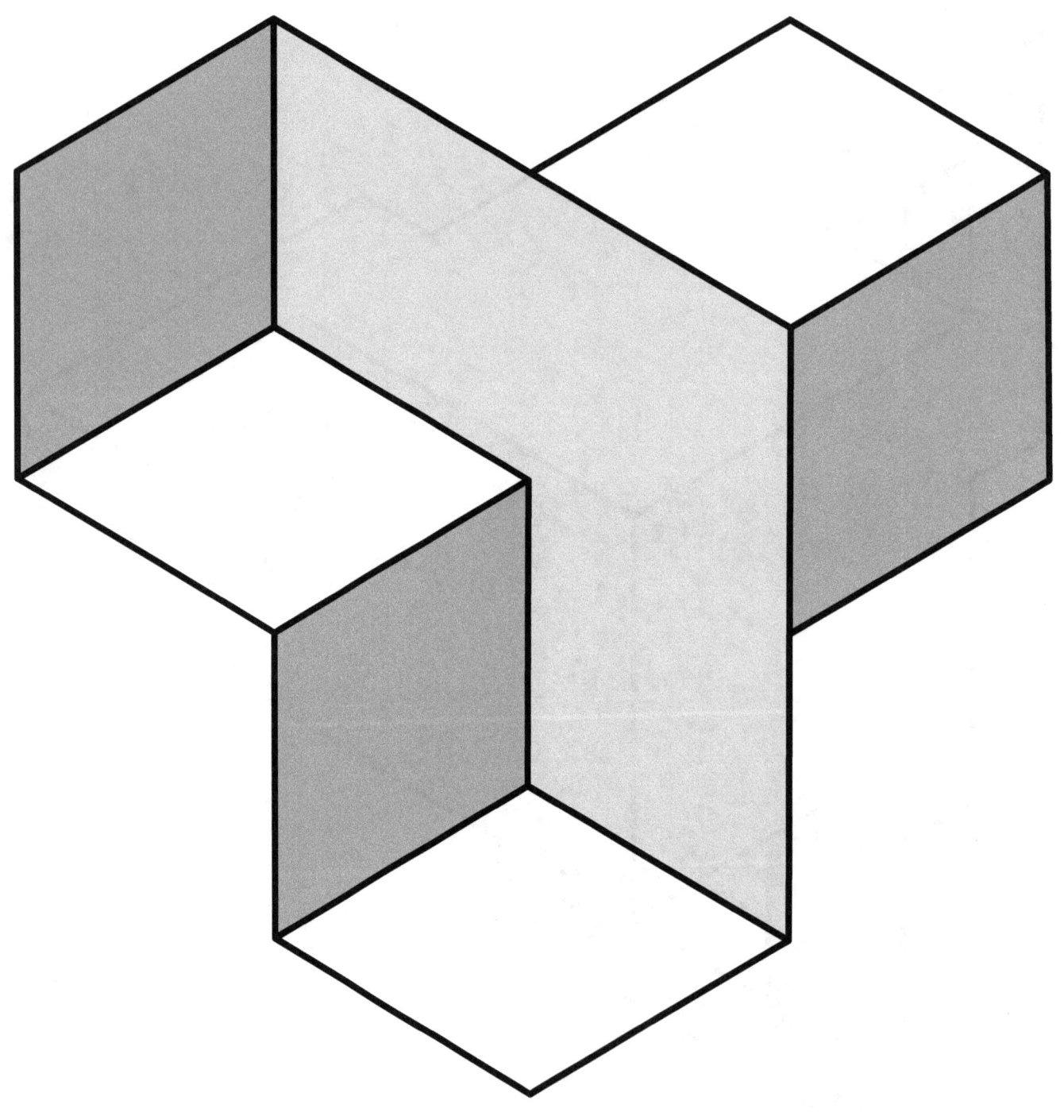

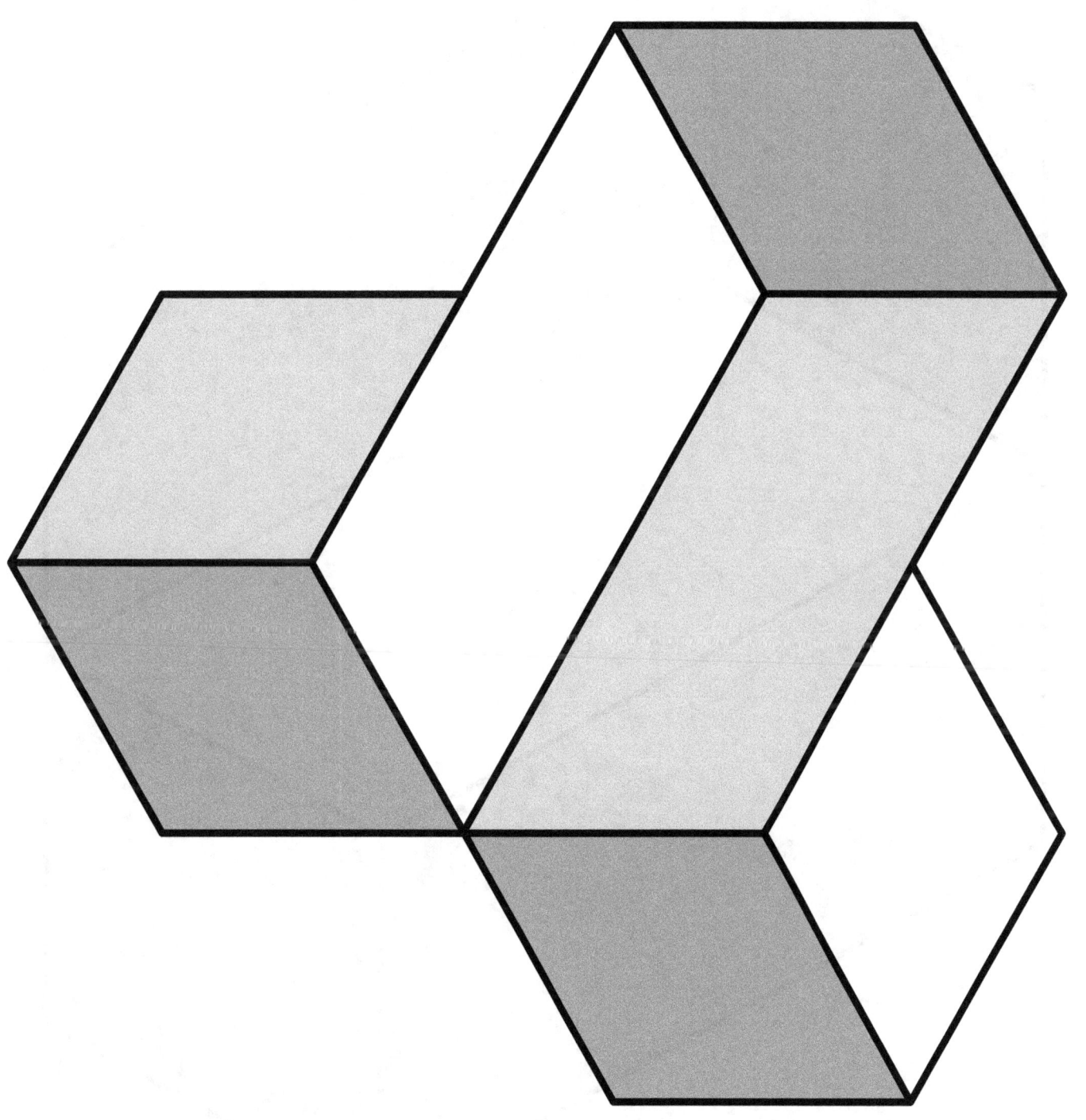

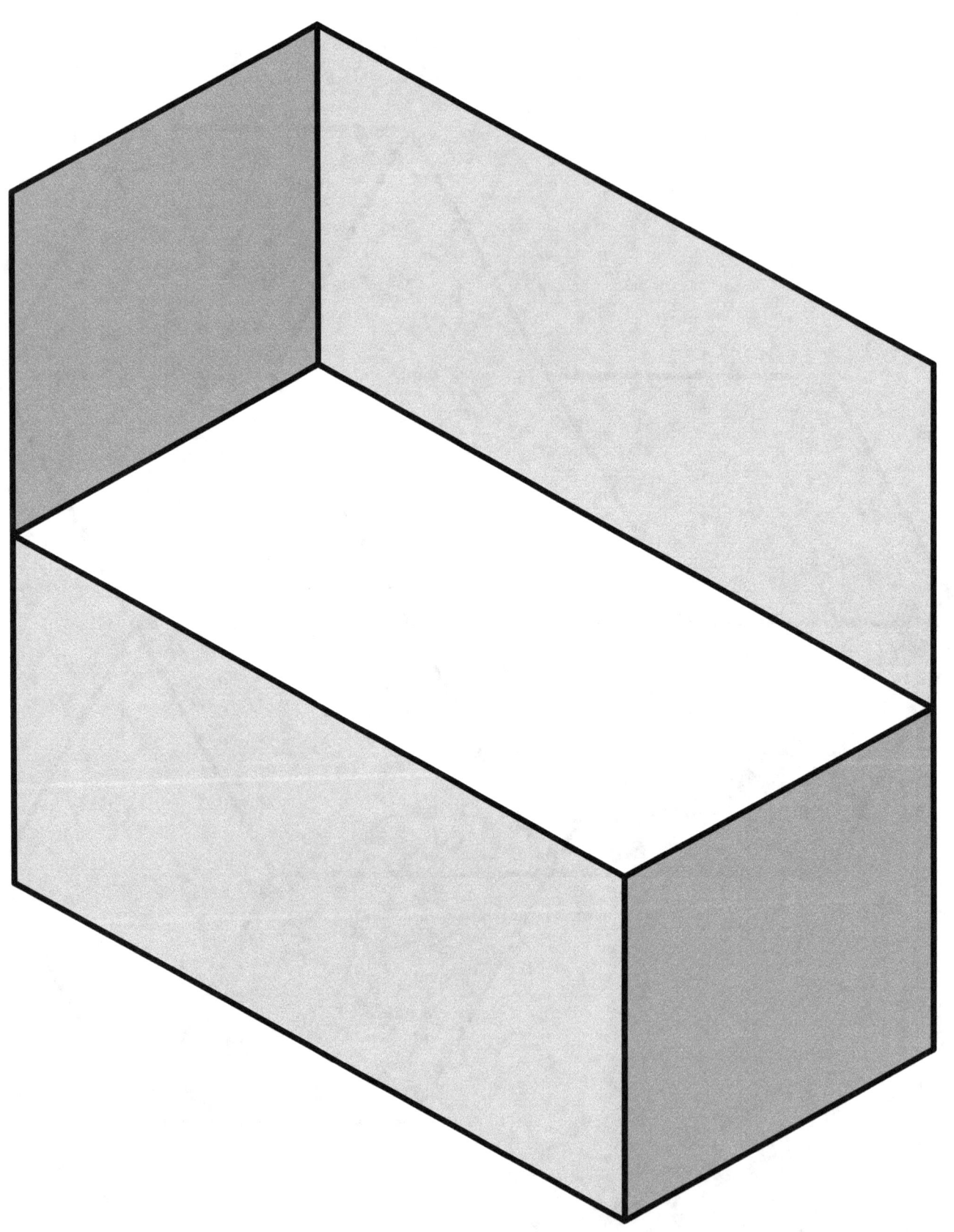

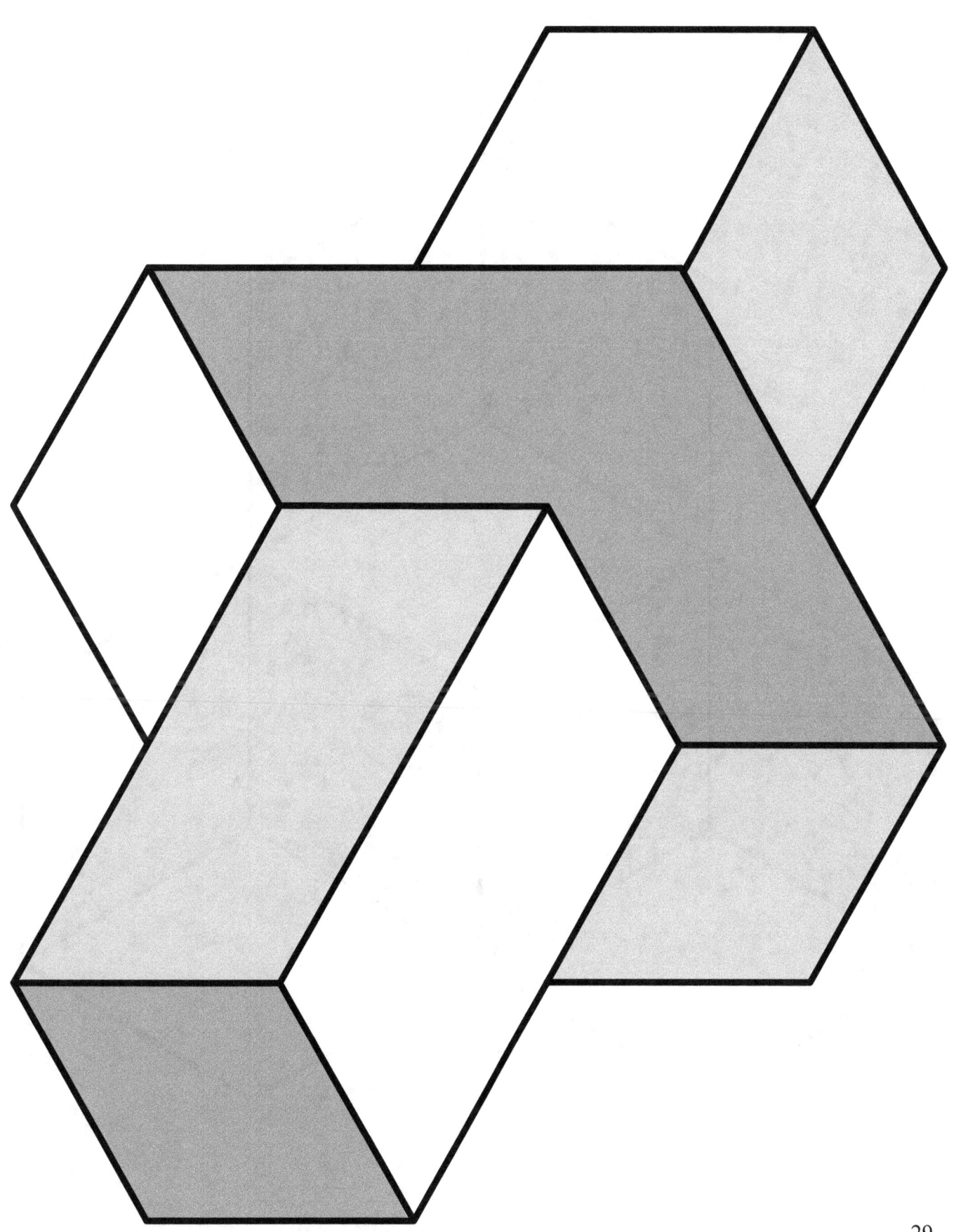

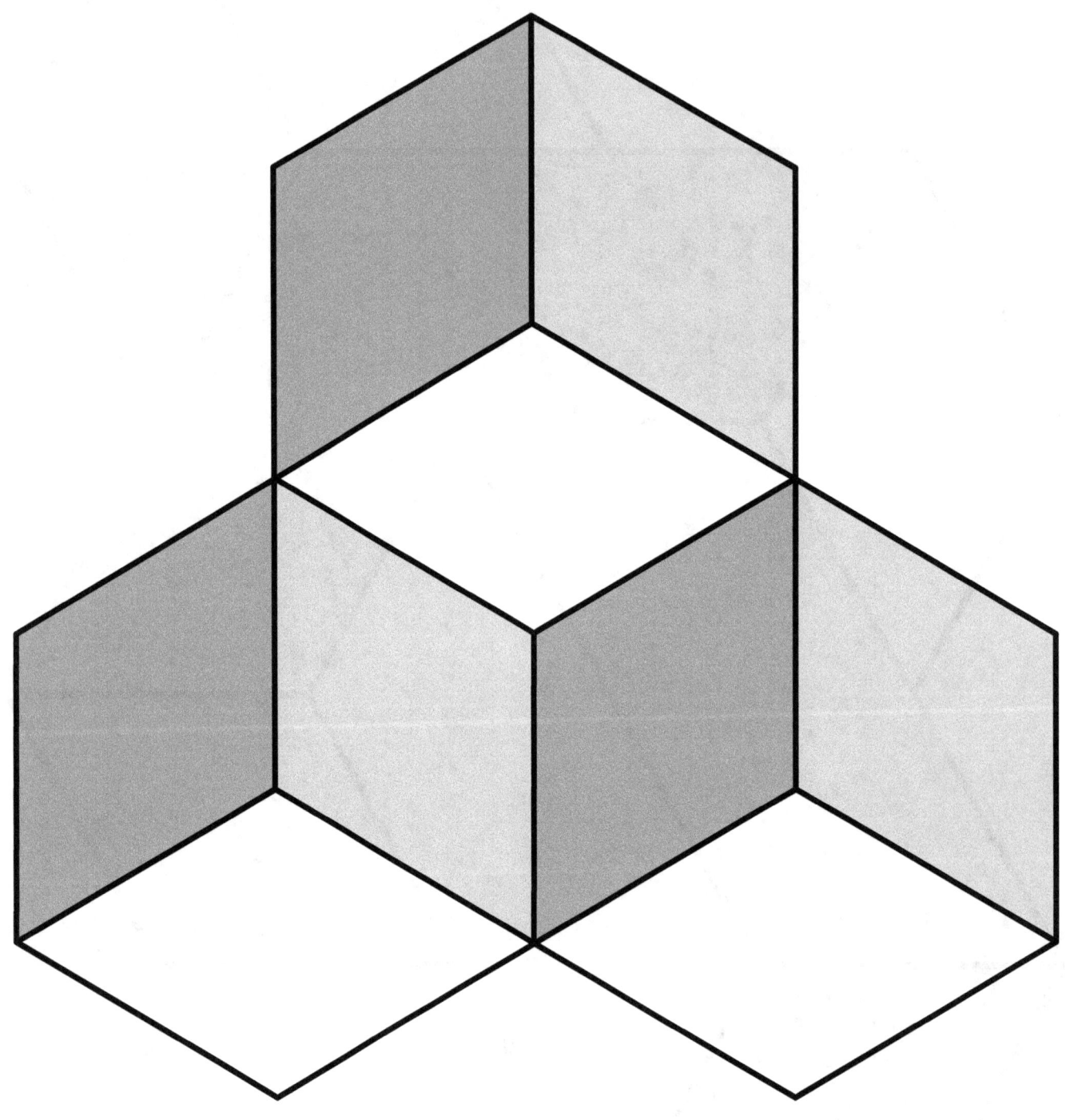

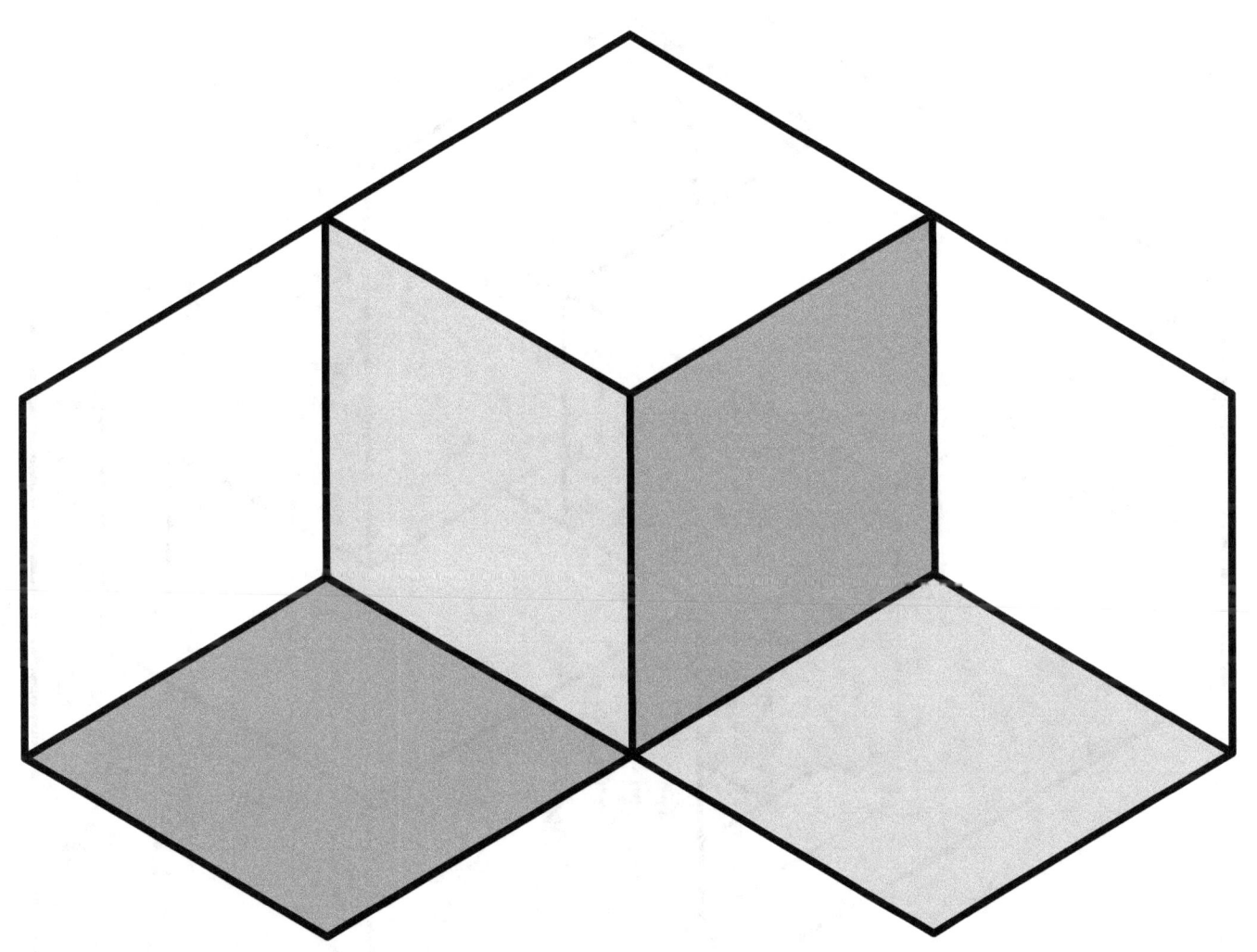

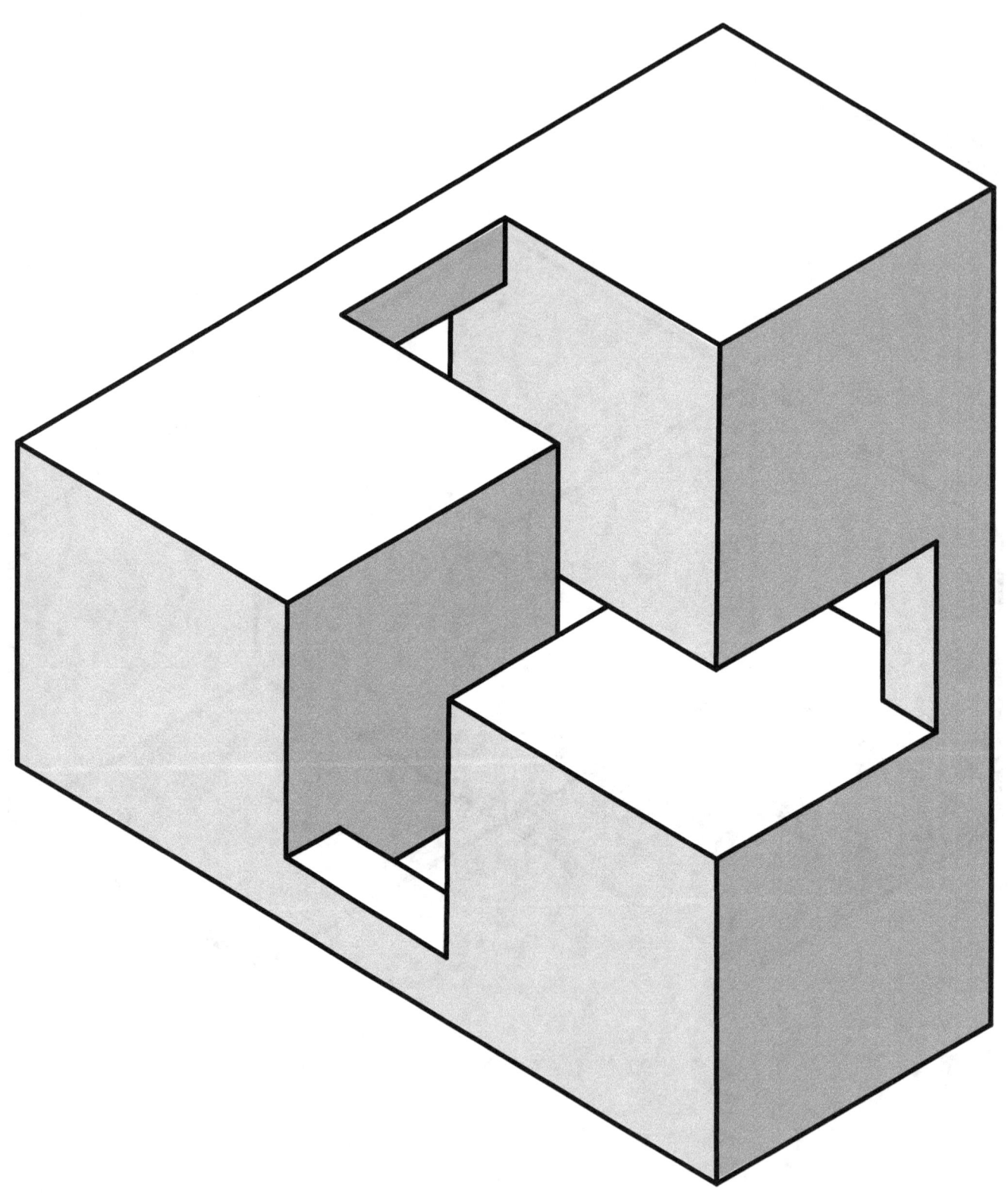

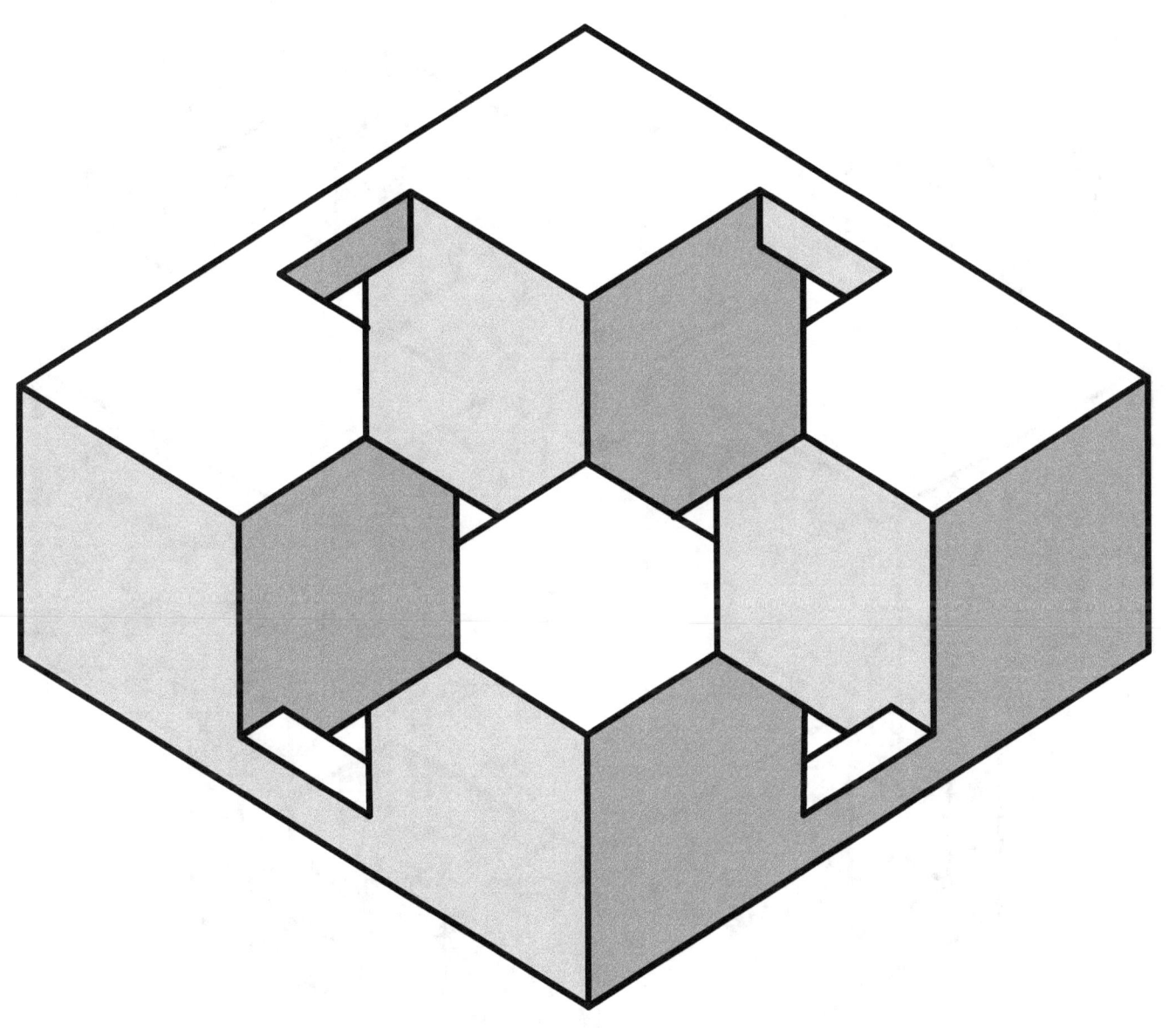

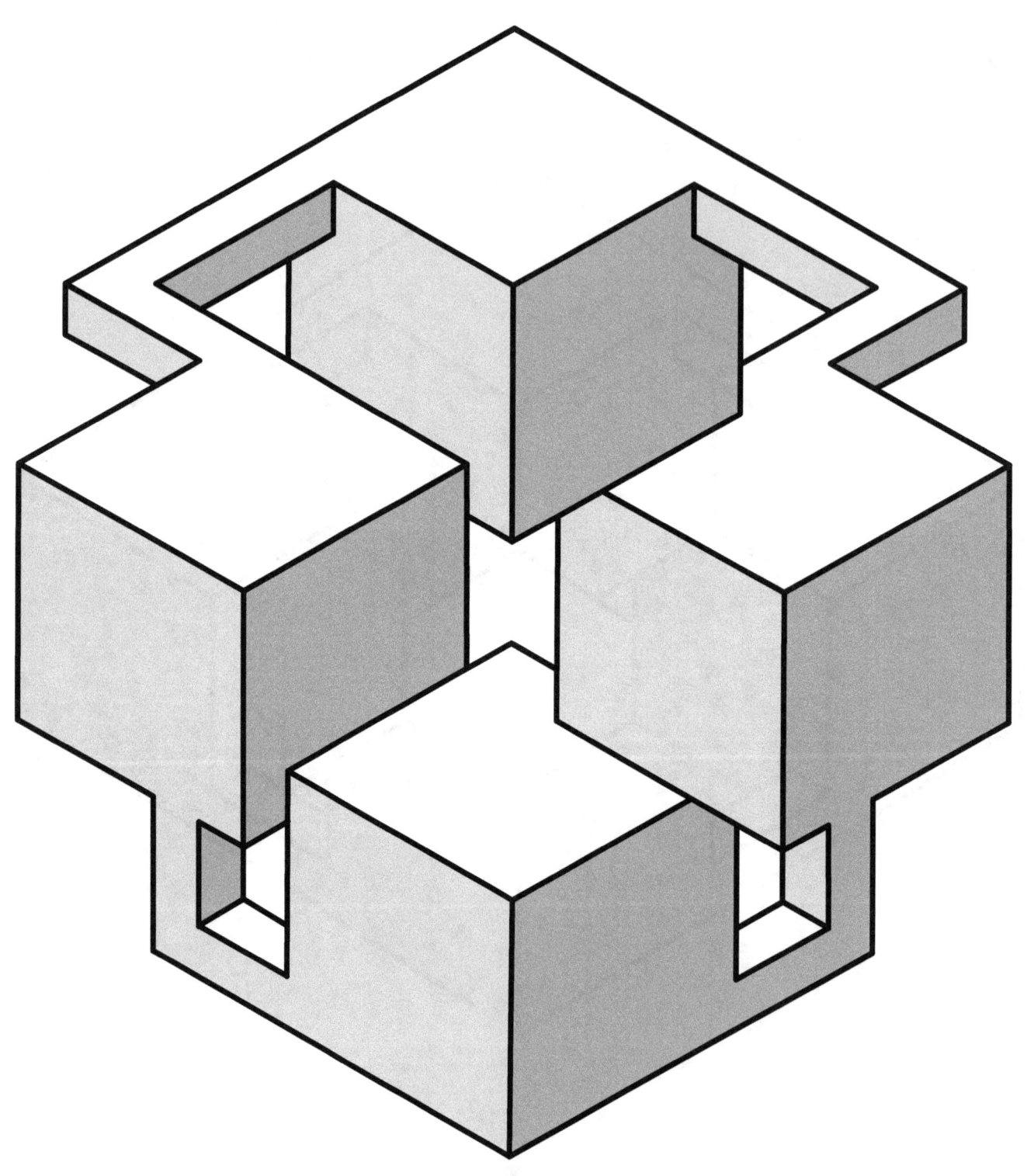

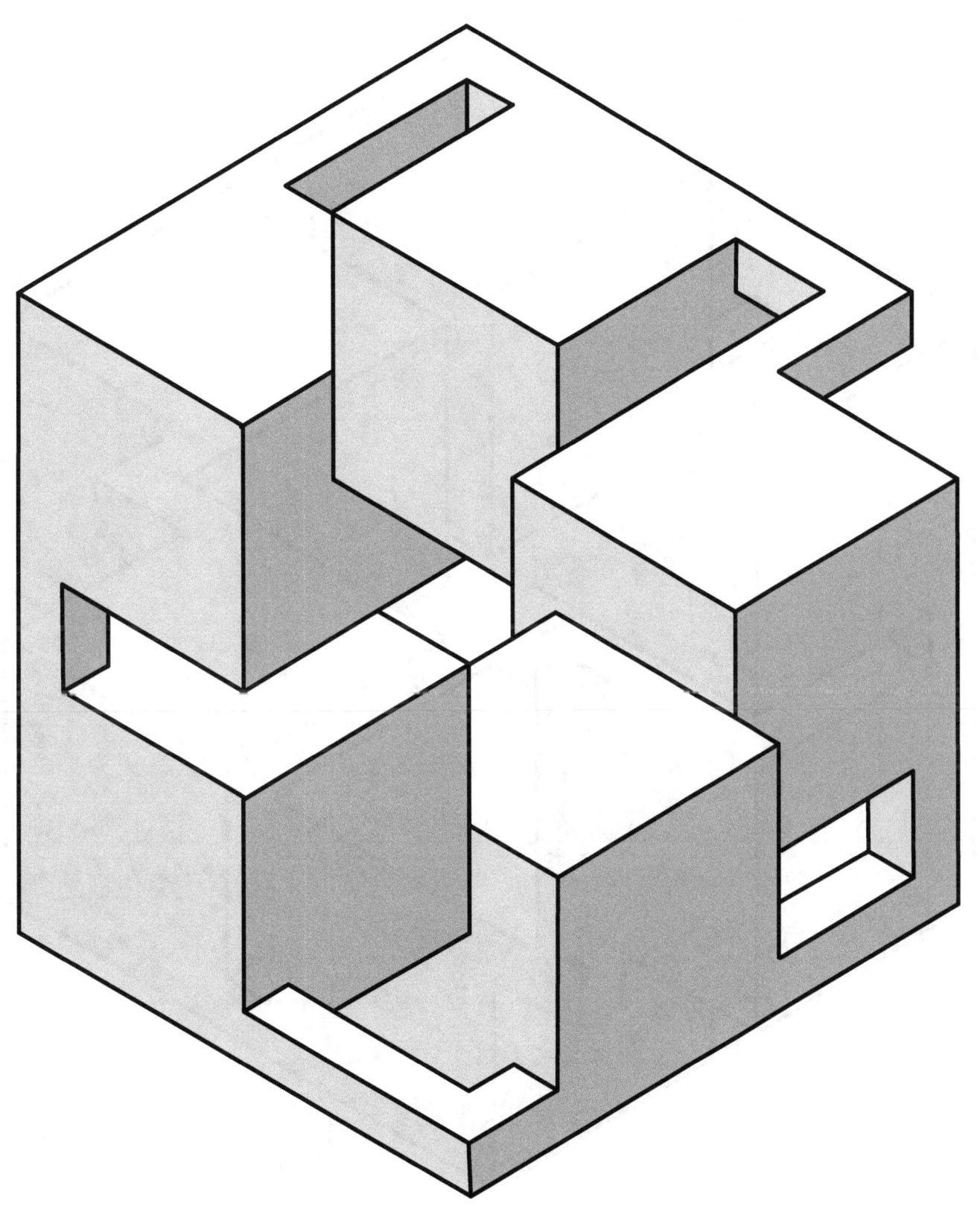

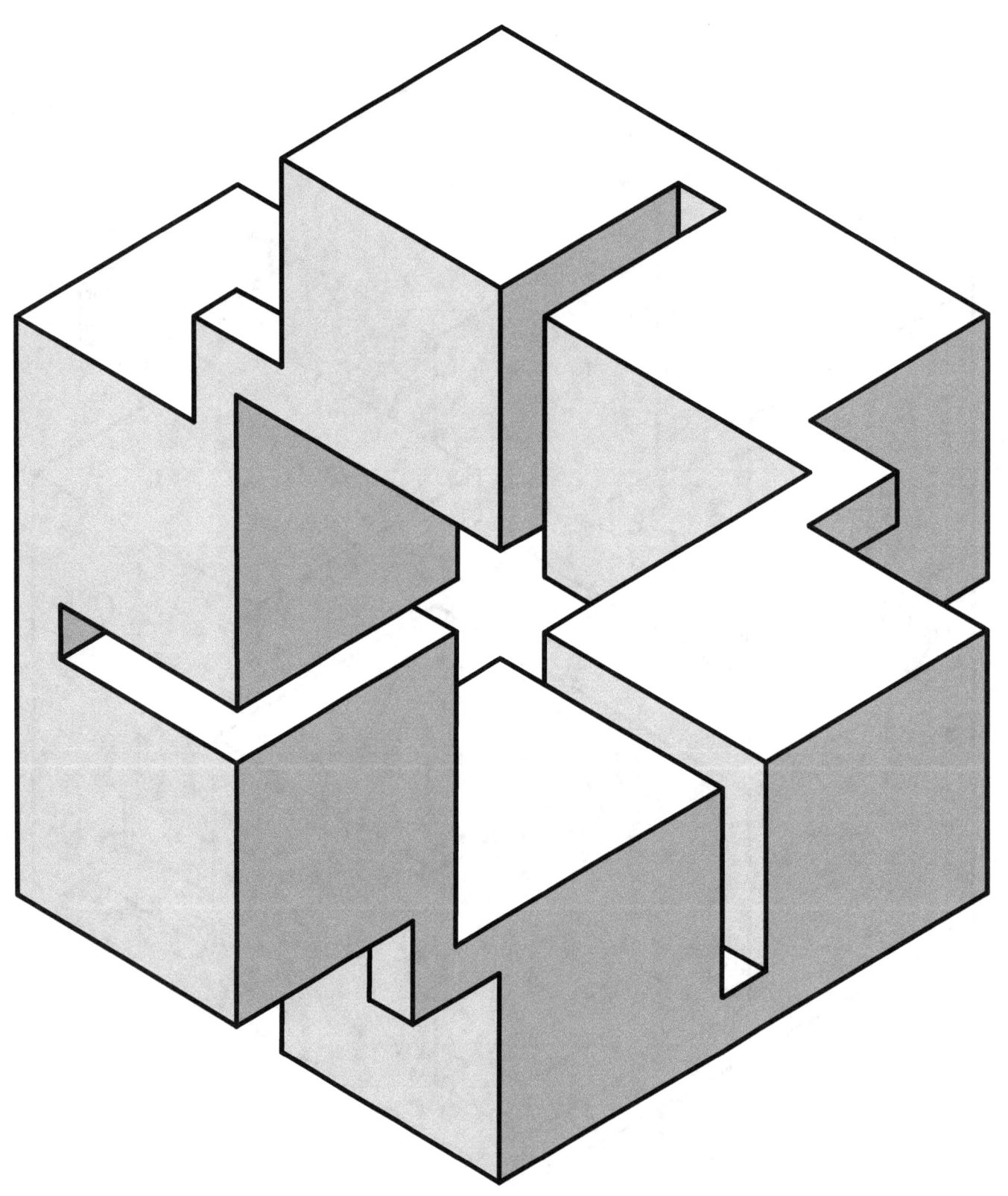

Nuts & Bolts

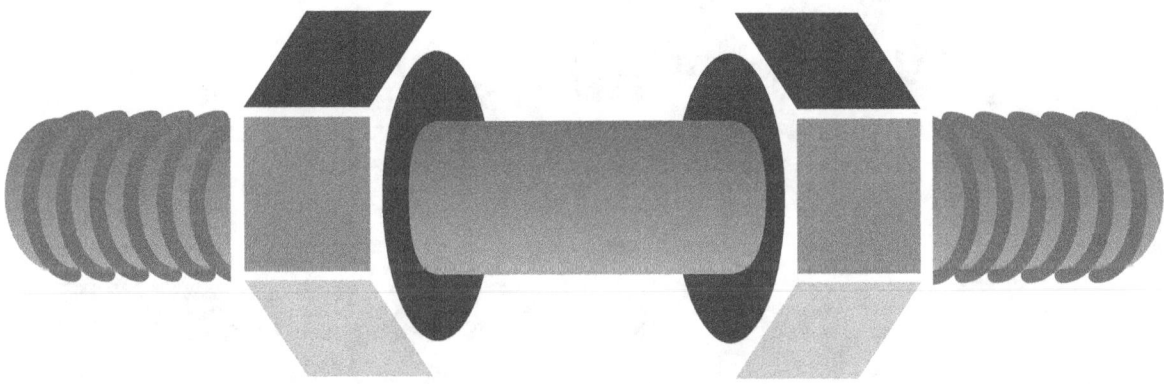

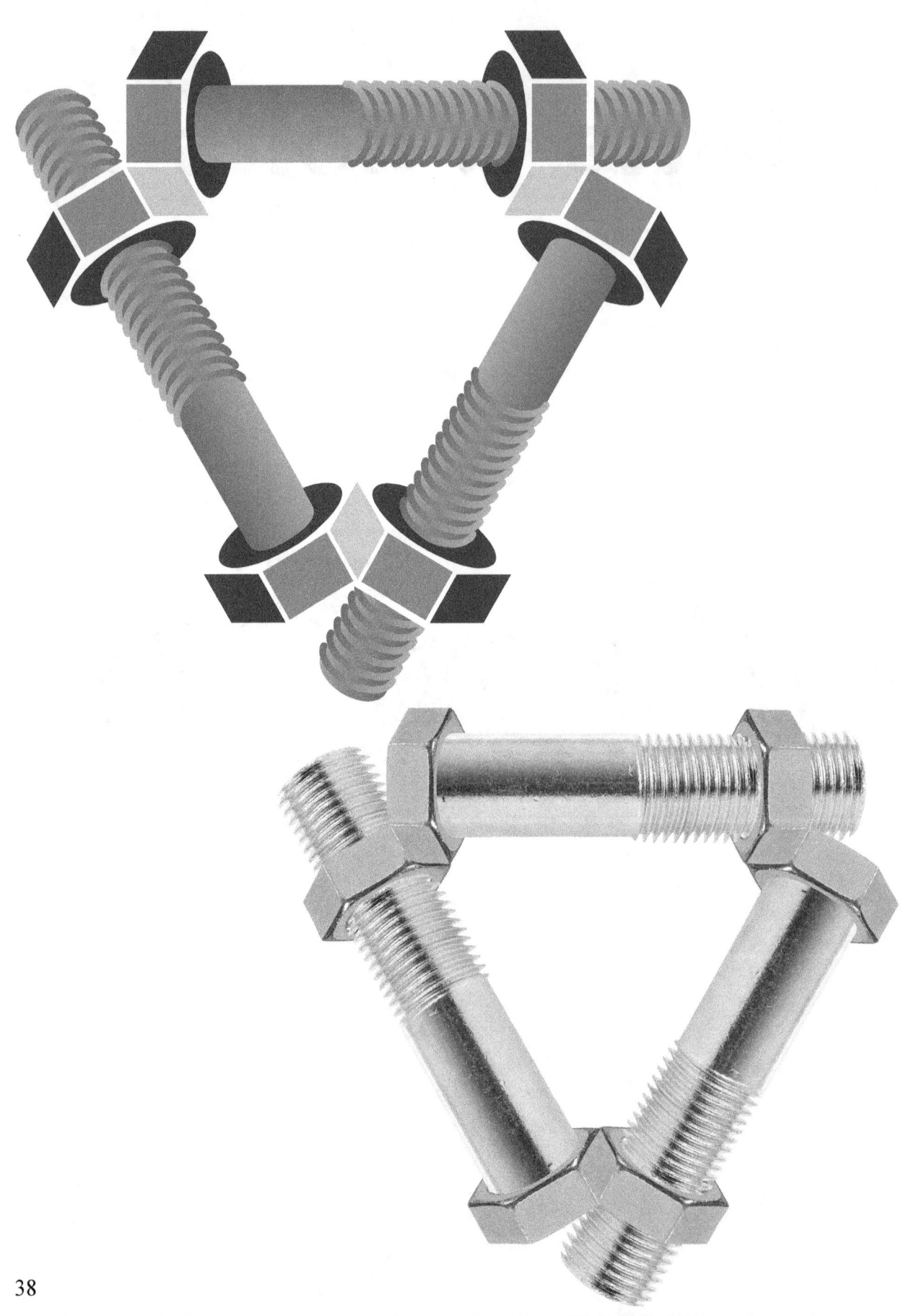

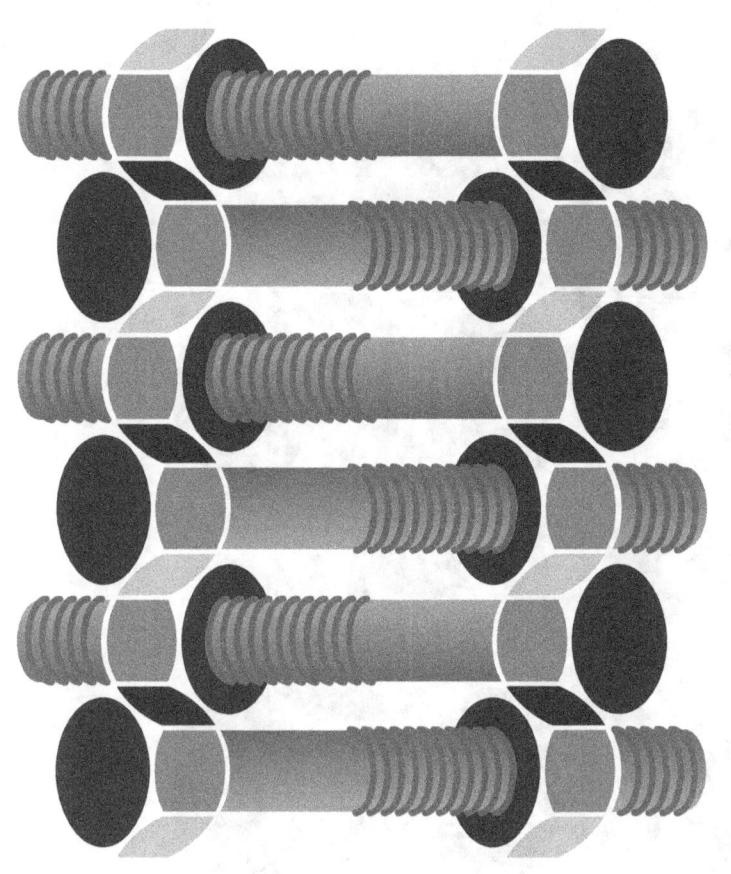

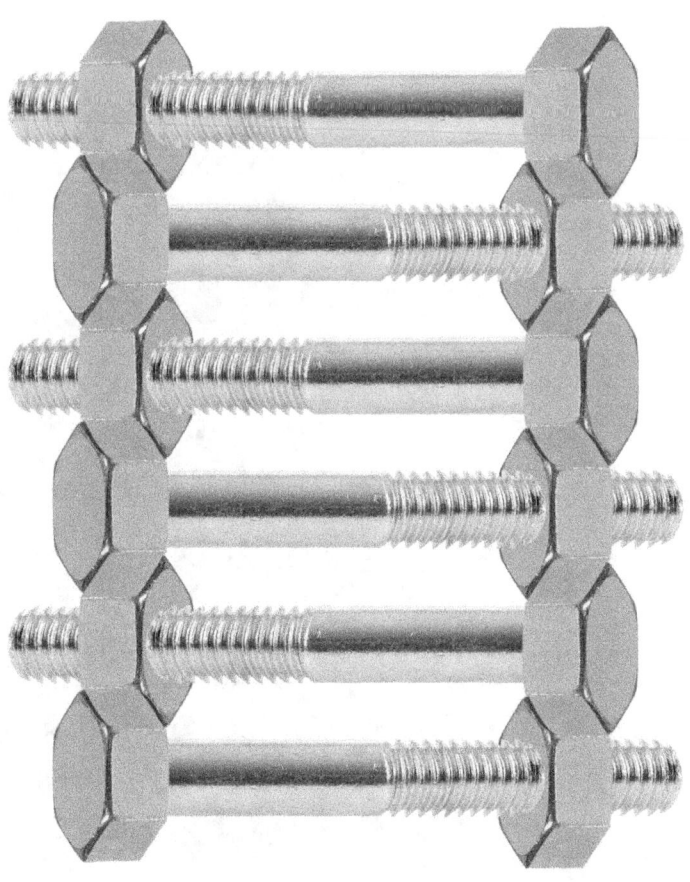

39

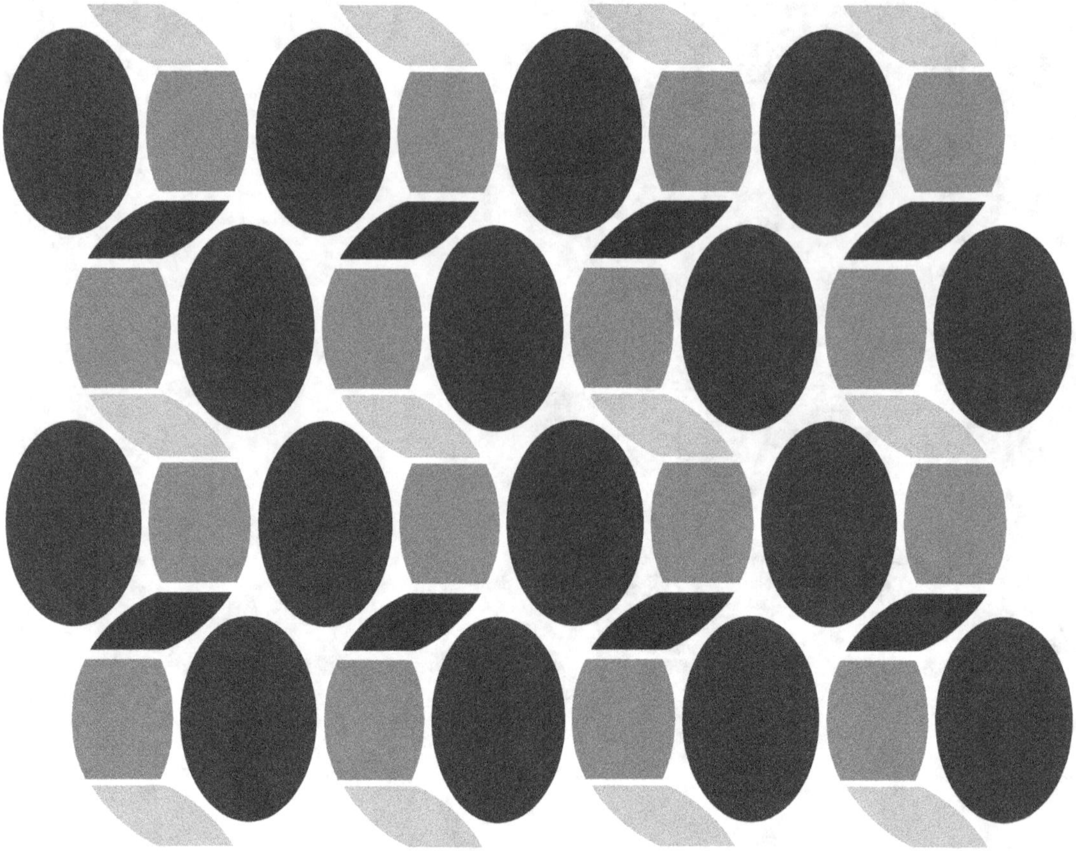

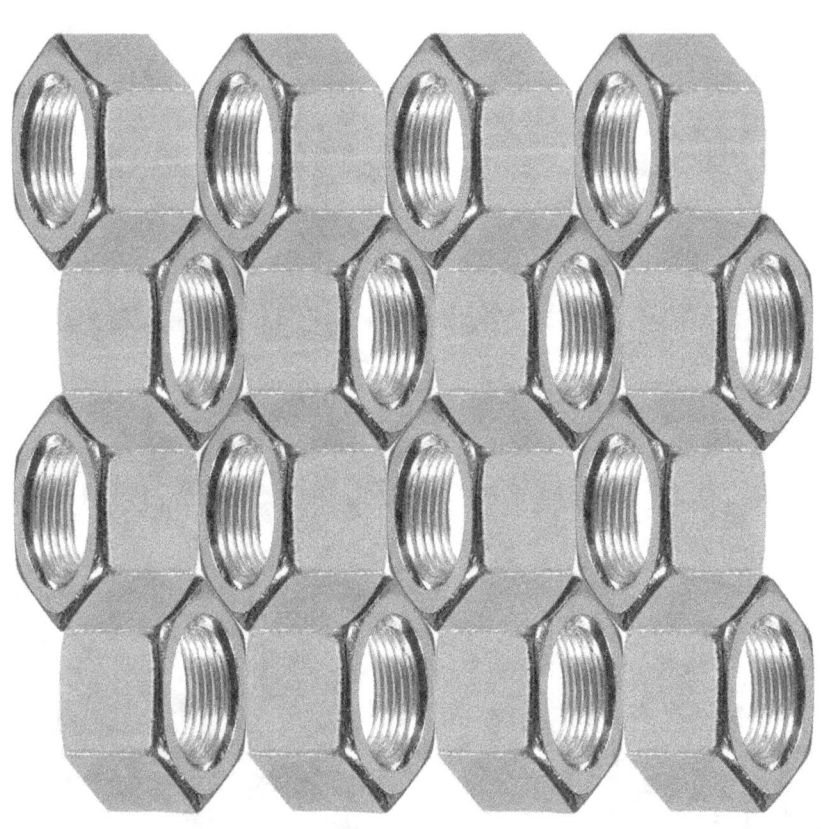

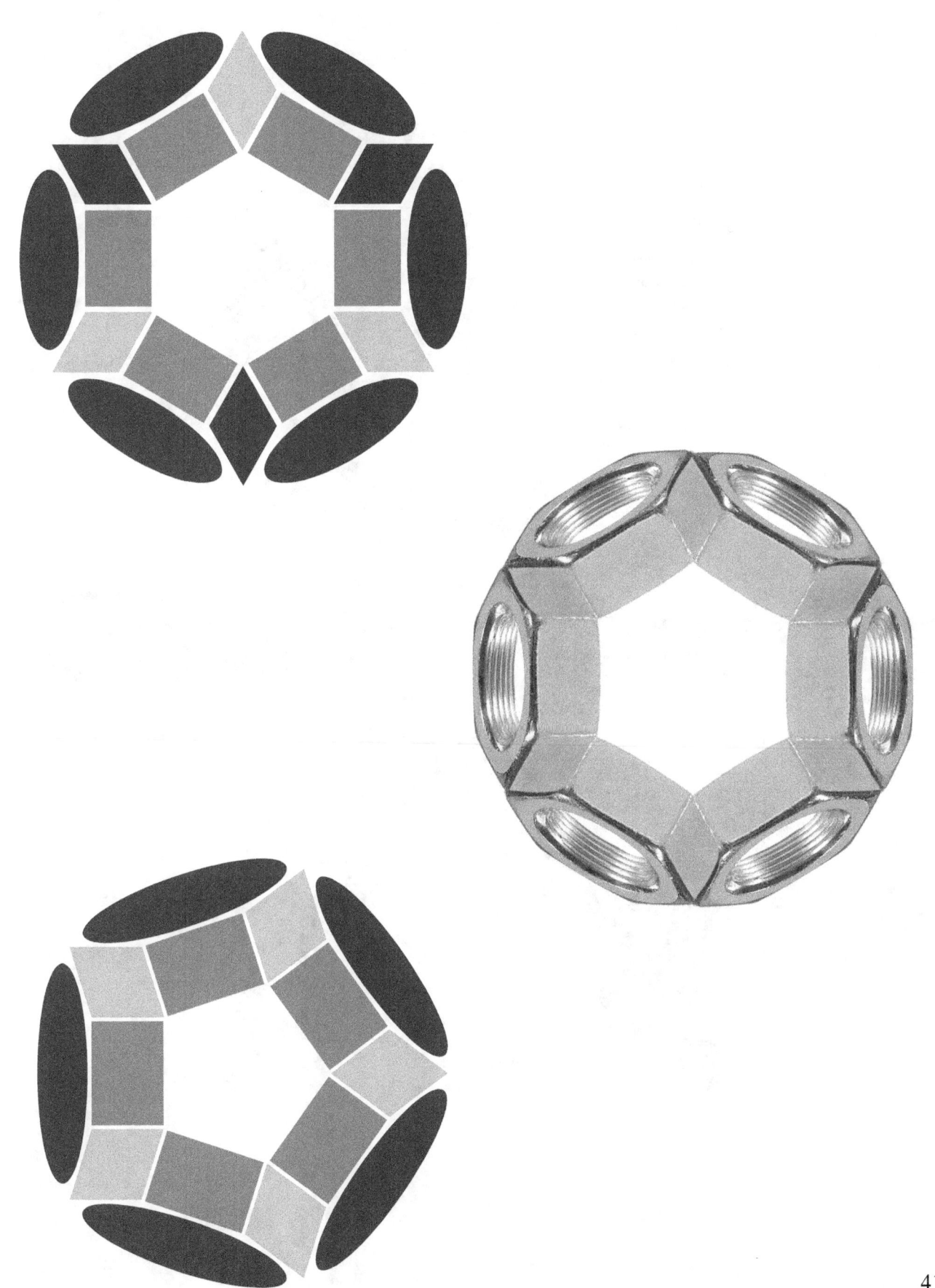

41

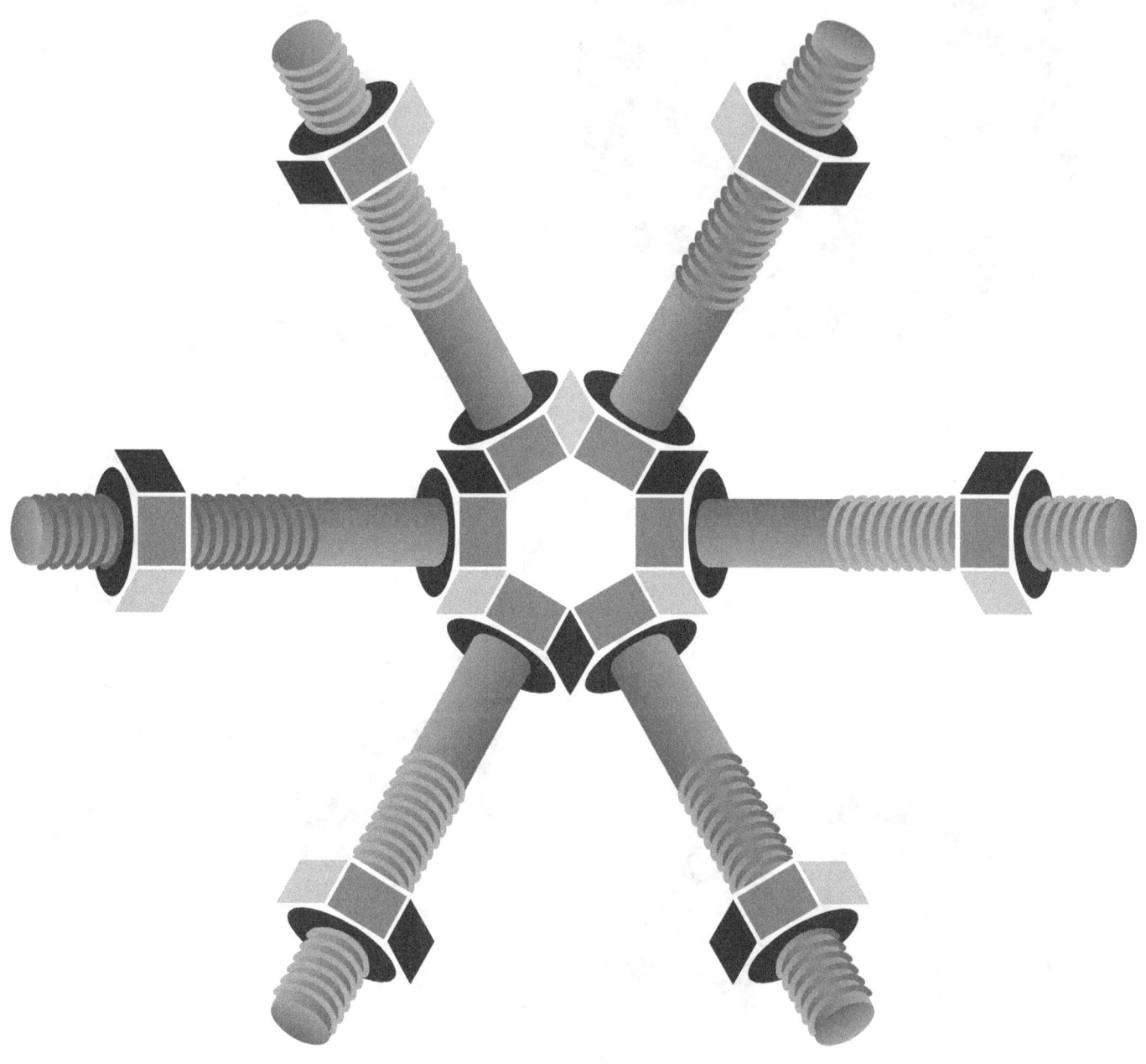

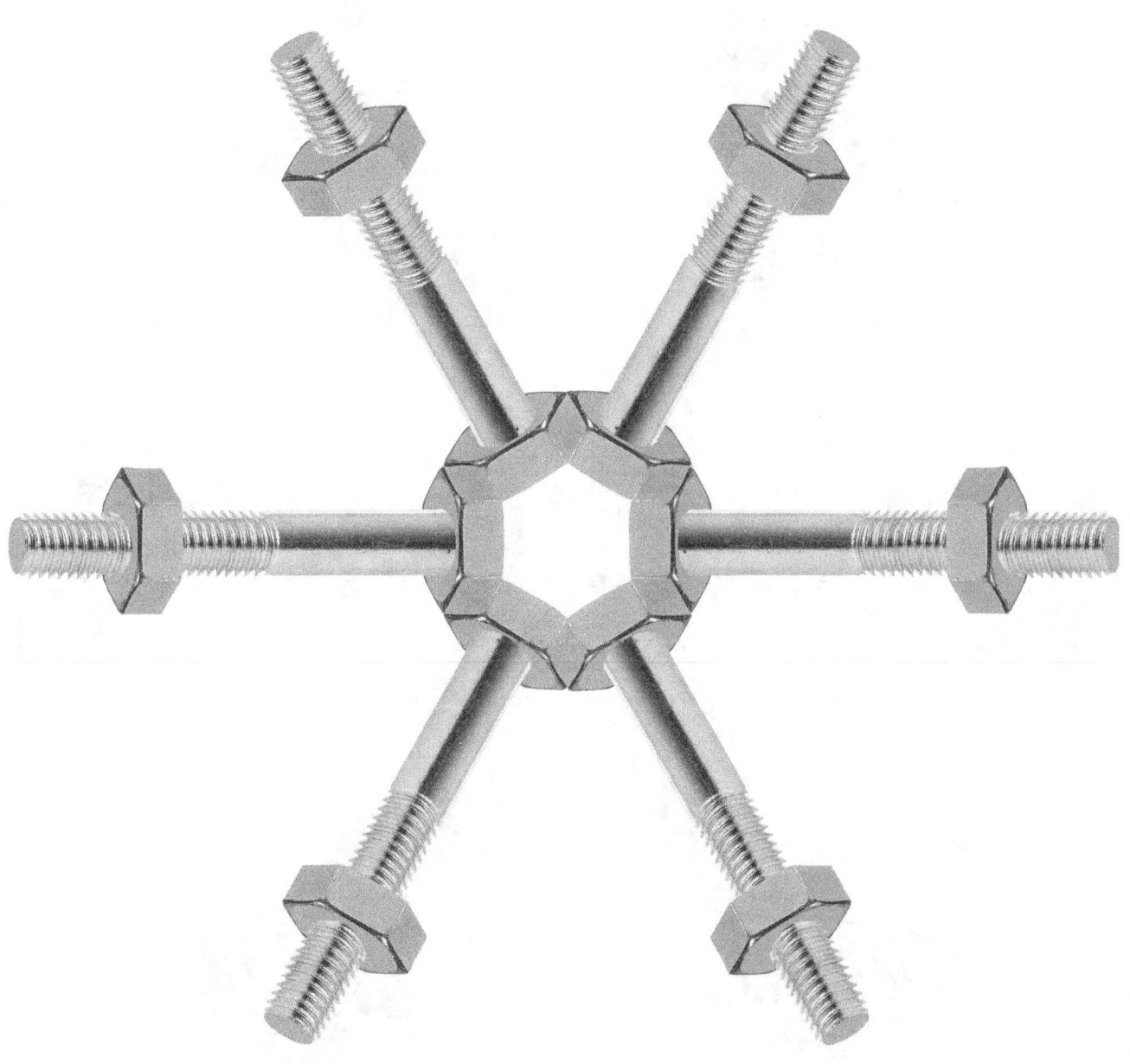

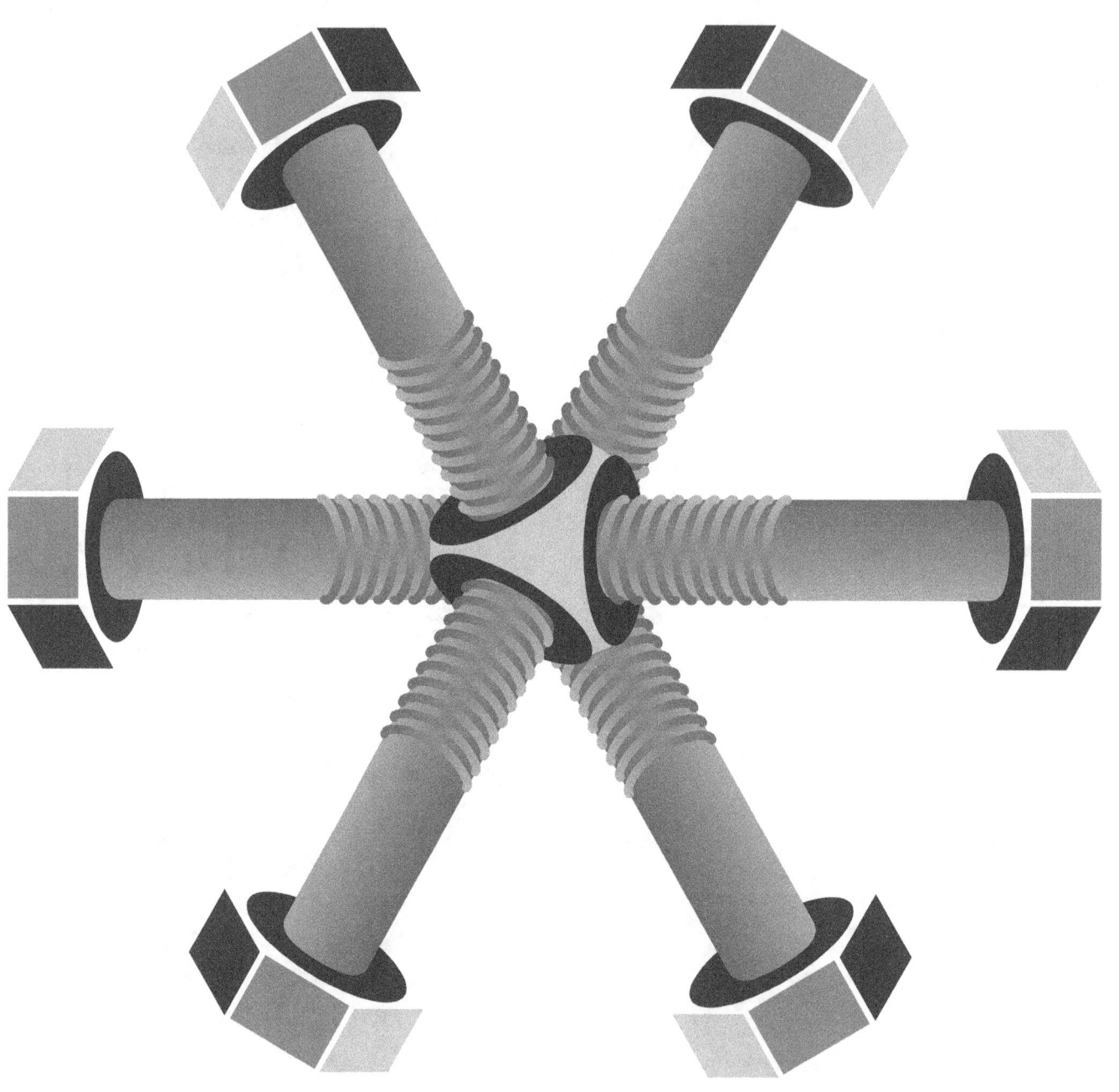

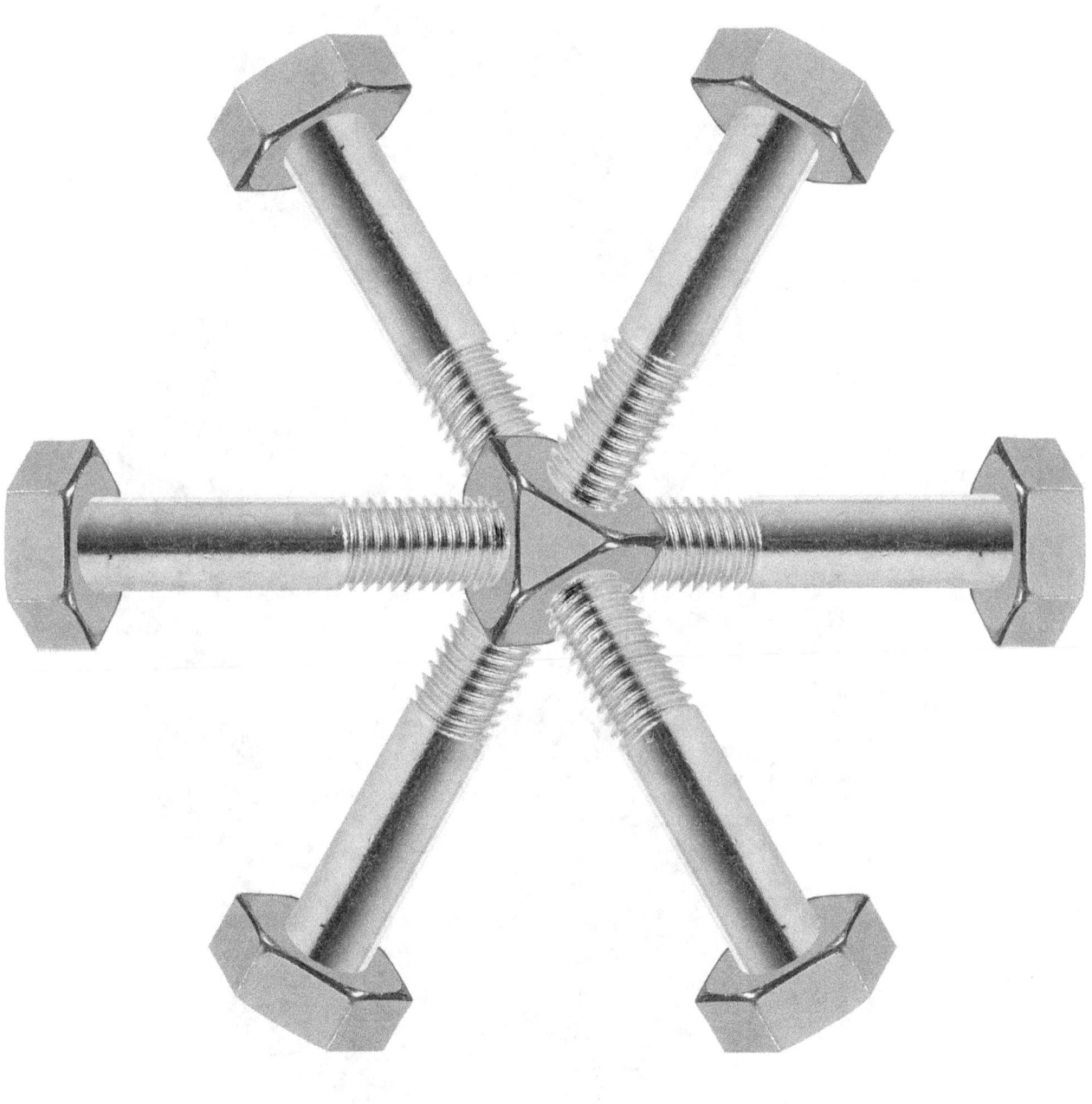

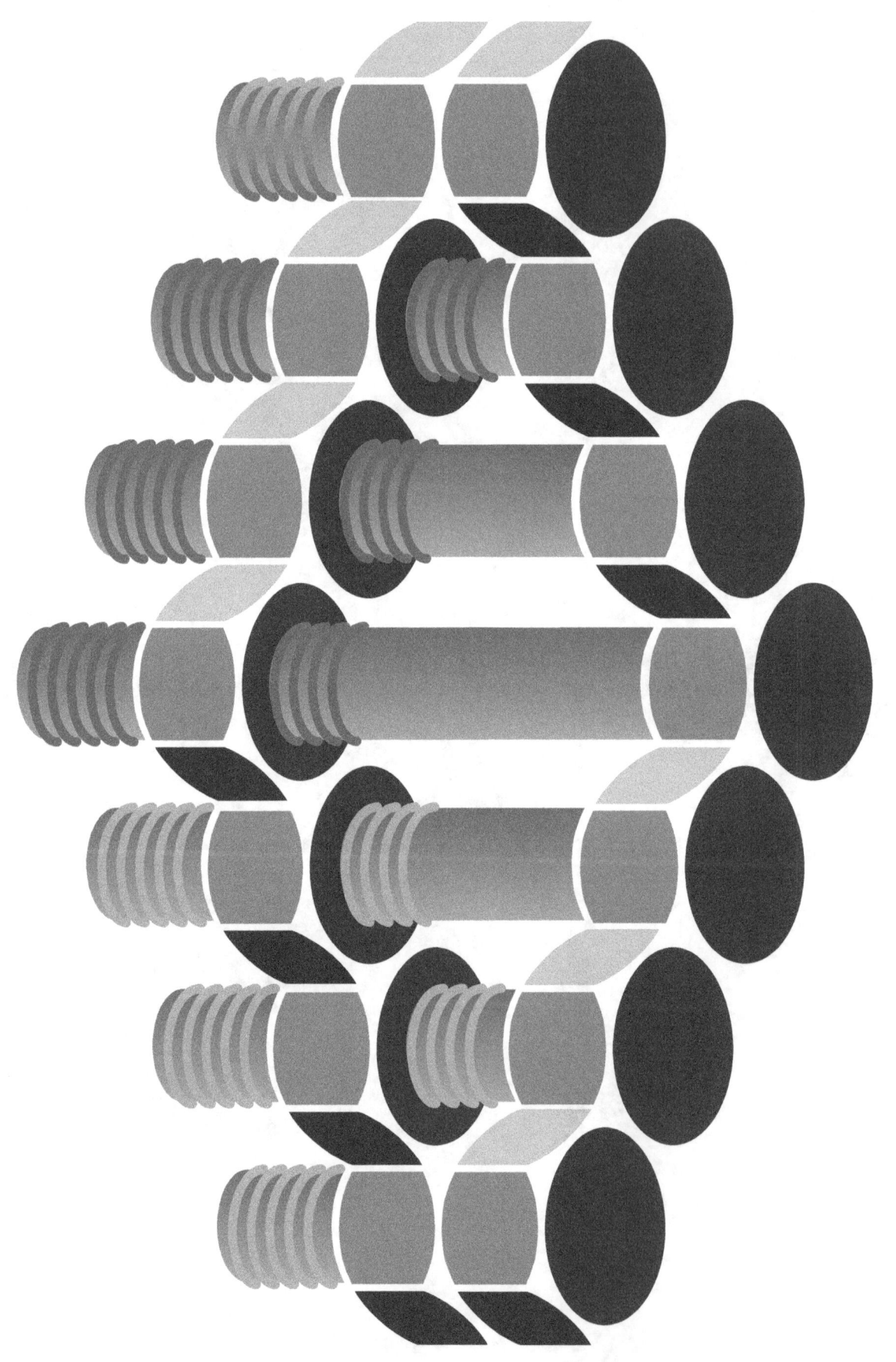

46

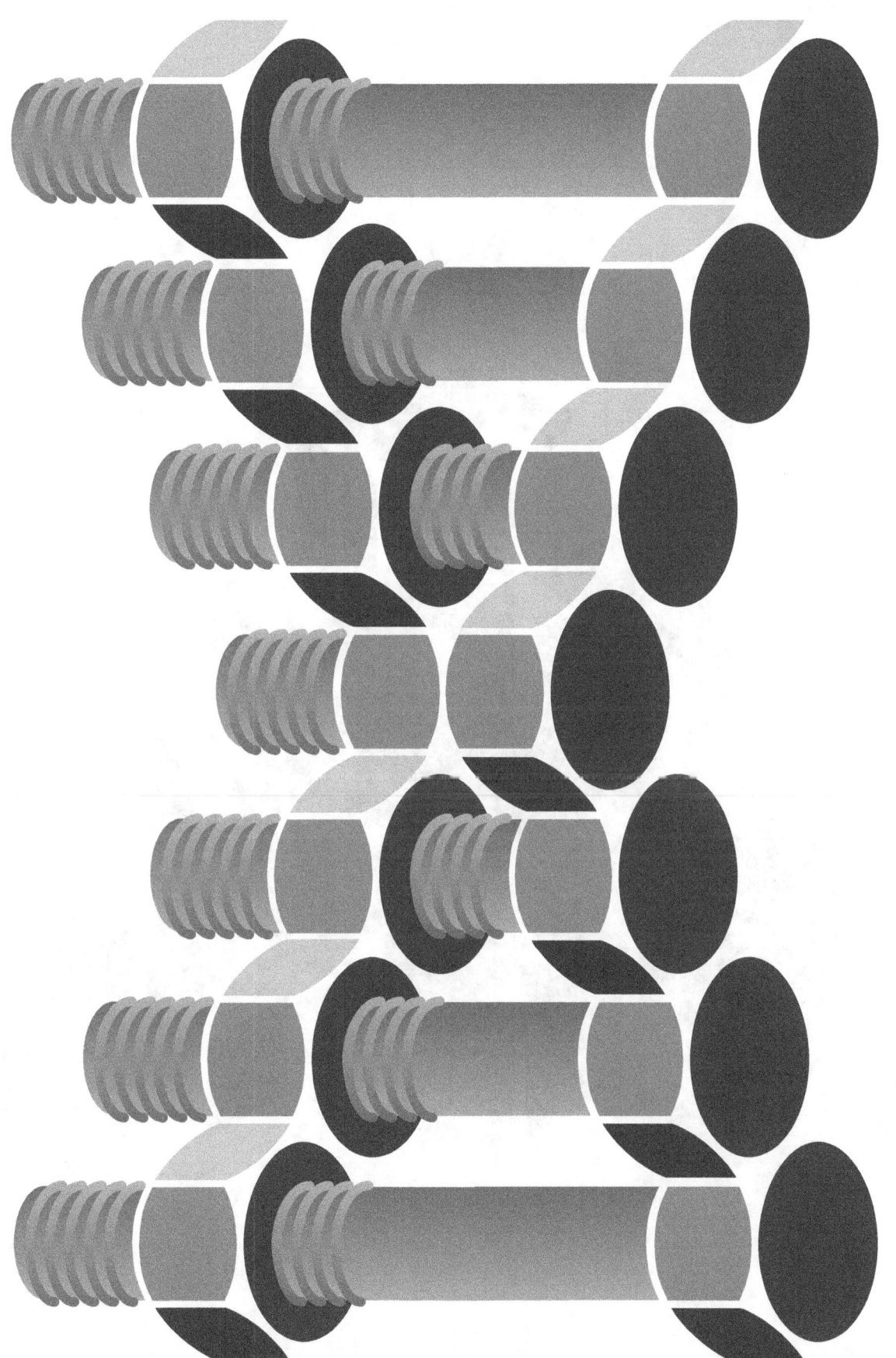

47

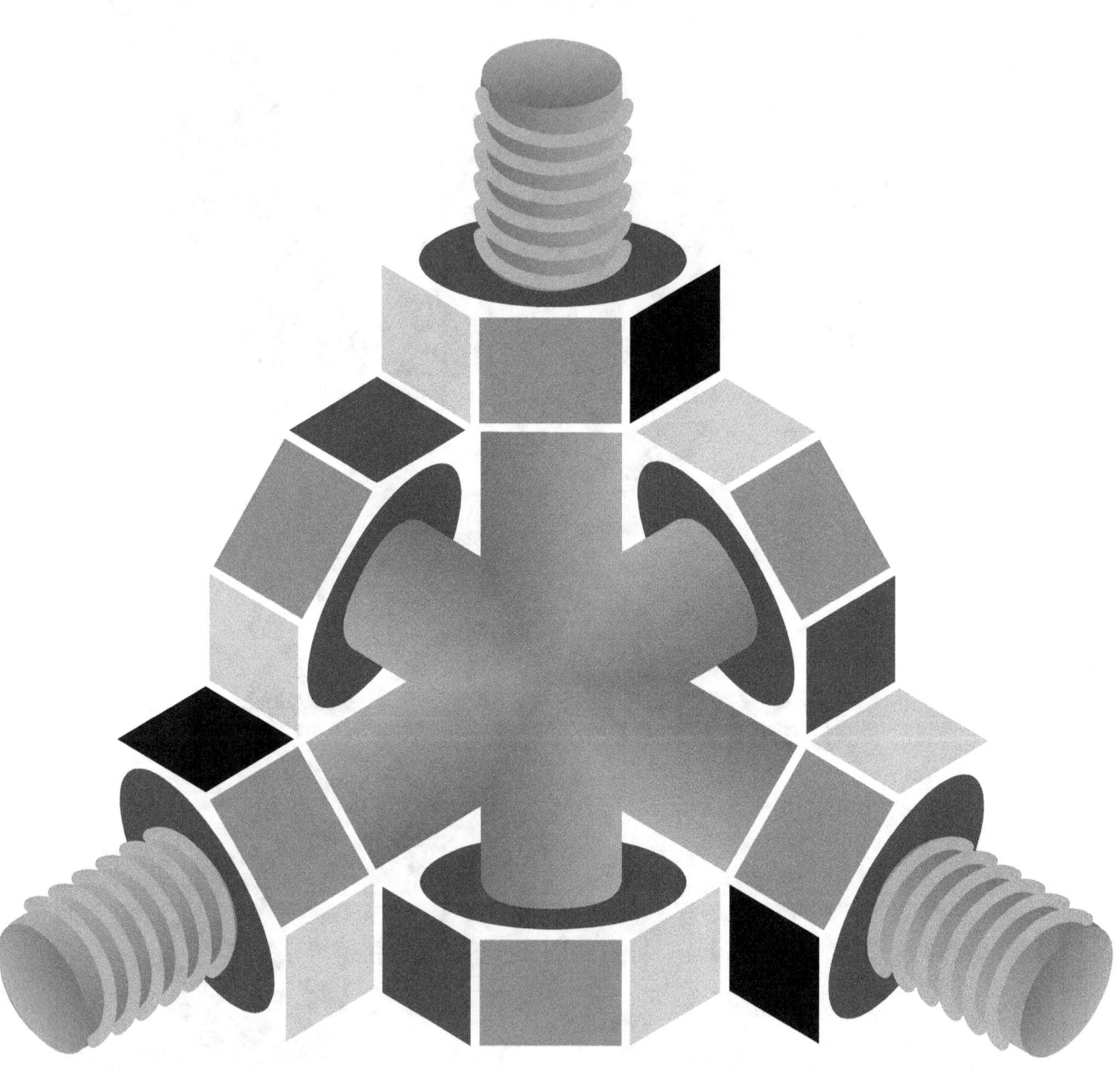

48

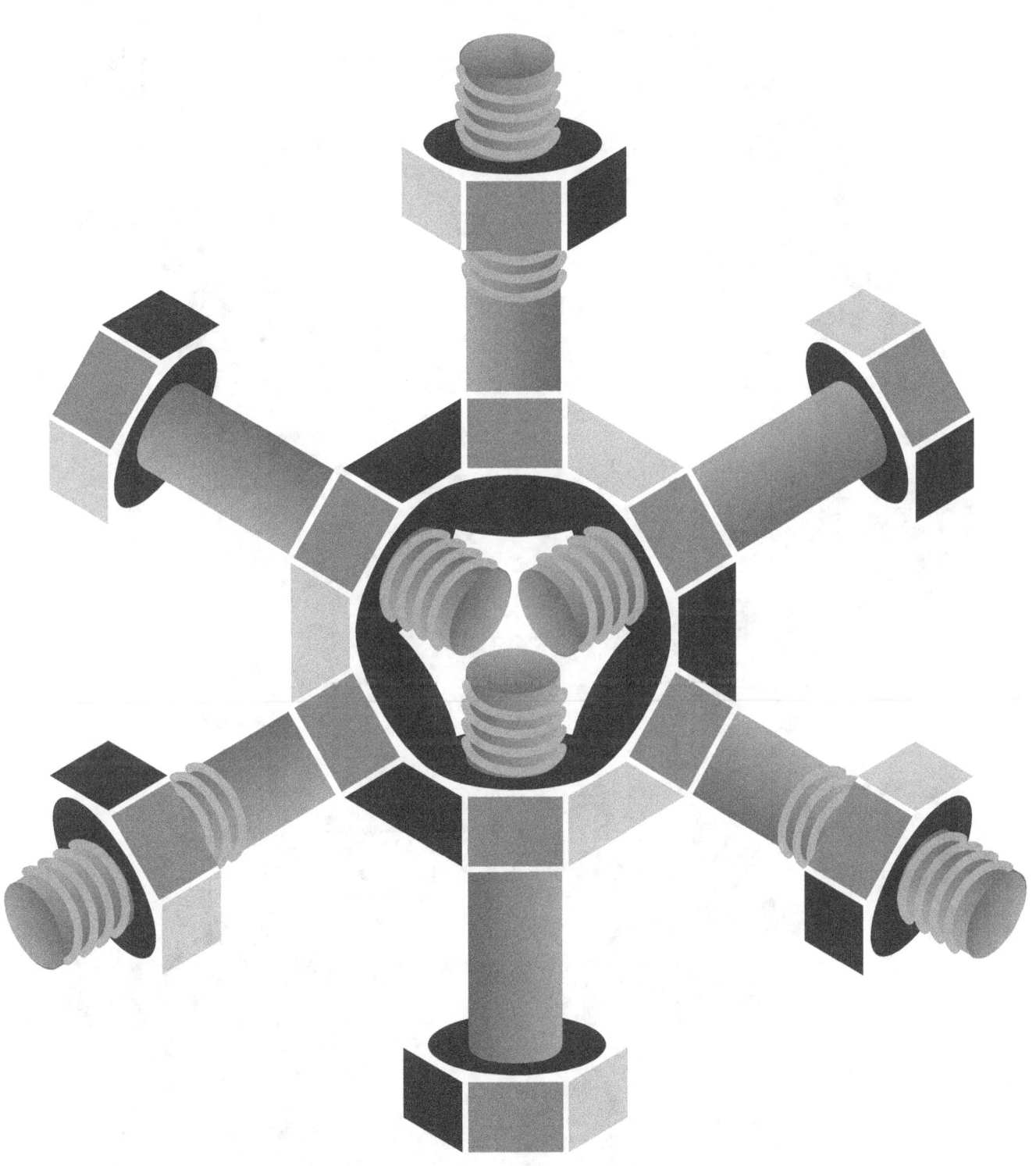

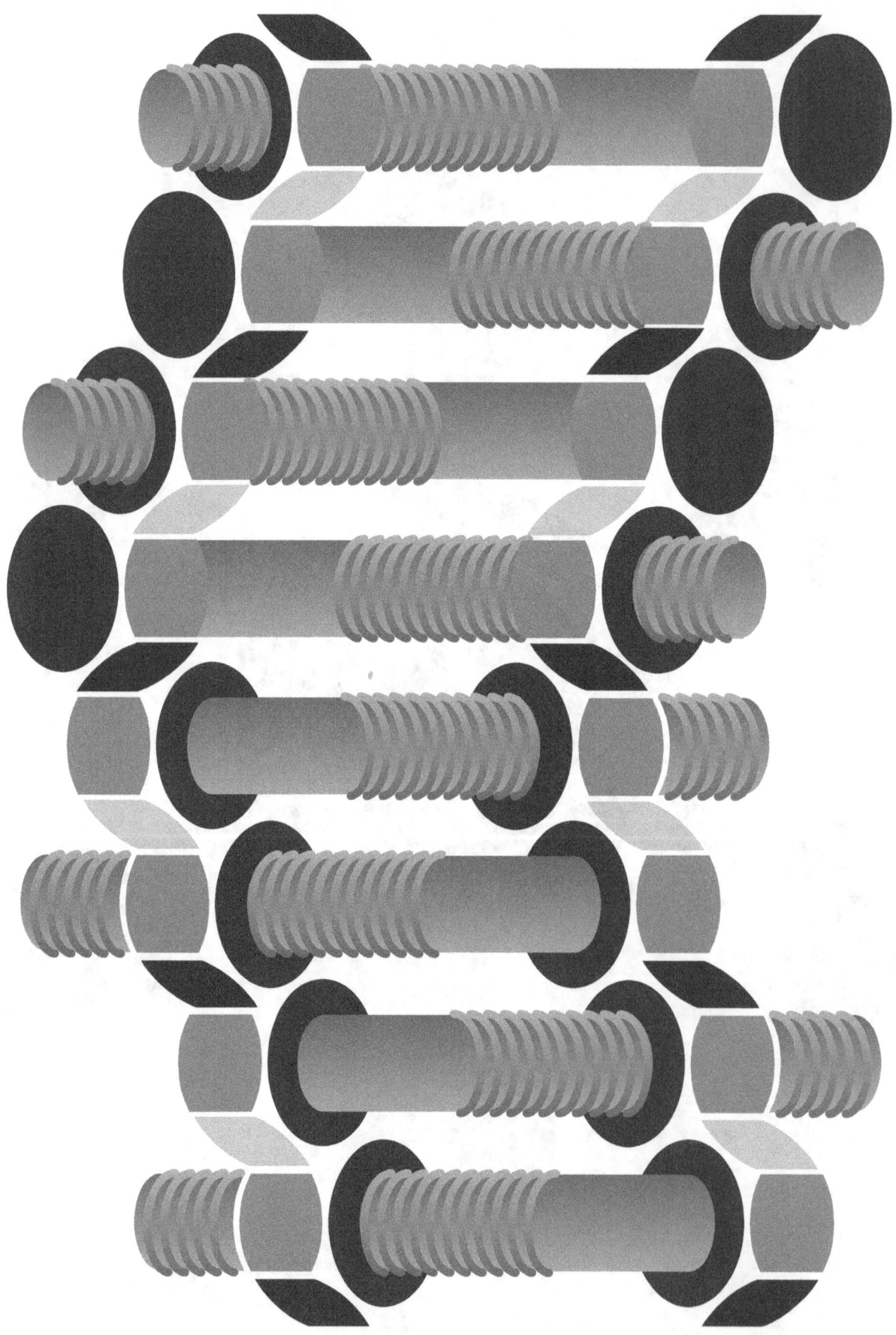

Shapes

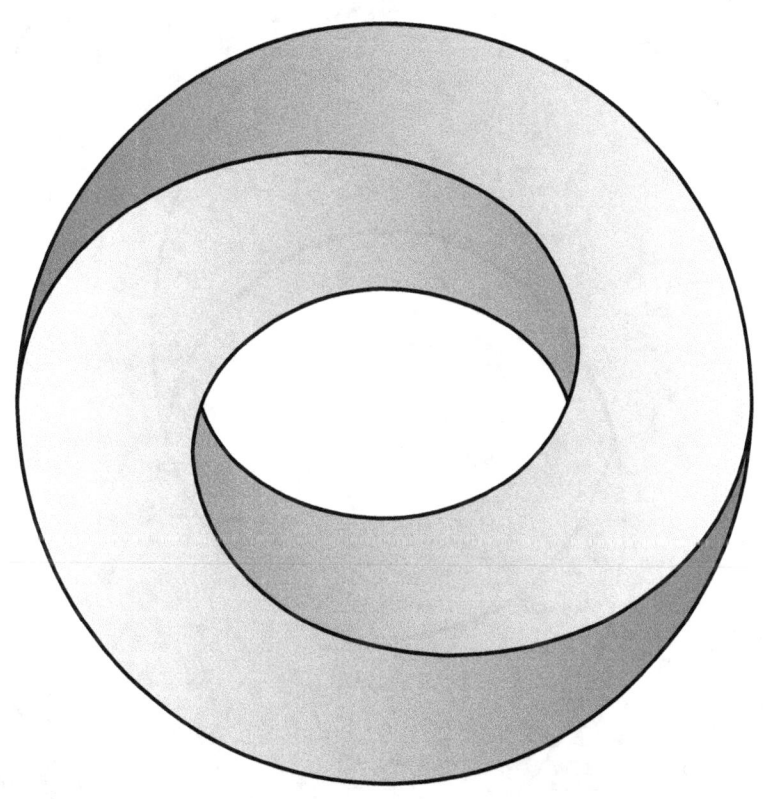

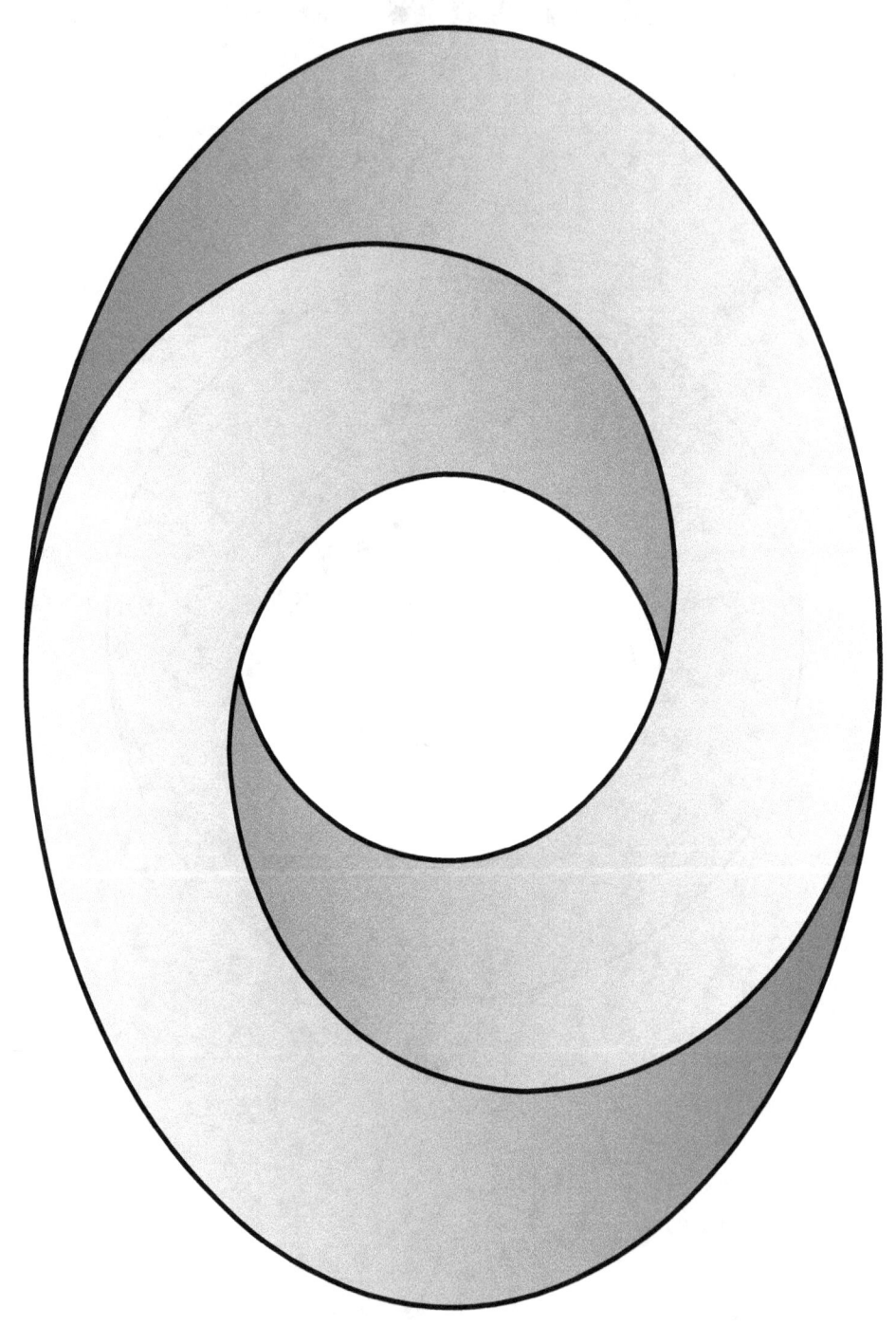

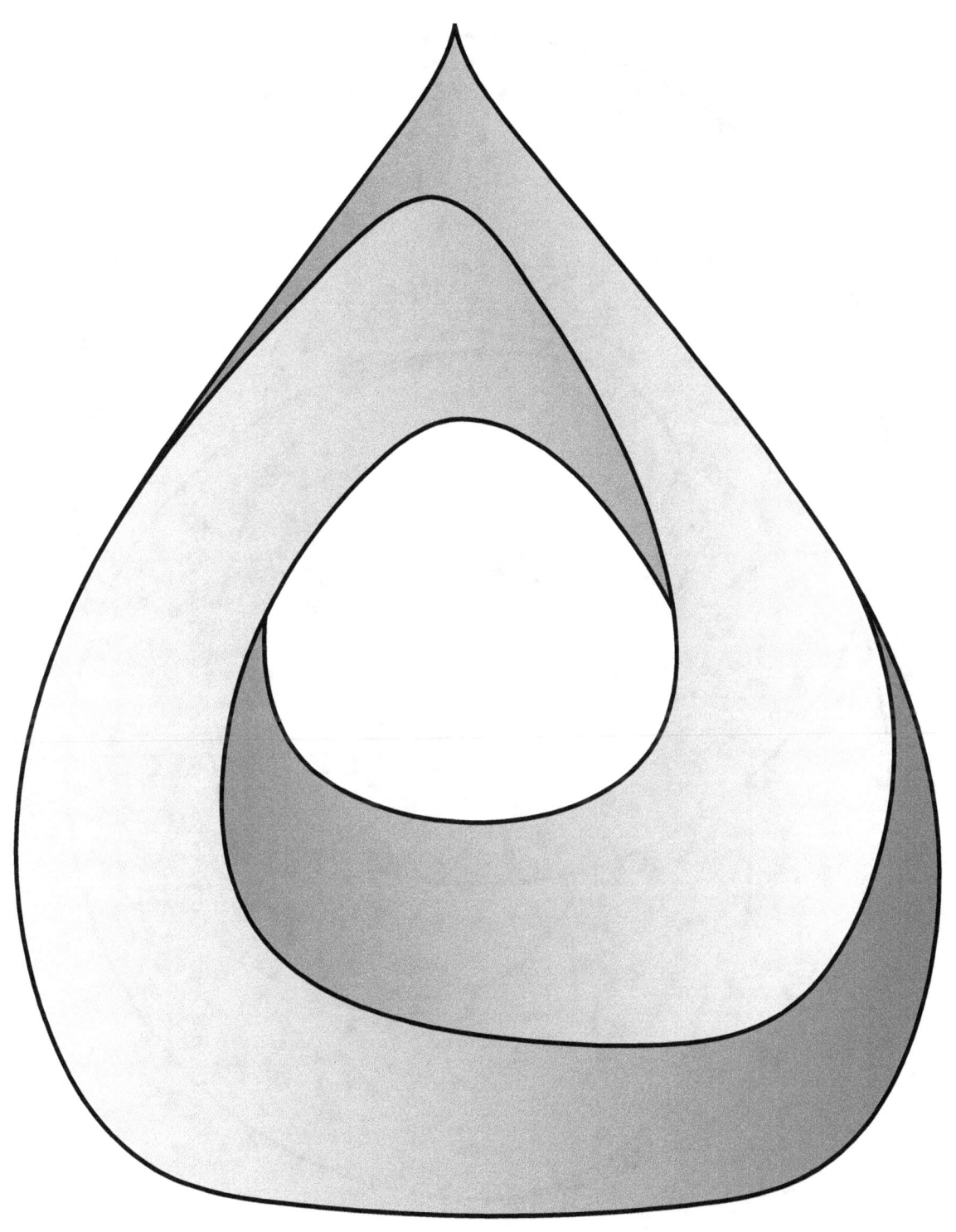

53

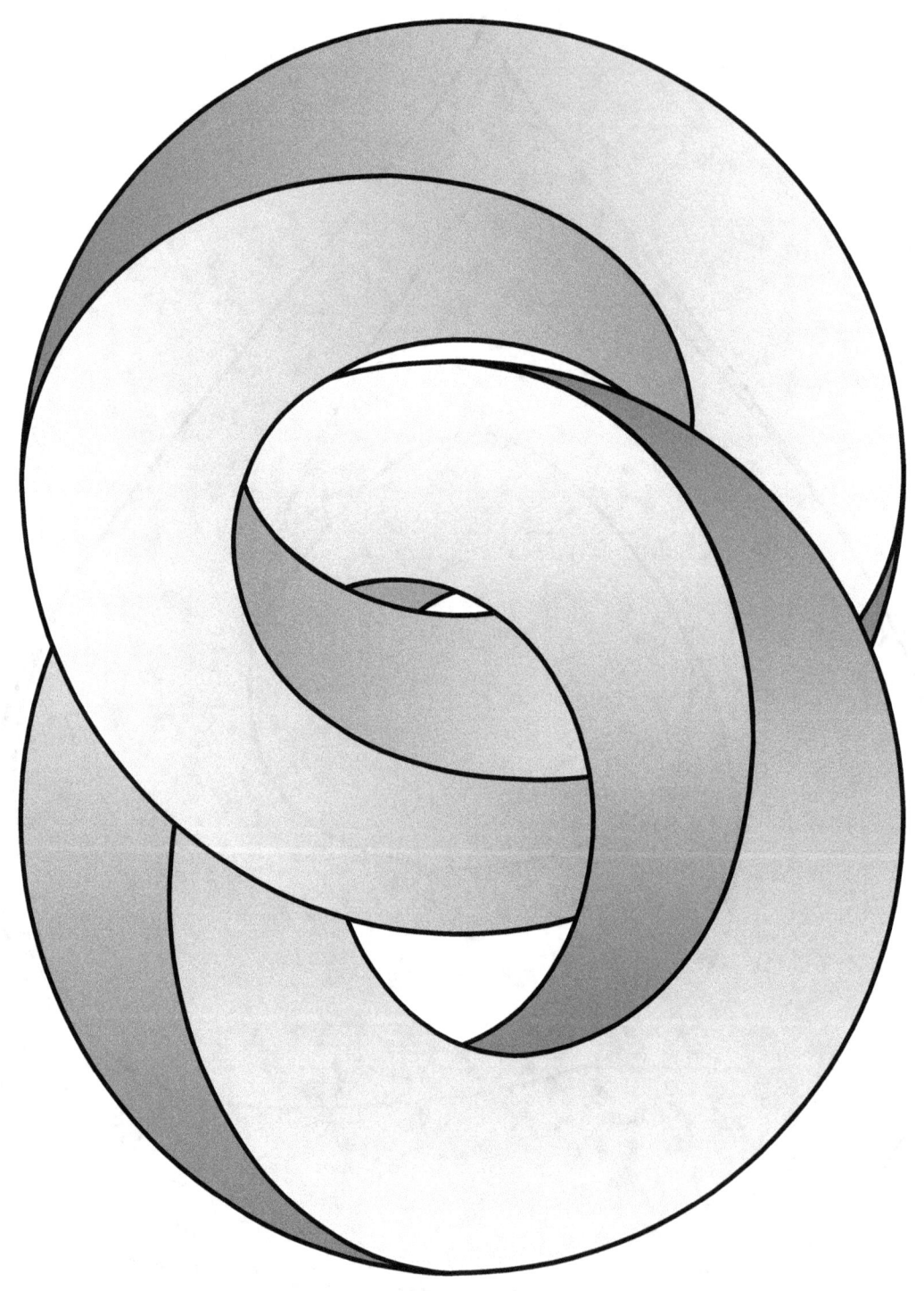

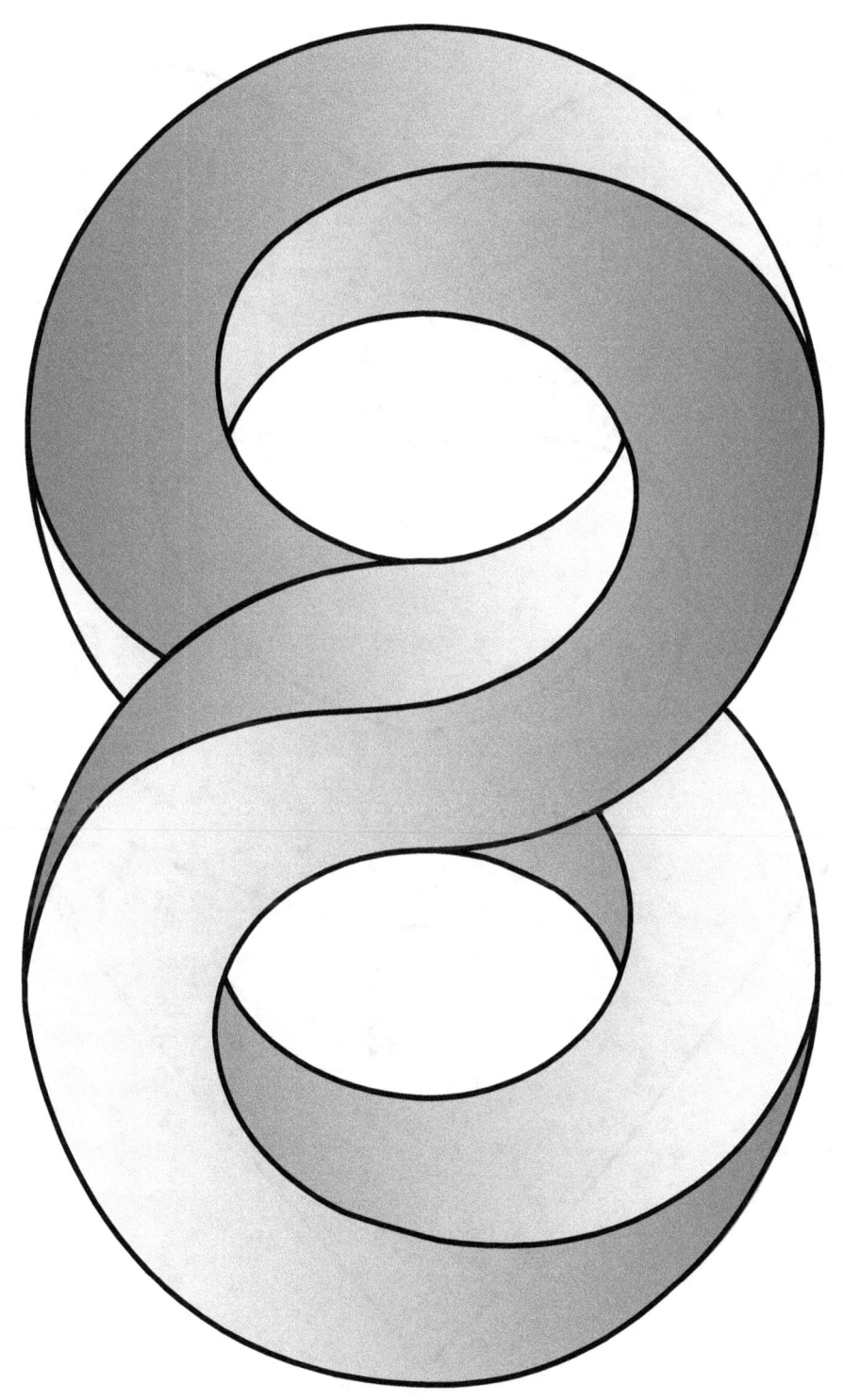

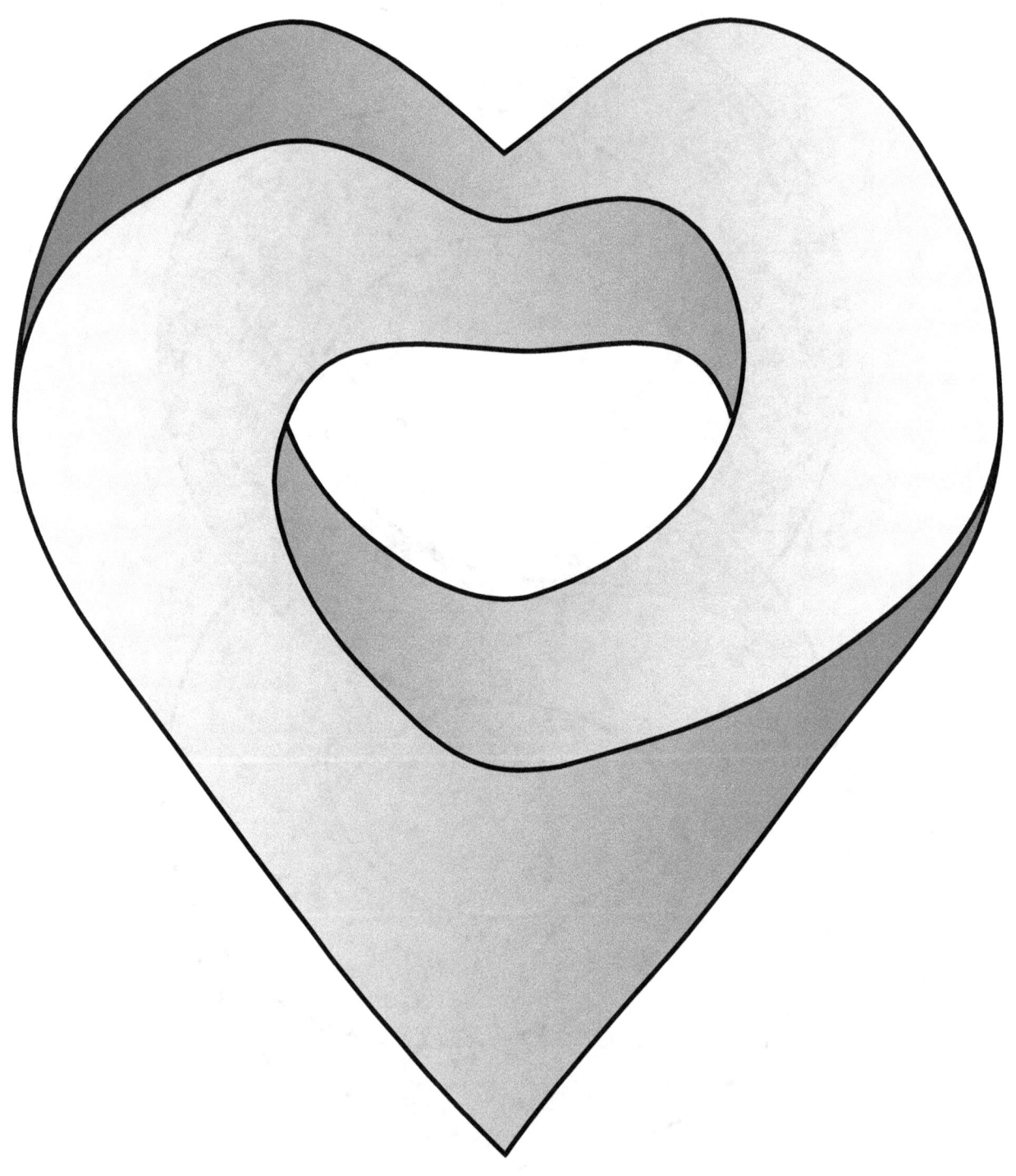

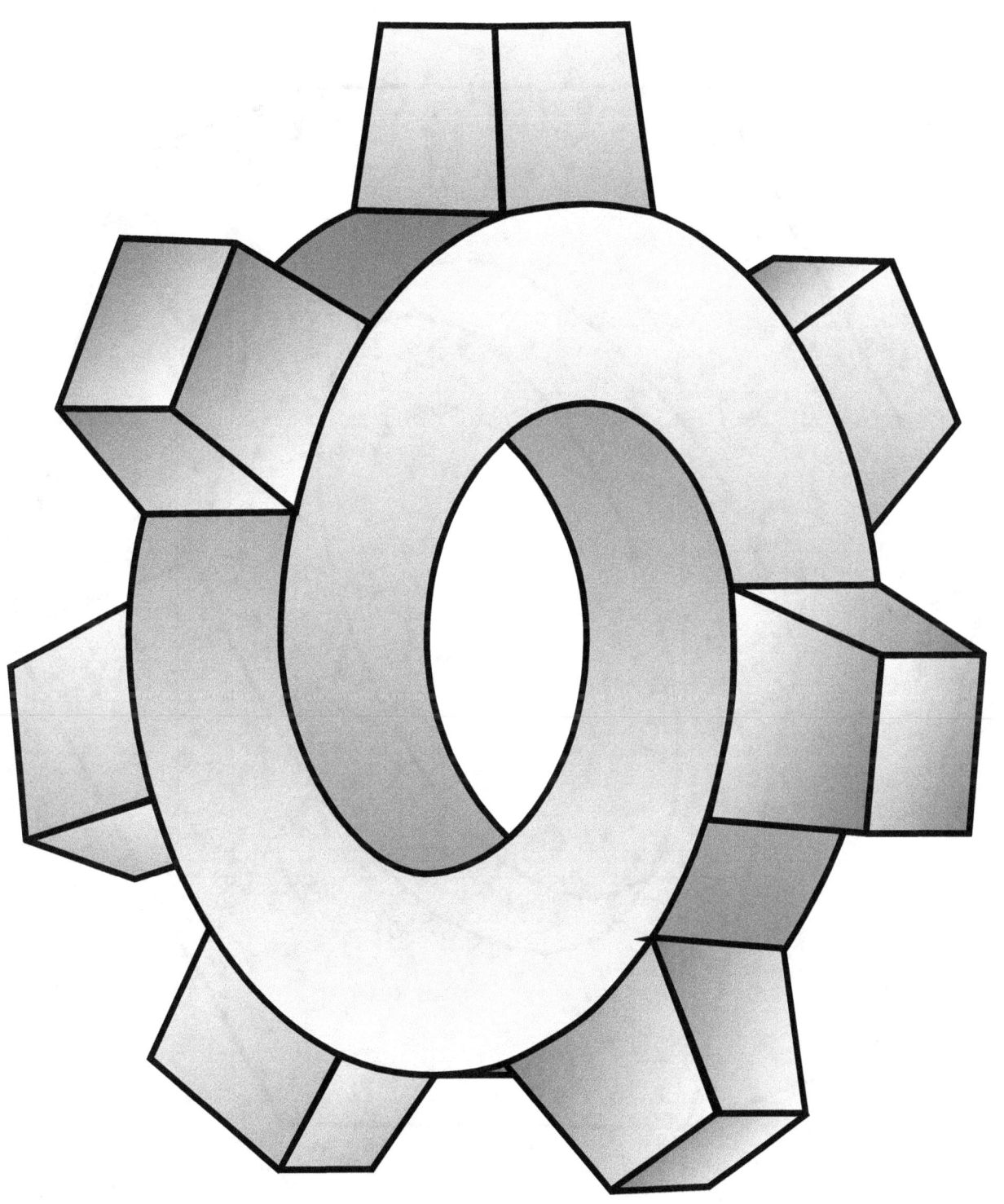

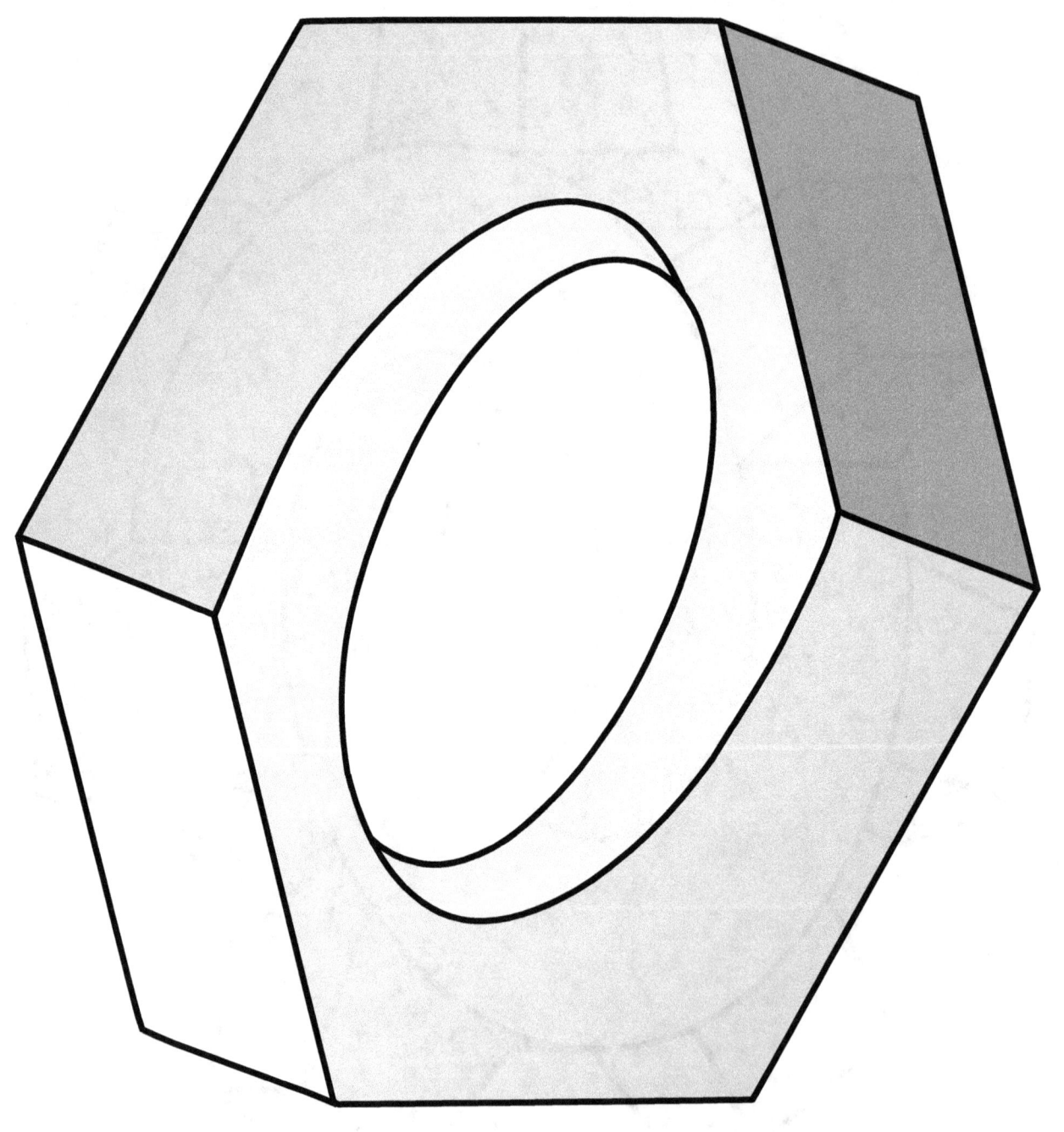

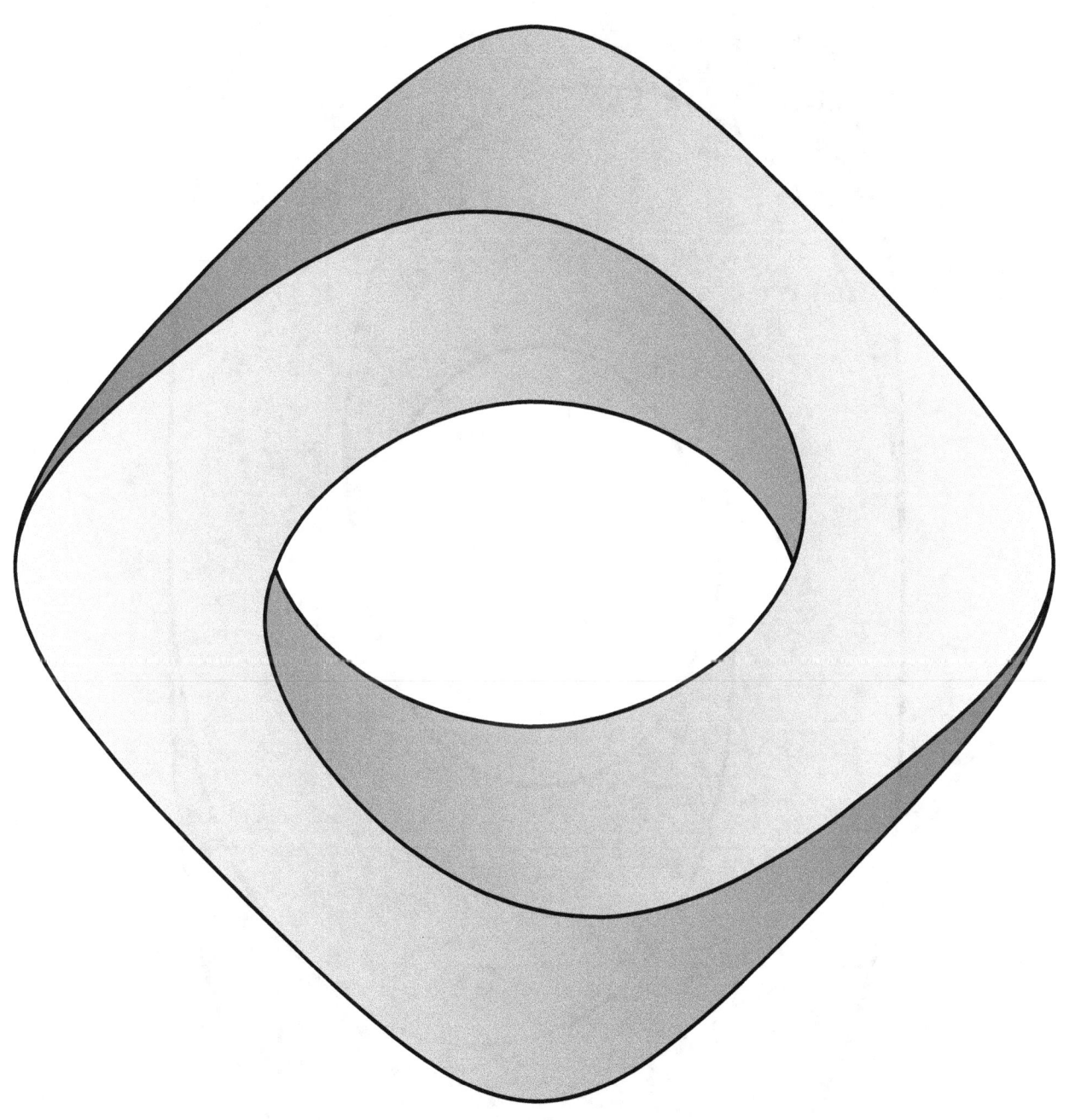

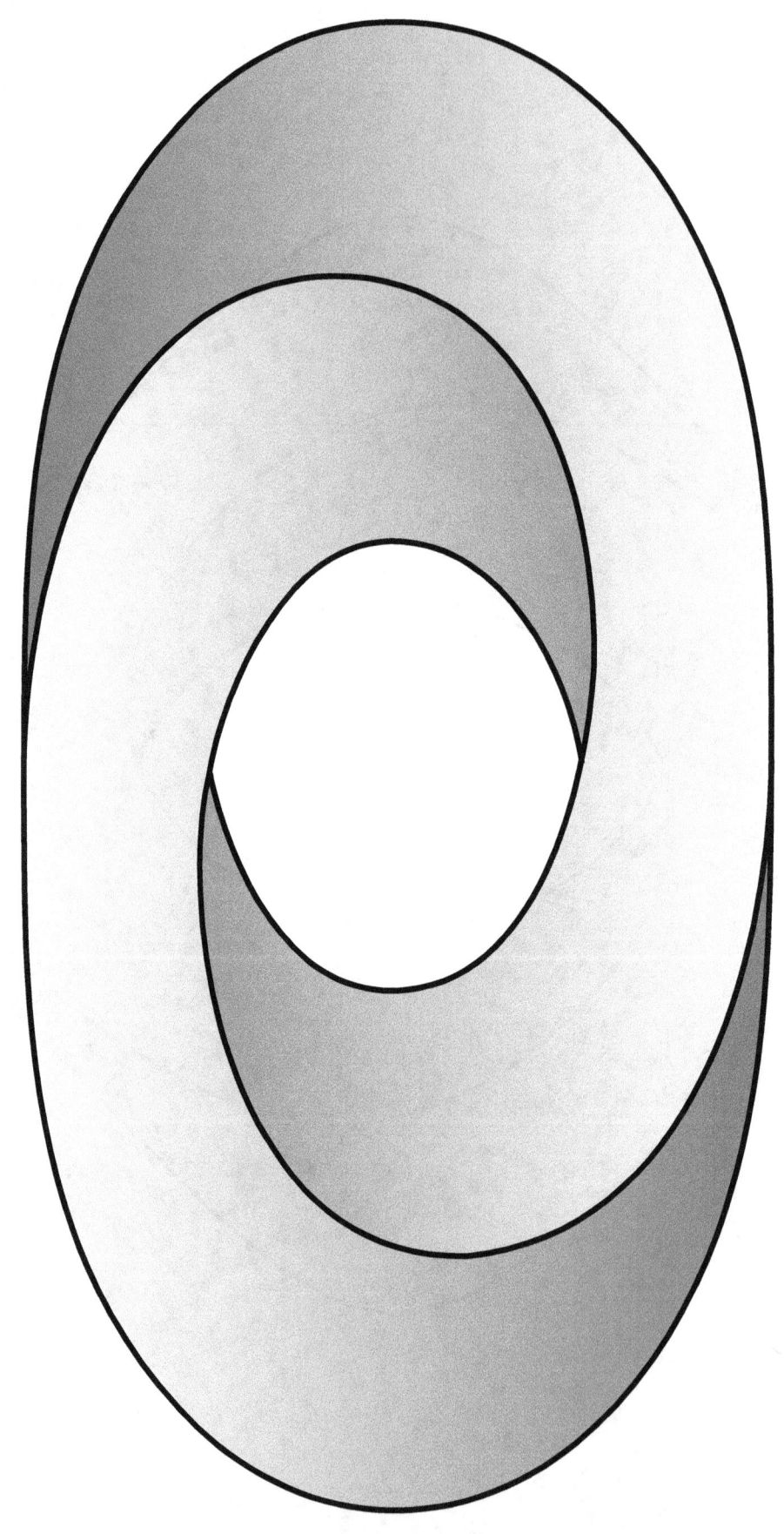

Patents Pending

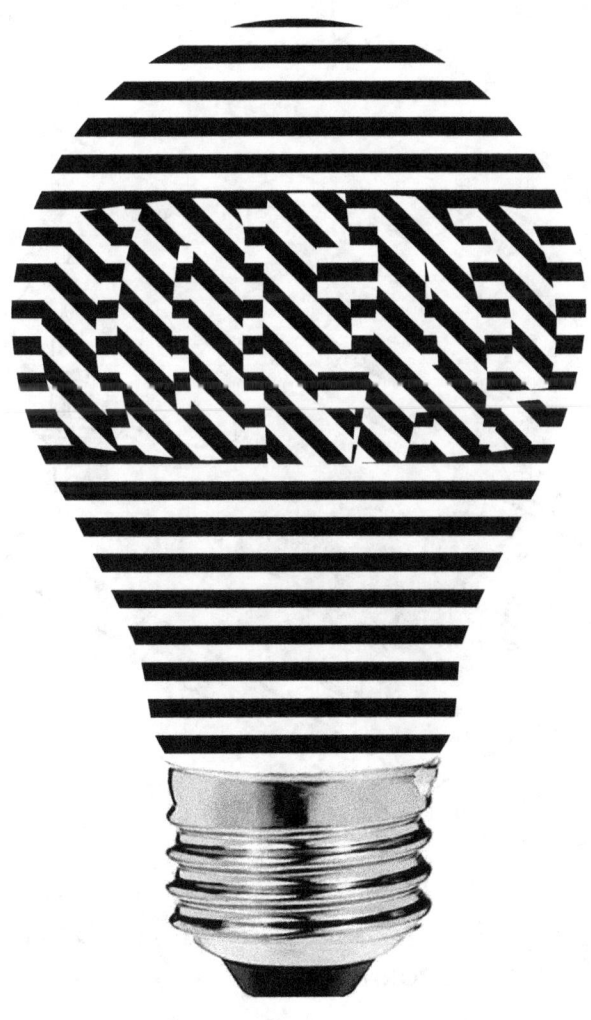

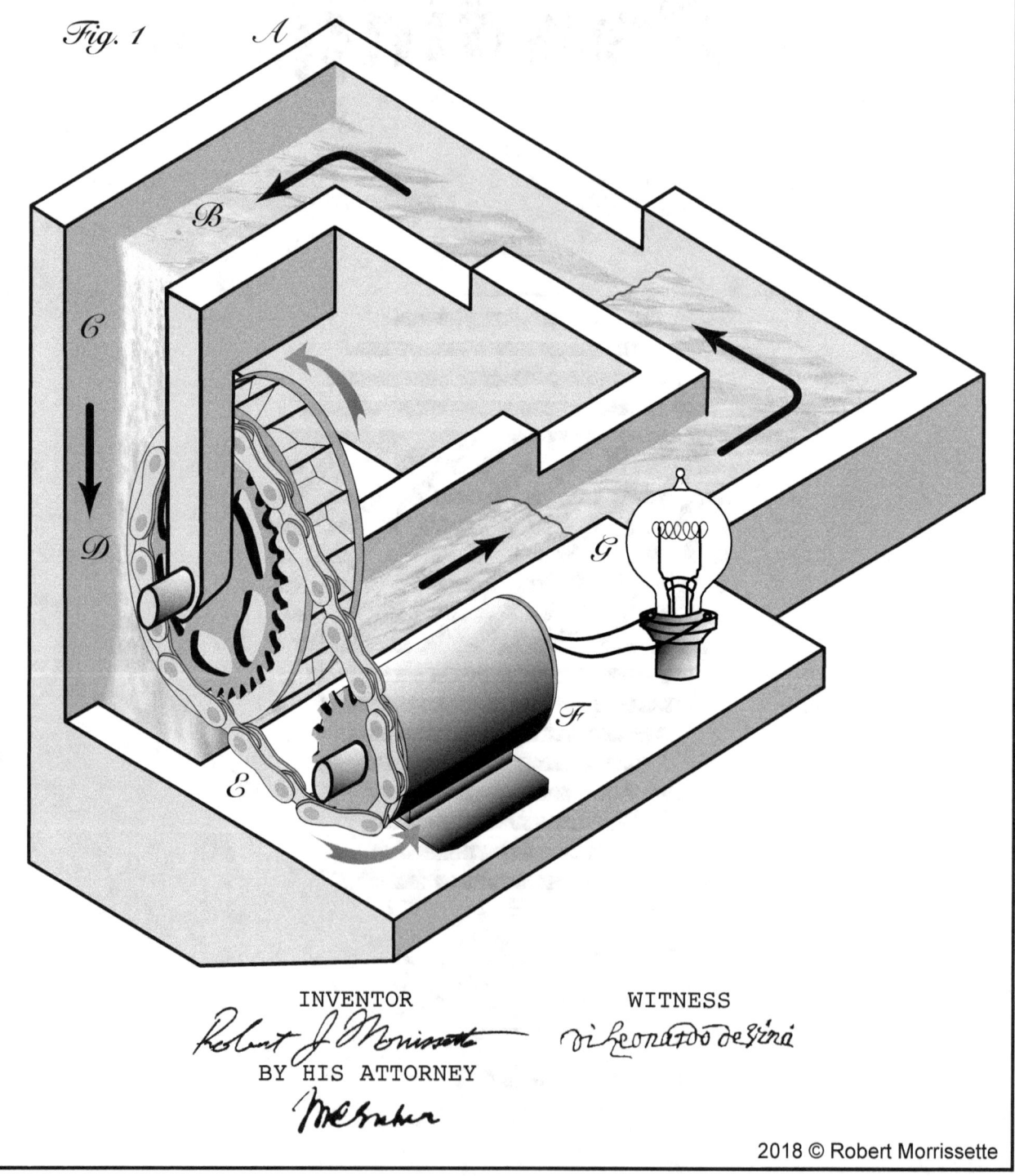

CHEESE SLICER TABLE

ROBERT JOHN MORRISSETTE
APRIL 01, 2018
PATENT PENDING

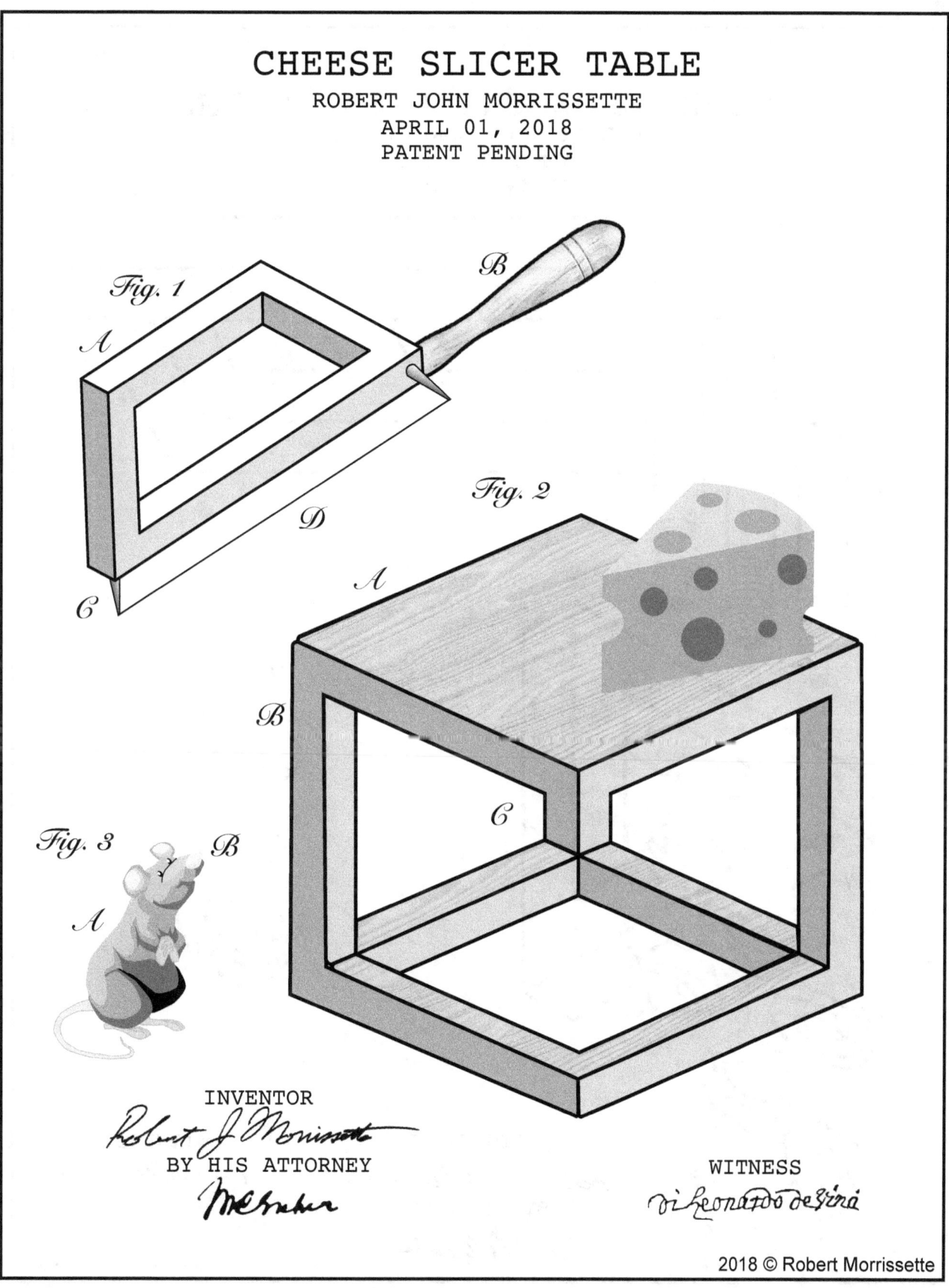

Fig. 1

Fig. 2

Fig. 3

INVENTOR

BY HIS ATTORNEY

WITNESS

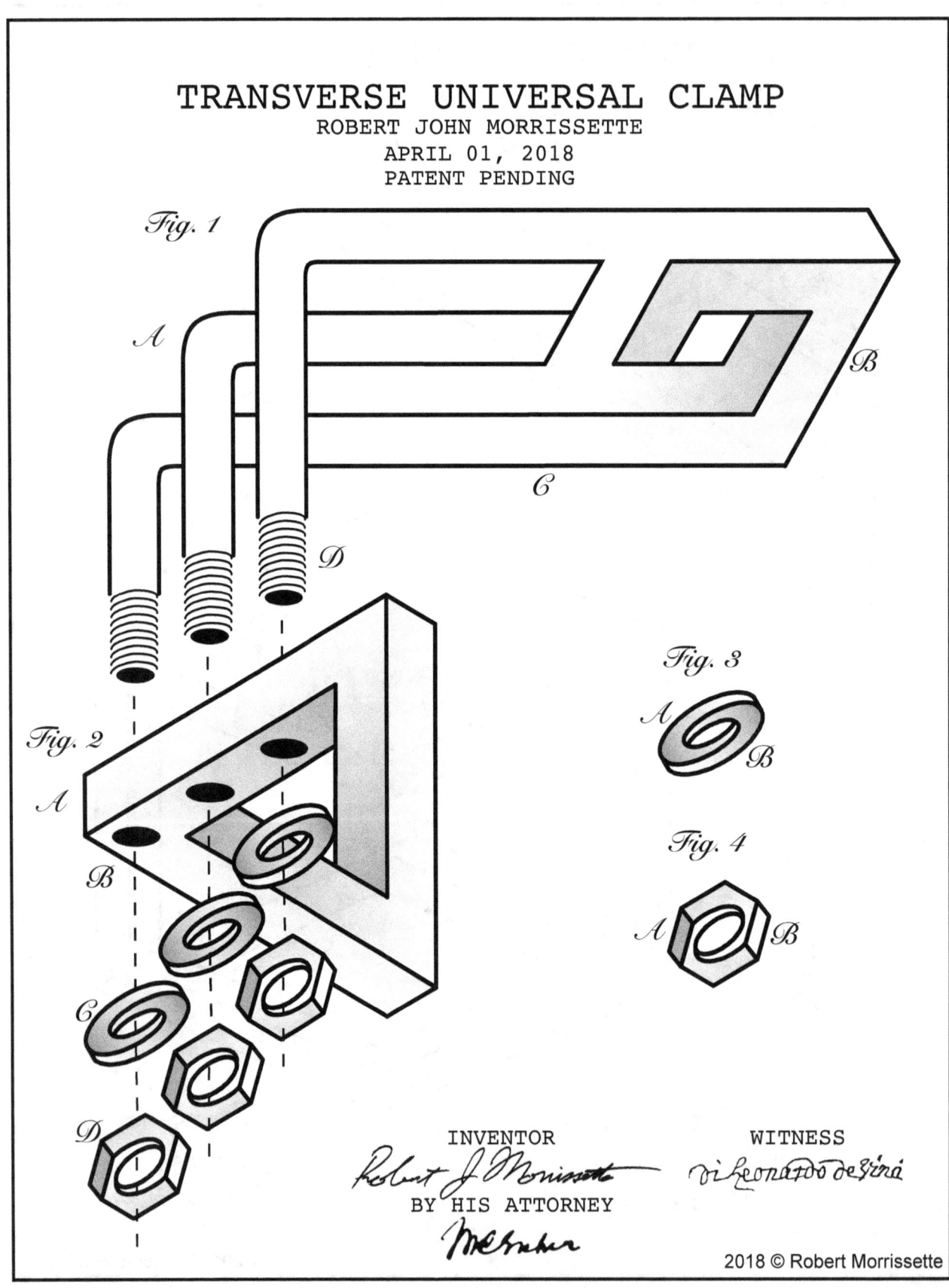

TRANSVERSE UNIVERSAL CLAMP
ROBERT JOHN MORRISSETTE
APRIL 01, 2018
PATENT PENDING

MULTIPLEX WATER FILTER SYSTEM

ROBERT JOHN MORRISSETTE
APRIL 01, 2018
PATENT PENDING

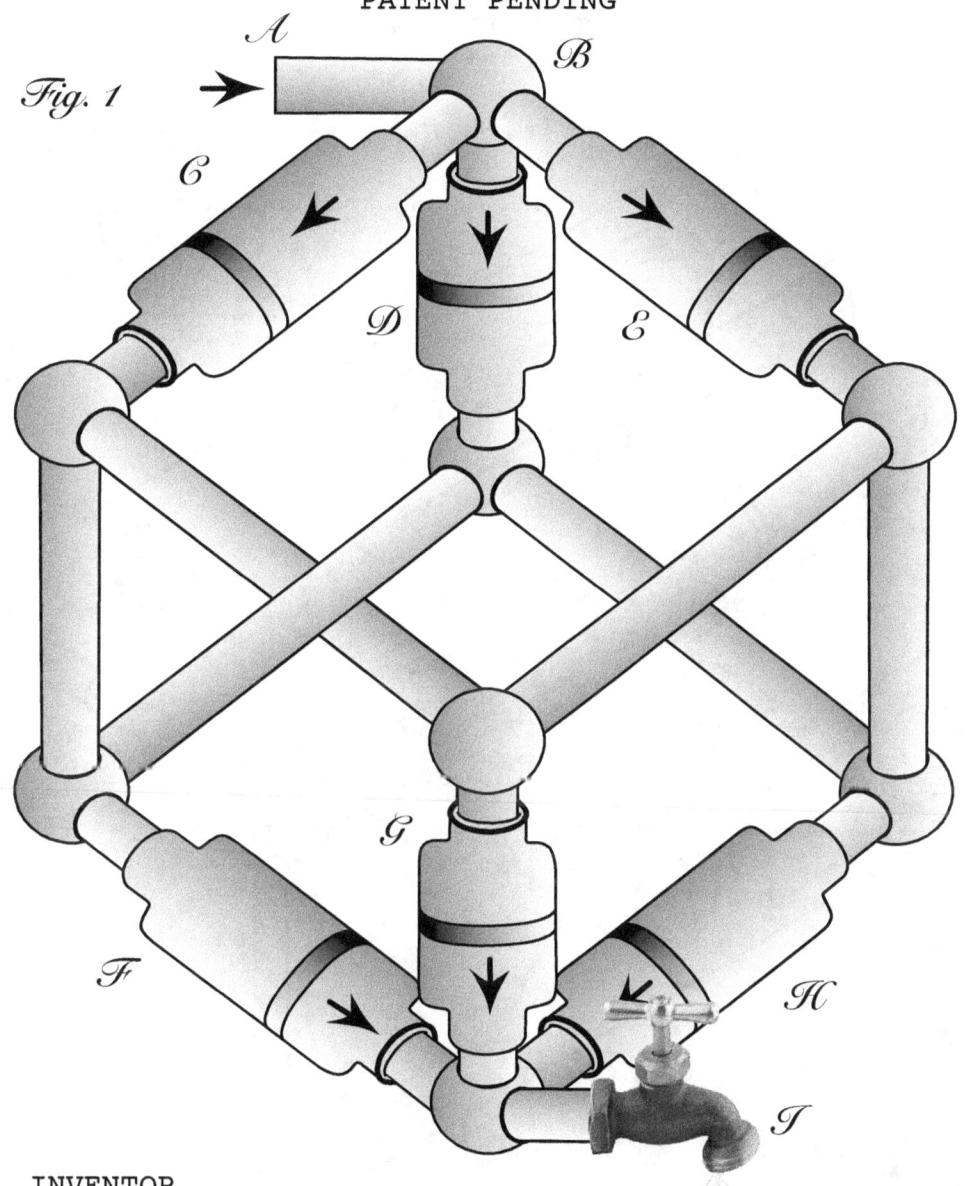

Fig. 1

INVENTOR

BY HIS ATTORNEY

WITNESS

INVERSABLE HINGE
ROBERT JOHN MORRISSETTE
APRIL 01, 2018
PATENT PENDING

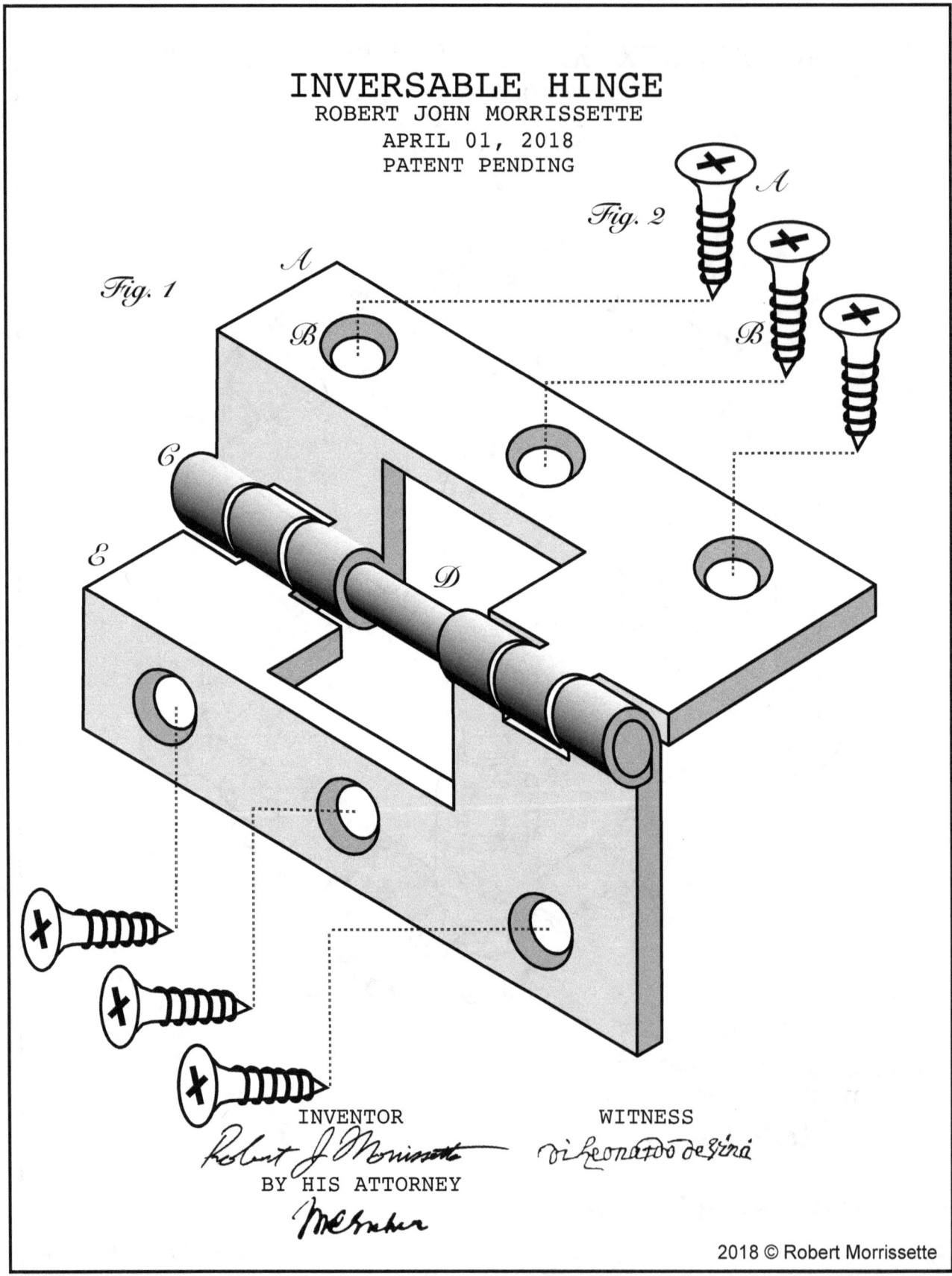

Fig. 2

Fig. 1

A

B

C

D

E

A

B

INVENTOR

WITNESS

BY HIS ATTORNEY

FLEX-STEP, FIVE-LEGGED LADDER

ROBERT JOHN MORRISSETTE
APRIL 01, 2018
PATENT PENDING

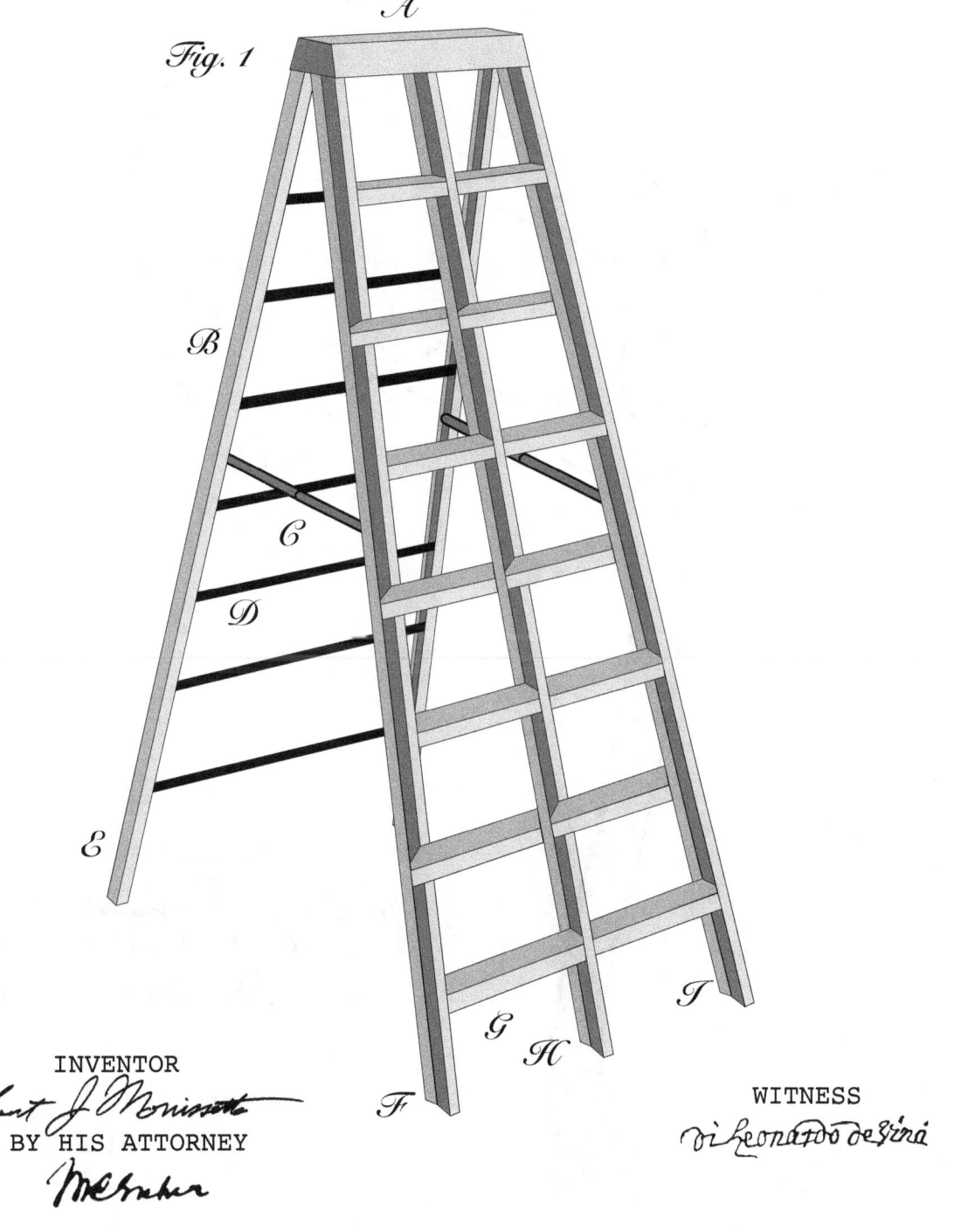

INVENTOR

BY HIS ATTORNEY

WITNESS

MAX–AXE
ROBERT JOHN MORRISSETTE
APRIL 01, 2018
PATENT PENDING

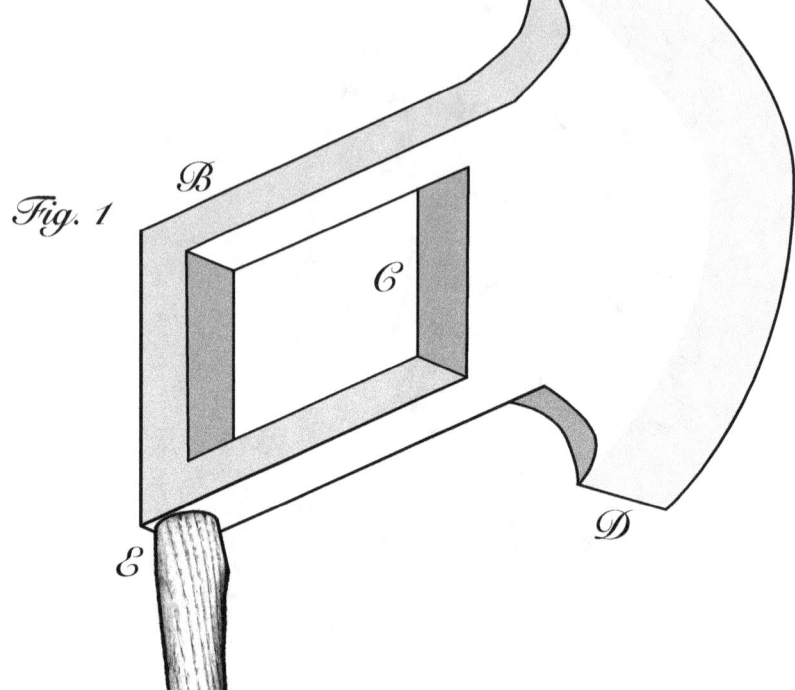

Fig. 1

INVENTOR

Robert J. Morrissette

BY HIS ATTORNEY

WITNESS

di Leonardo de Vinci

ELECTRONIC ADJUSTABLE TUNING FORK

ROBERT JOHN MORRISSETTE
APRIL 01, 2018
PATENT PENDING

Fig. 1

Fig. 2

Frequencies

Note	Hz	Note	Hz
A	220.00	$D_4^\#$ E_4^b	311.13
$A_3^\#$ B_3^b	233.08	E_4	329.63
B_3	246.94	F_4	349.99
C_4	261.63	$F_4^\#$ G_4^b	369.99
$C_4^\#$ D_4^b	277.18	G_4	392.00
D_4	293.66	$G_4^\#$ A_4^b	415.30

Fig. 3

INVENTOR

Robert J. Morrissette

BY HIS ATTORNEY

WITNESS

di Leonardo de Grá

2018 © Robert Morrissette

69

SOLAR-POWERED BARRICADE

ROBERT JOHN MORRISSETTE
APRIL 01, 2018
PATENT PENDING

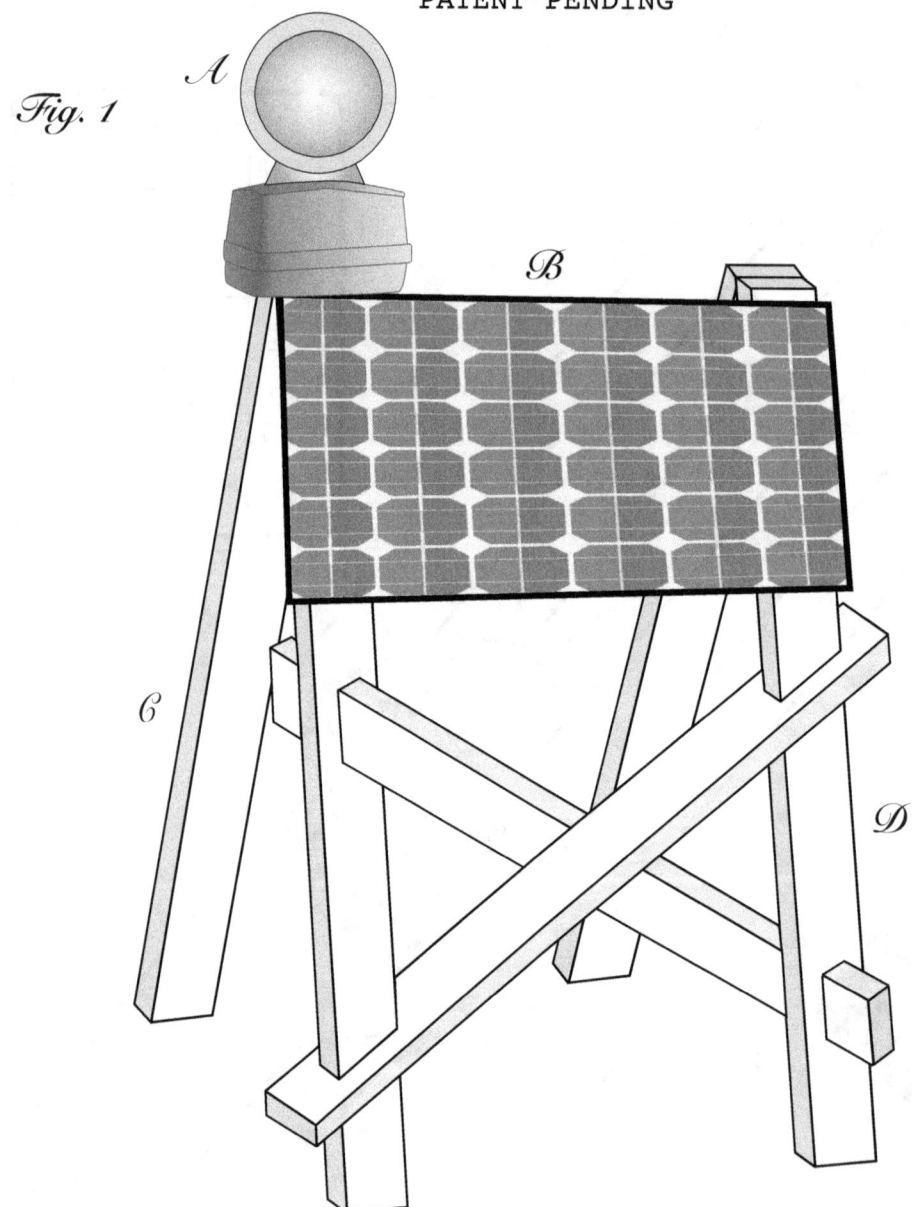

Fig. 1

INVENTOR

BY HIS ATTORNEY

WITNESS

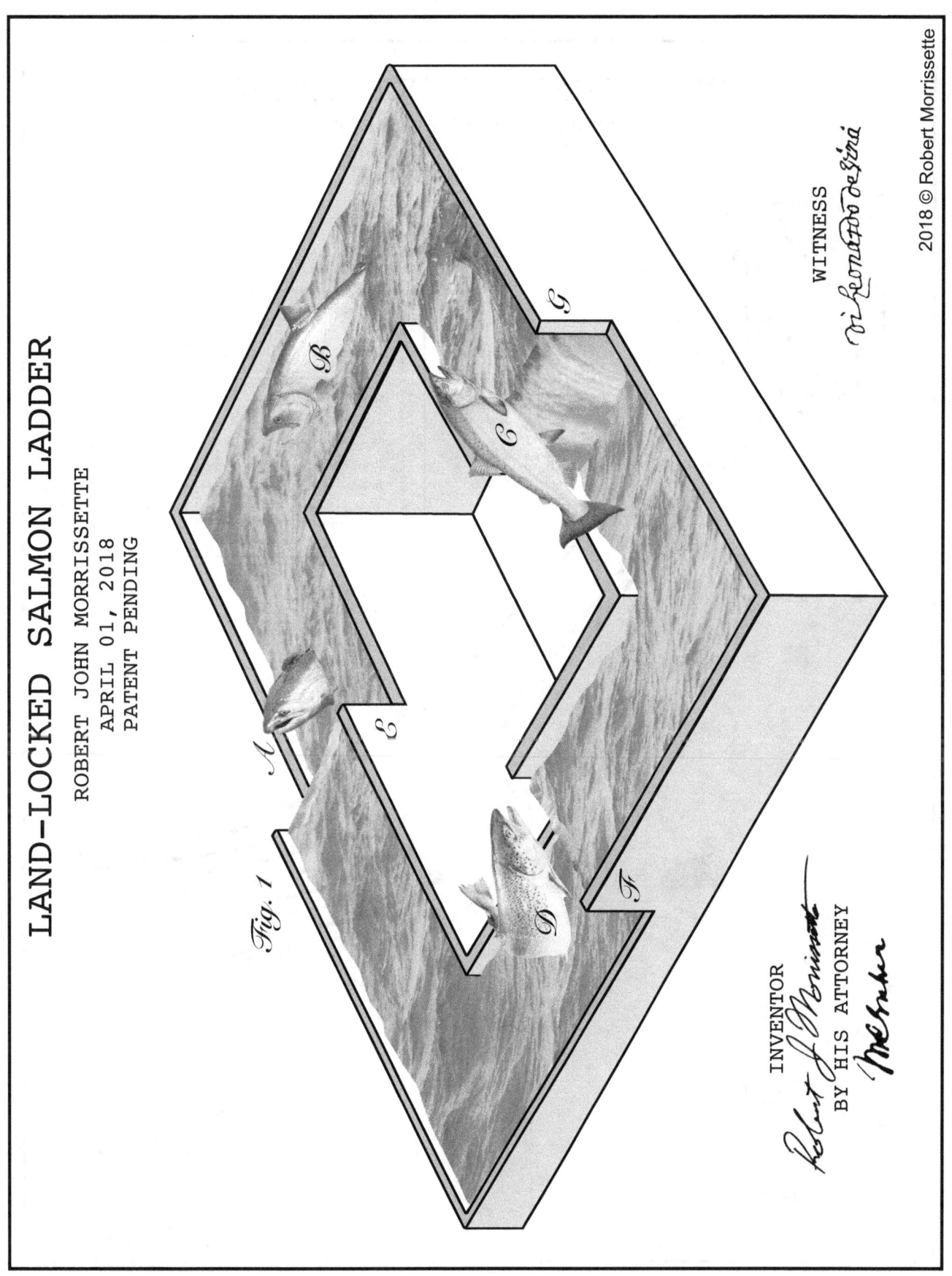

LAND–LOCKED SALMON LADDER

ROBERT JOHN MORRISSETTE

APRIL 01, 2018
PATENT PENDING

Fig. 1

INVENTOR
Robert J. Morrissette
BY HIS ATTORNEY

WITNESS
vi Leonardo deSitra

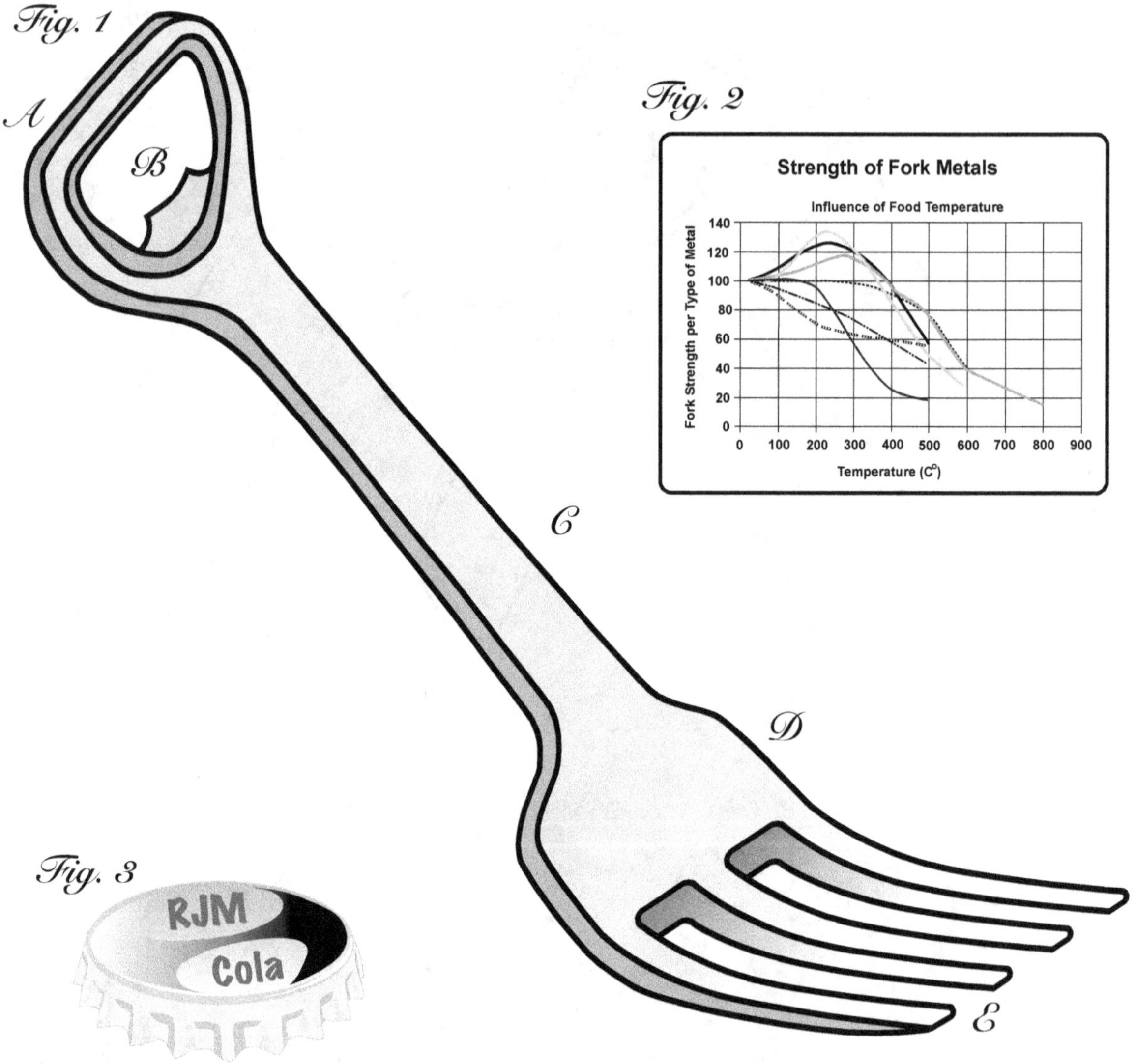

COMBO FORK–BOTTLE OPENER

ROBERT JOHN MORRISSETTE
APRIL 01, 2018
PATENT PENDING

Fig. 1

A

B

Fig. 2

Strength of Fork Metals

Influence of Food Temperature

Fork Strength per Type of Metal

140
120
100
80
60
40
20
0

0 100 200 300 400 500 600 700 800 900

Temperature (C°)

C

D

Fig. 3

RJM
Cola

E

INVENTOR

Robert J. Morrissette

BY HIS ATTORNEY

WITNESS

di Leonardo de Vinci

Frames

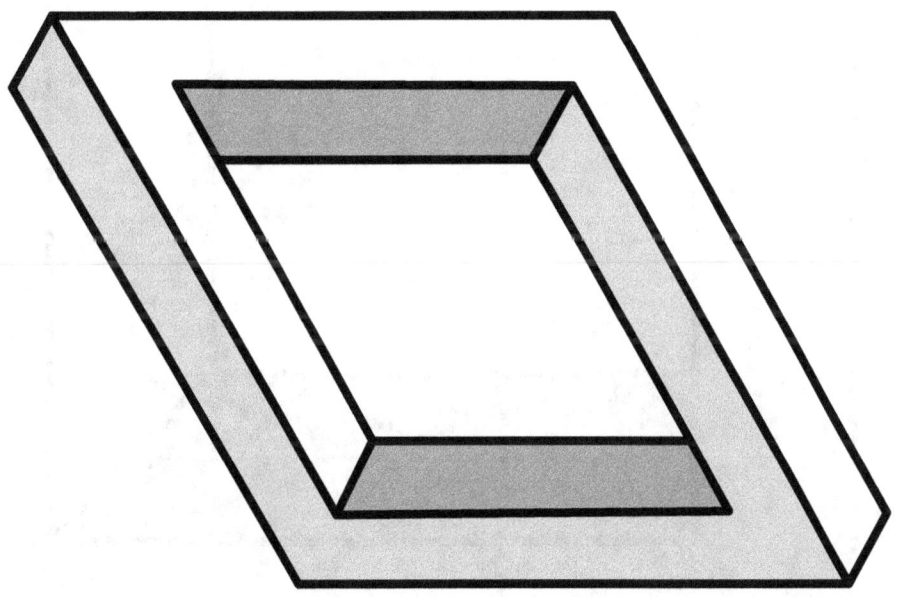

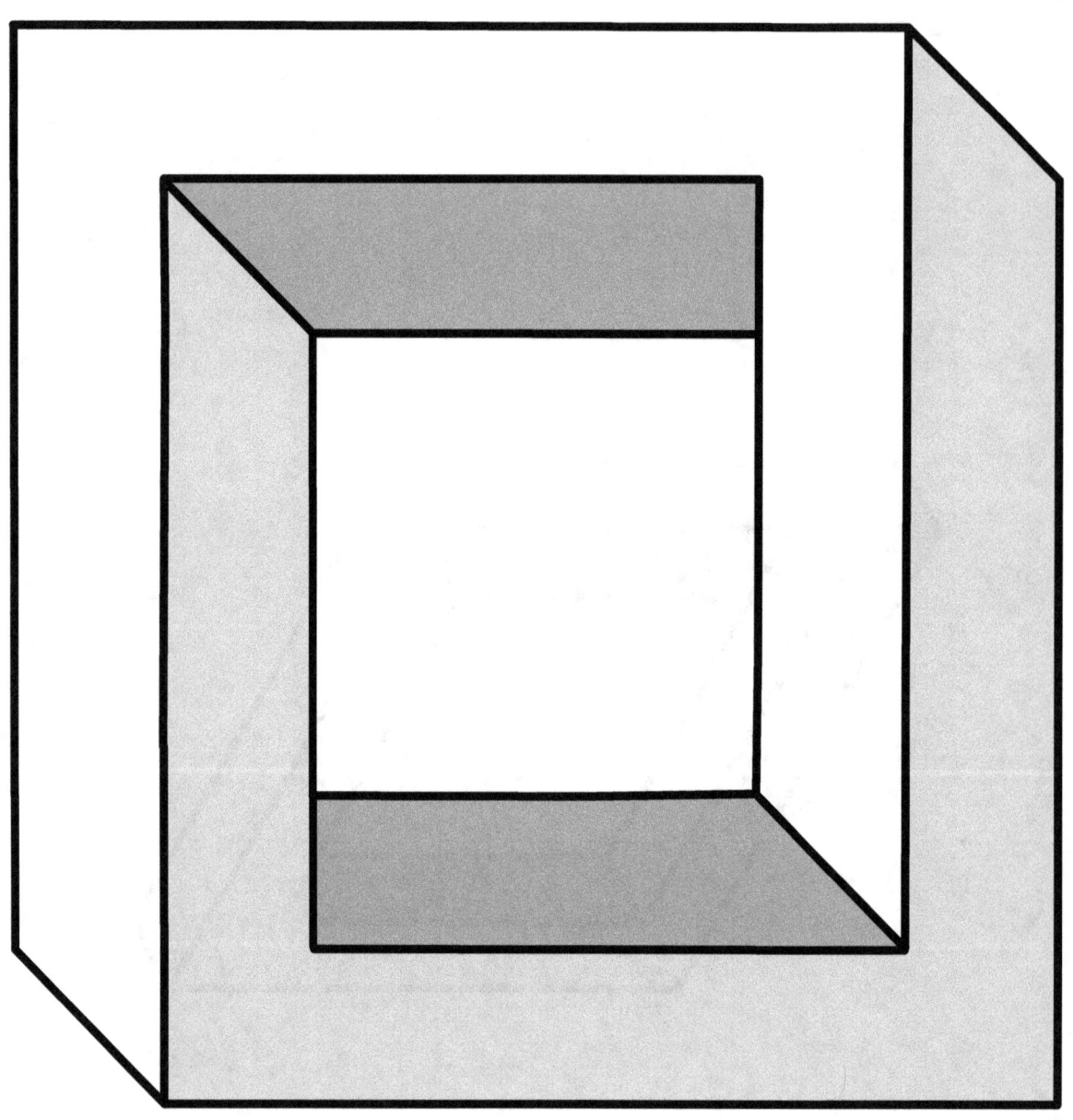

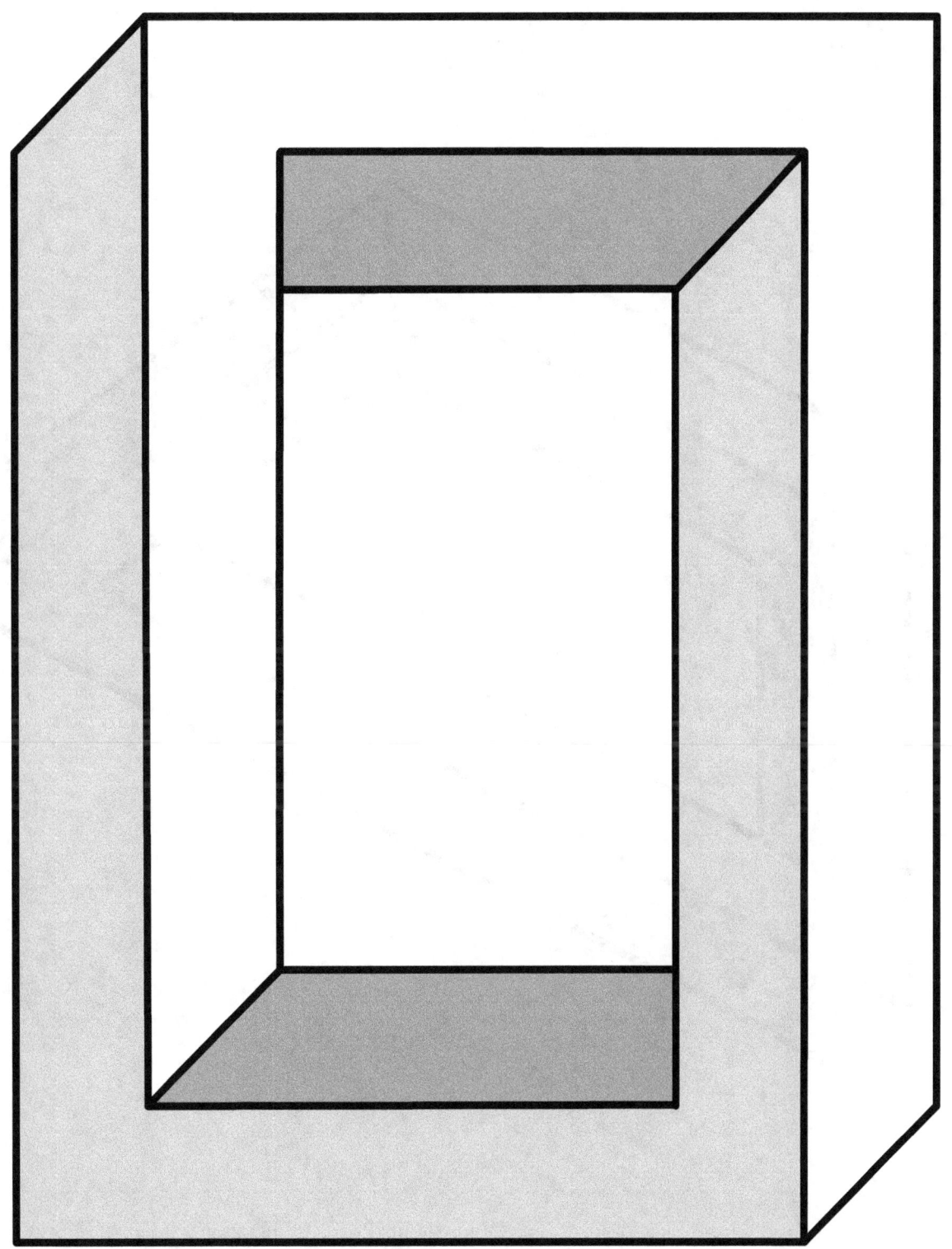

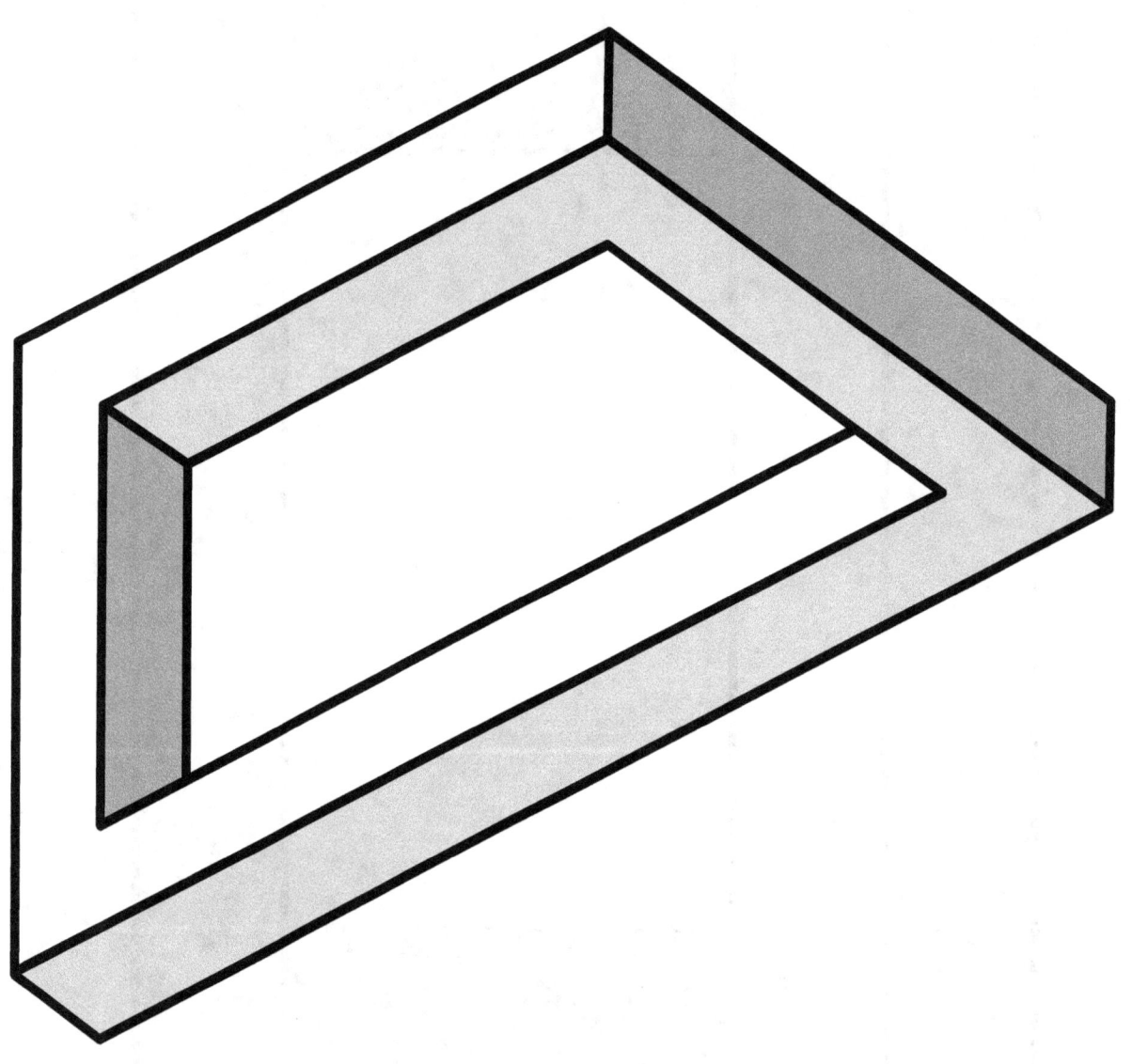

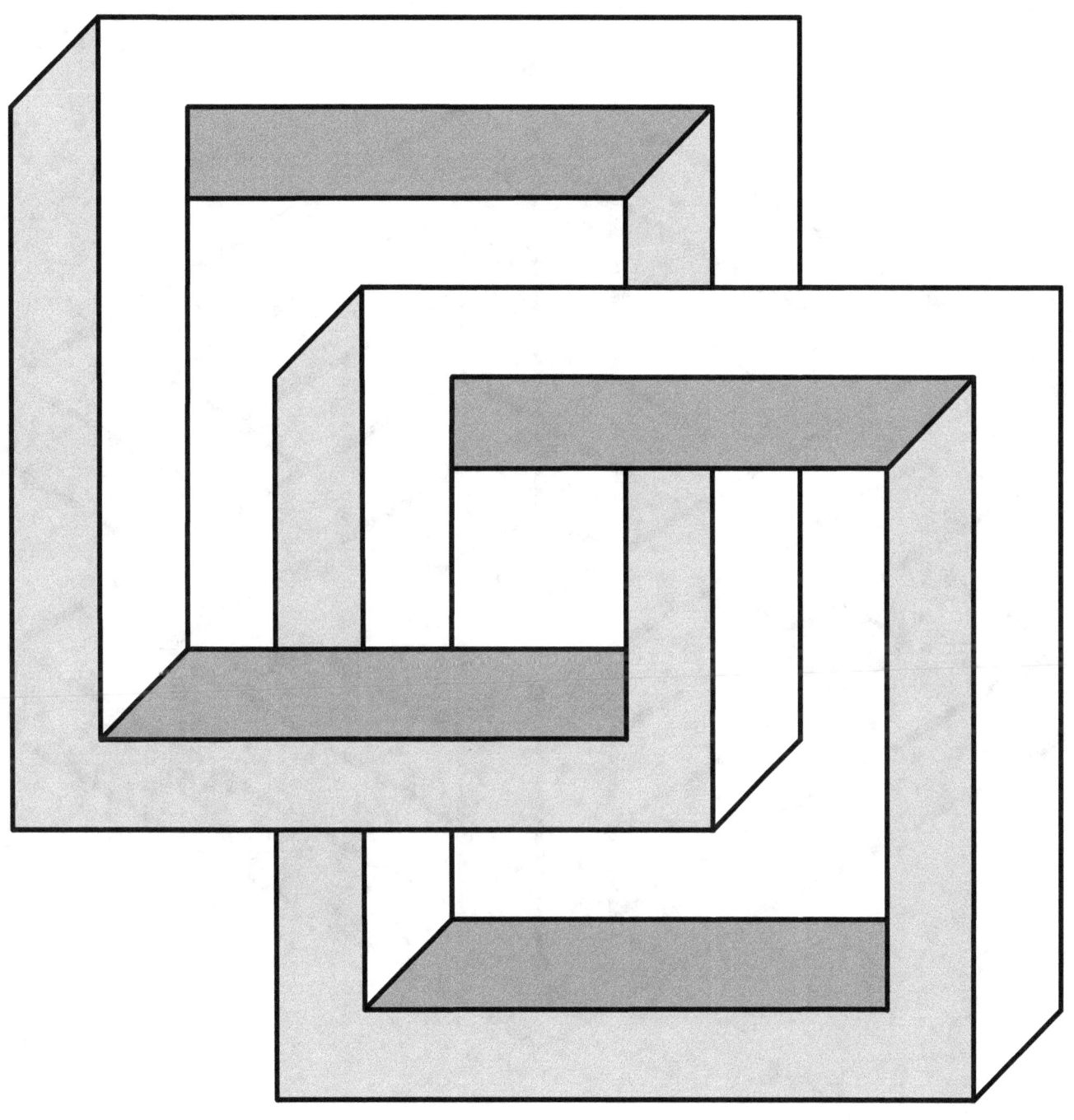

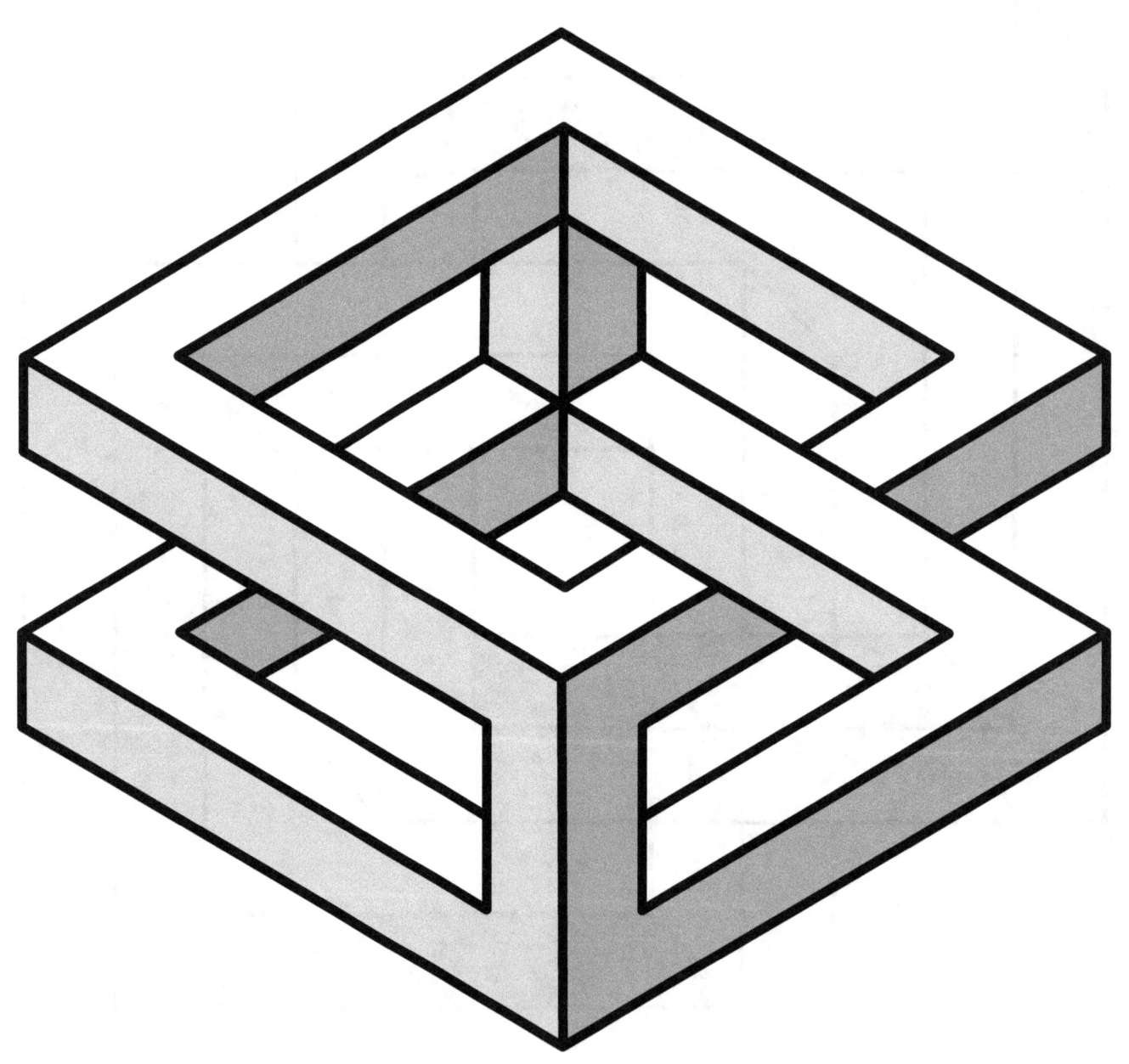

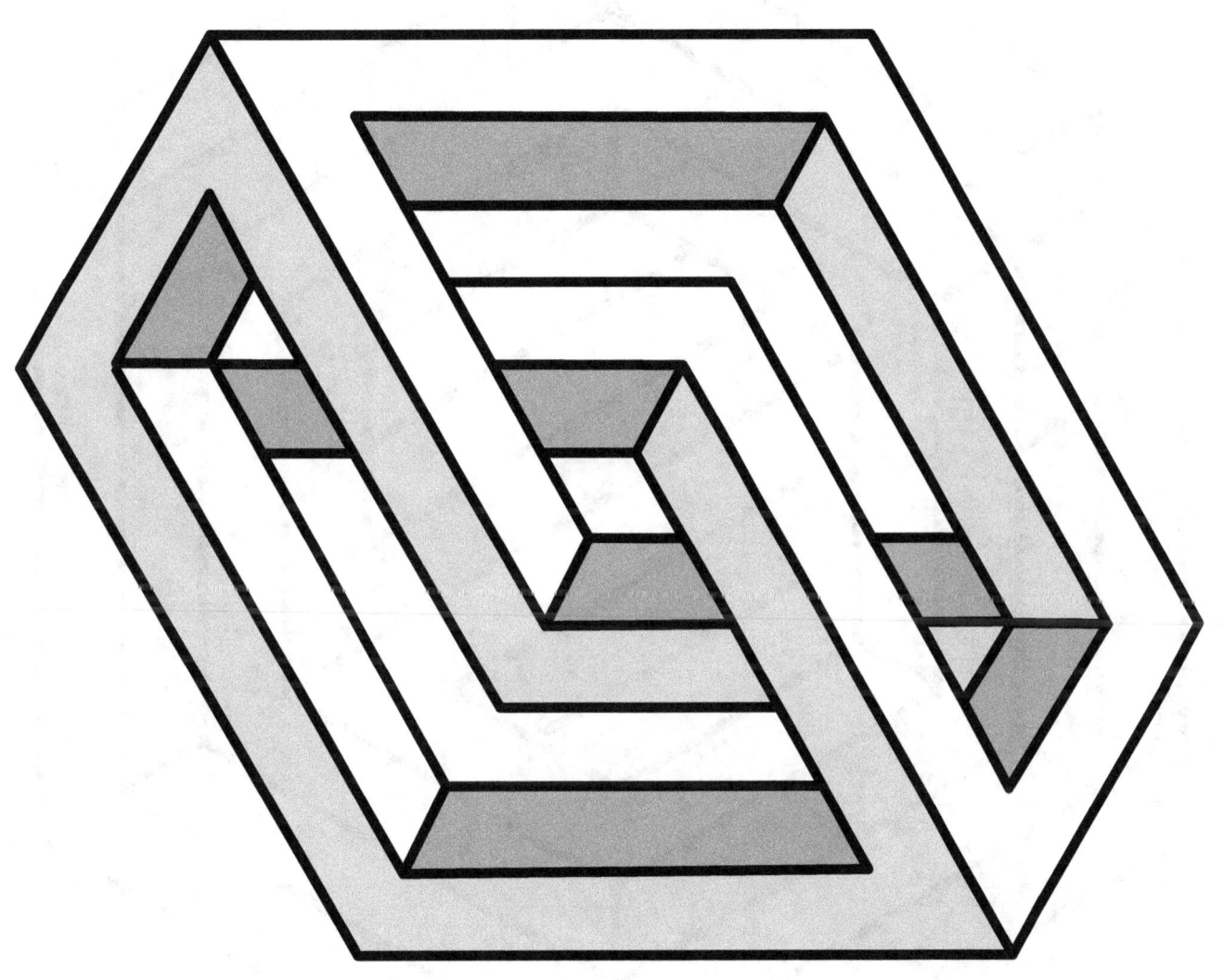

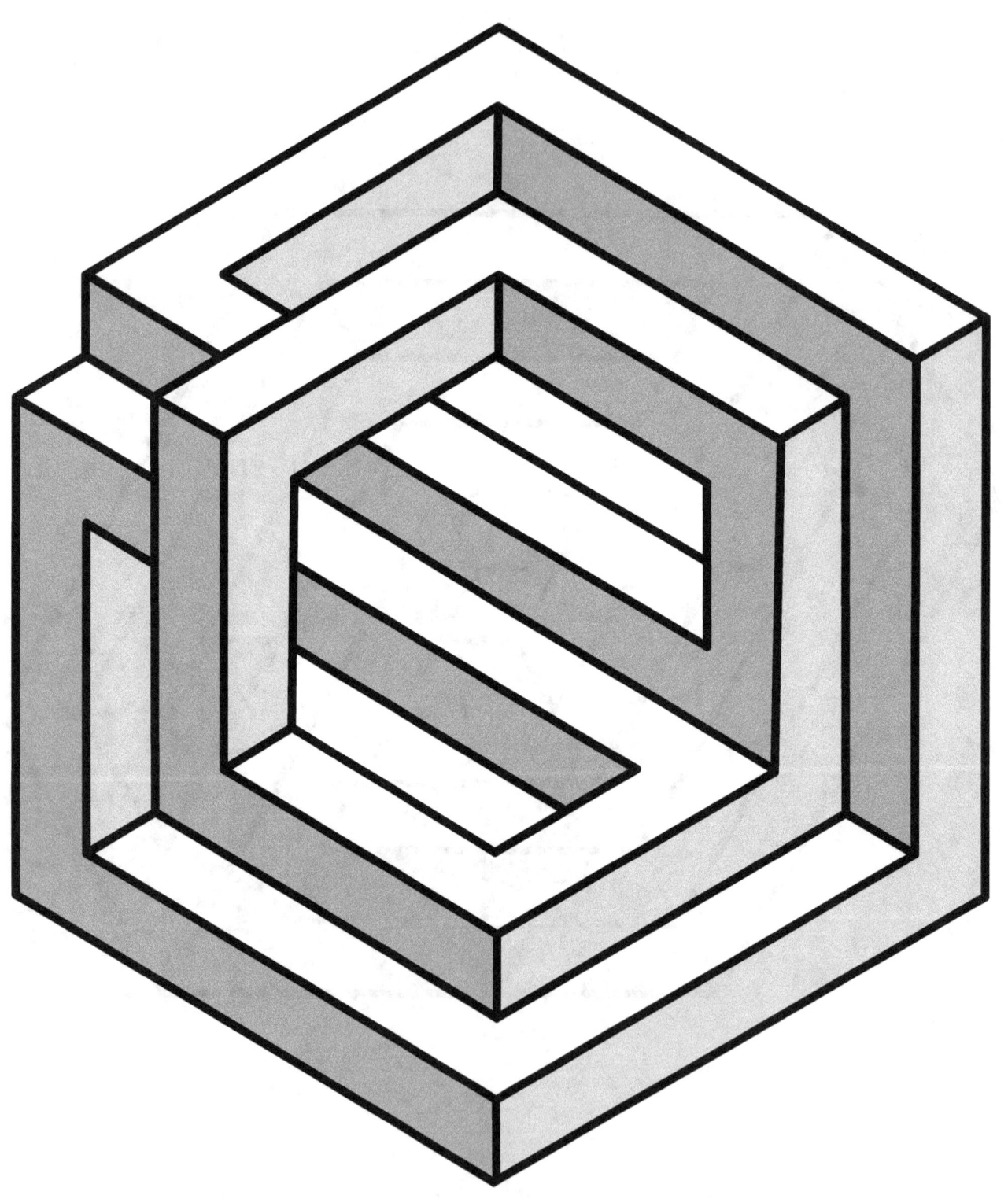

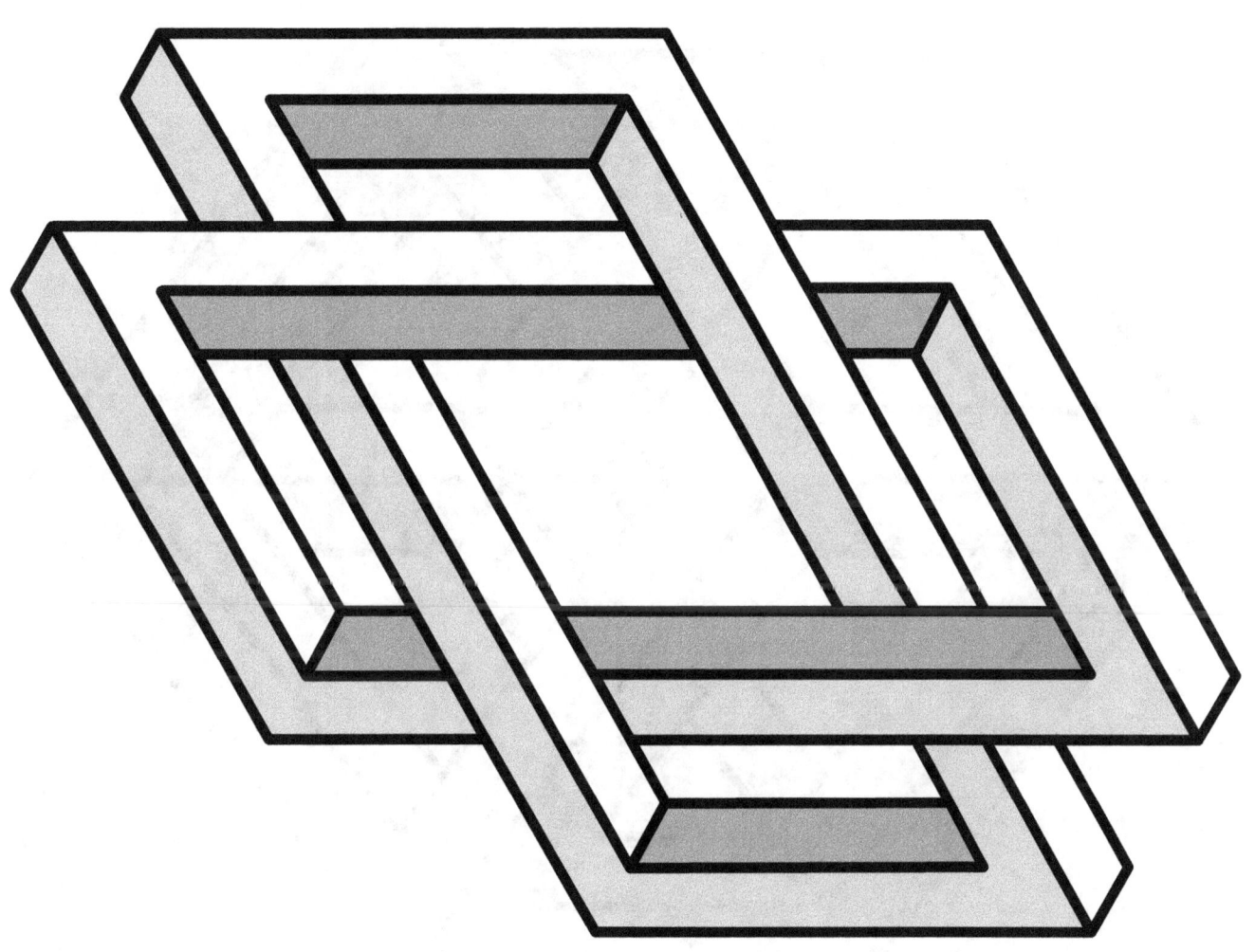

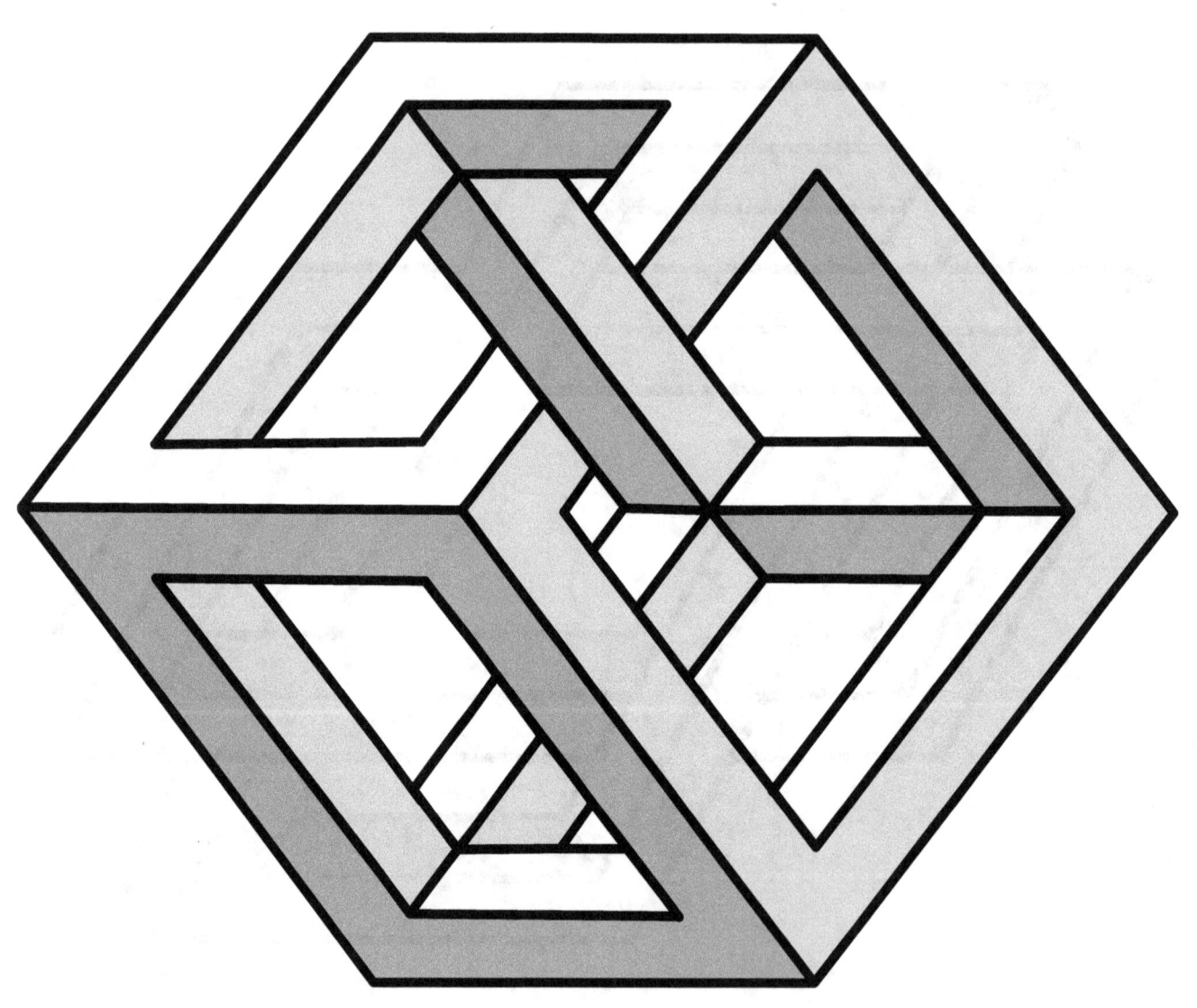

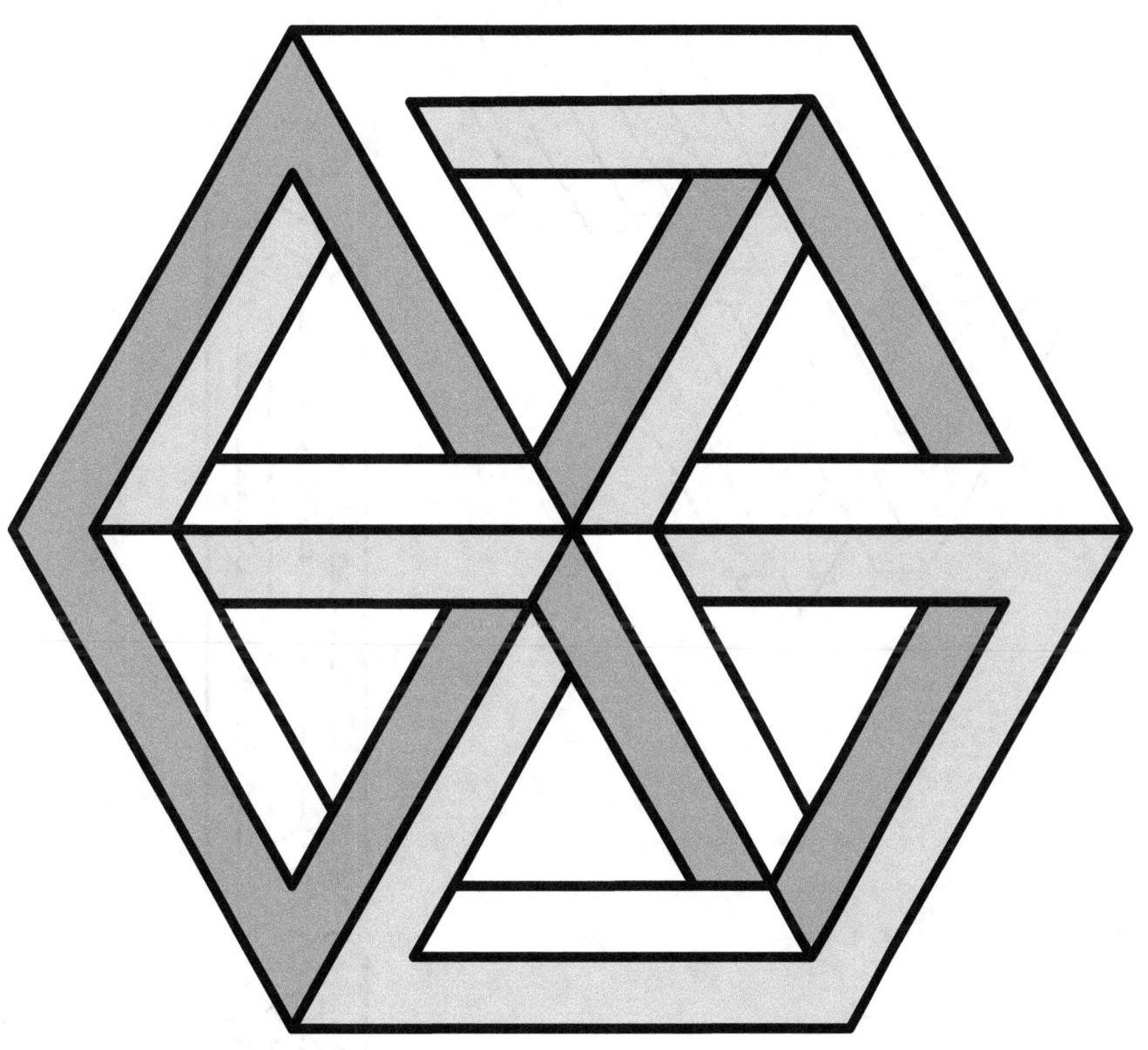

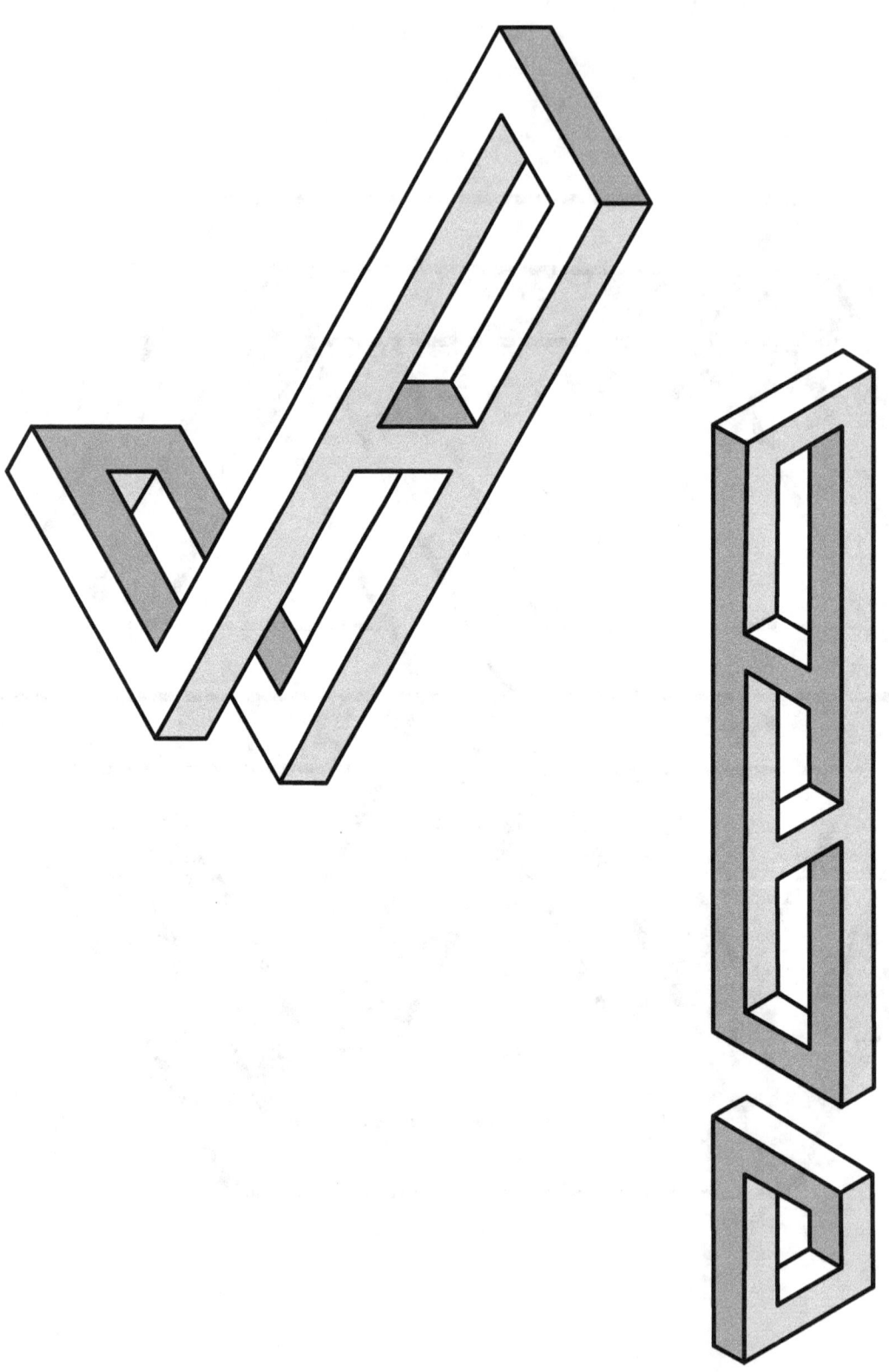

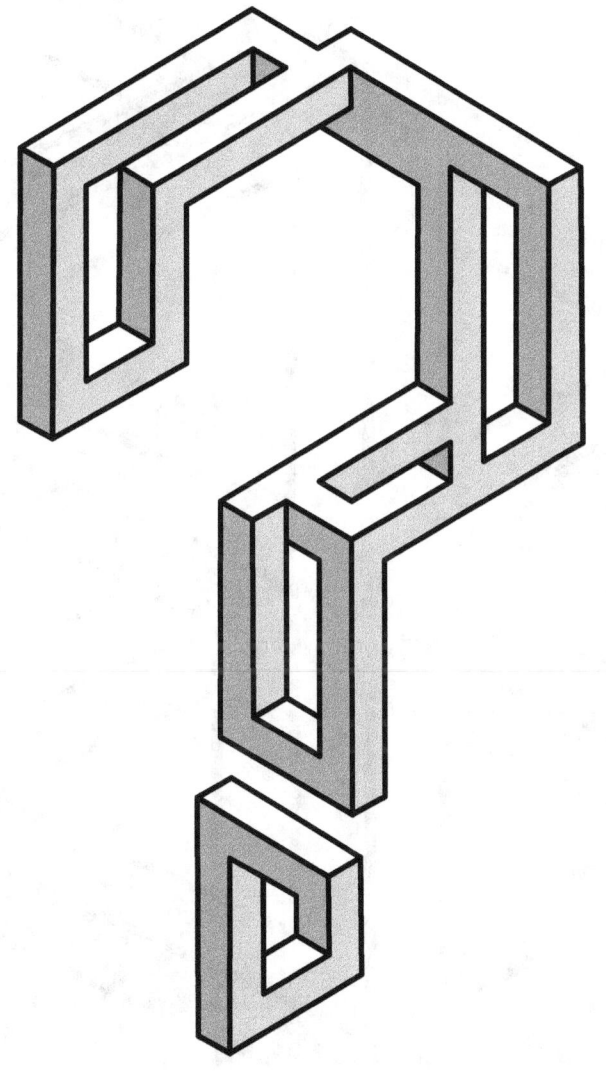

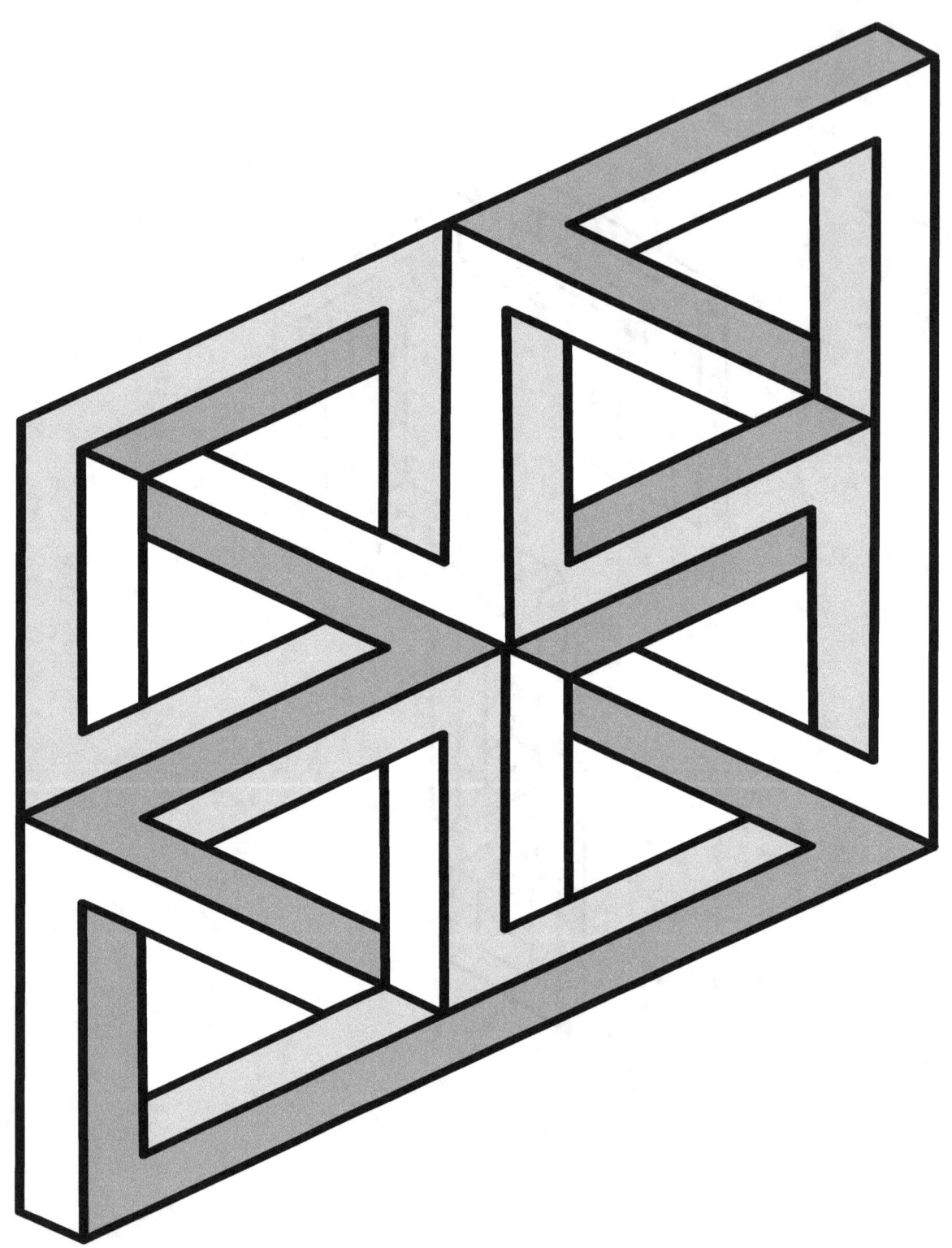

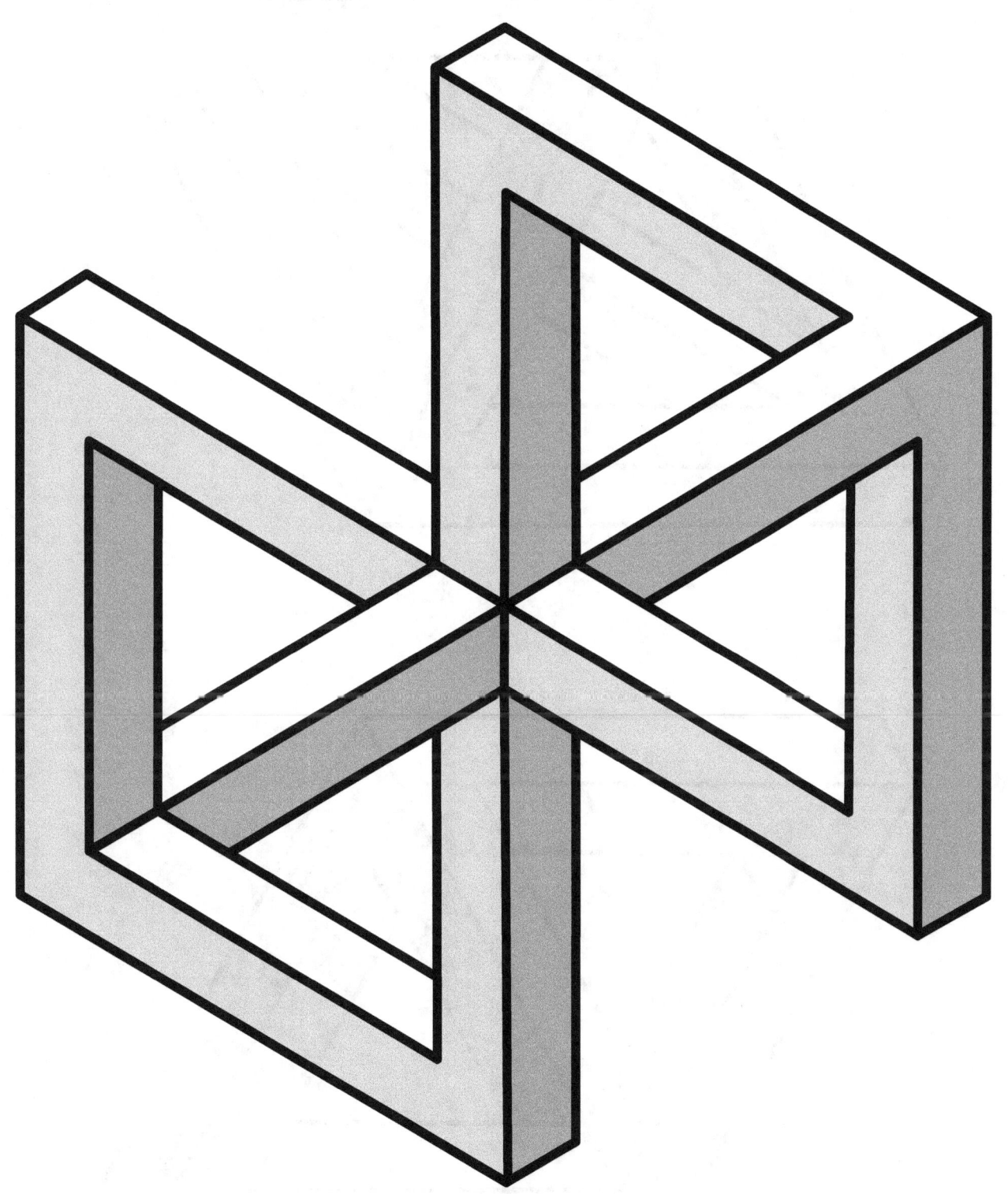

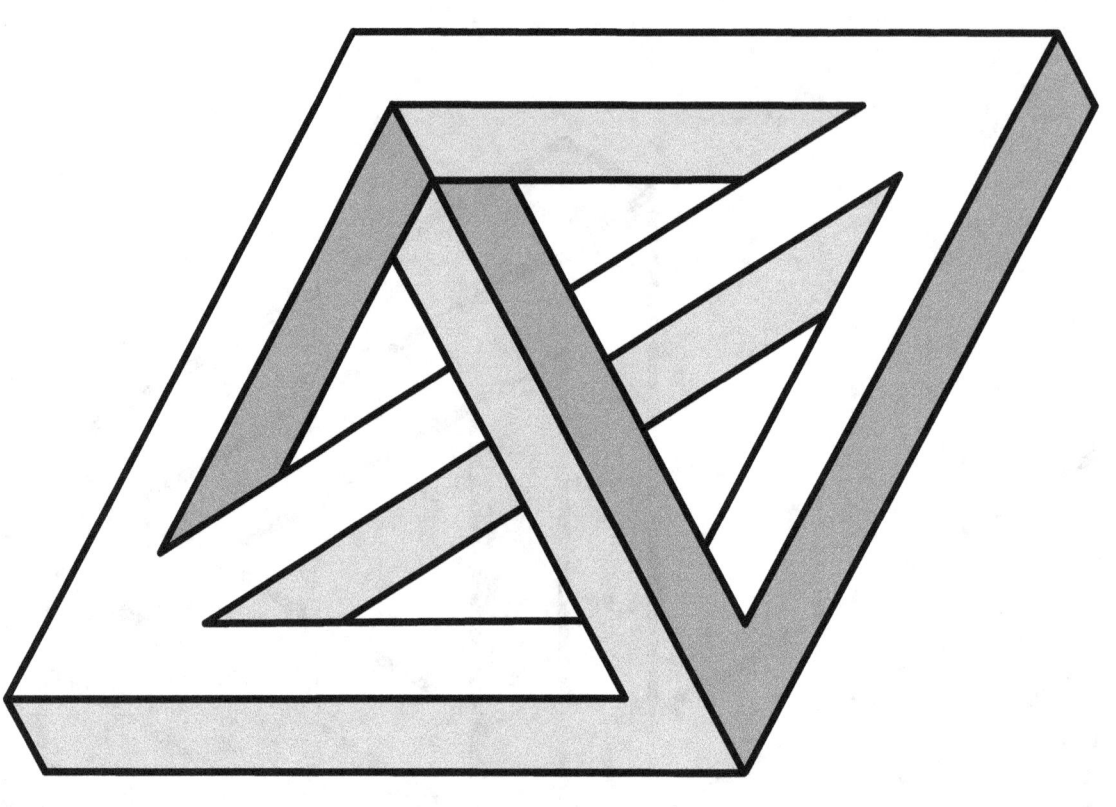

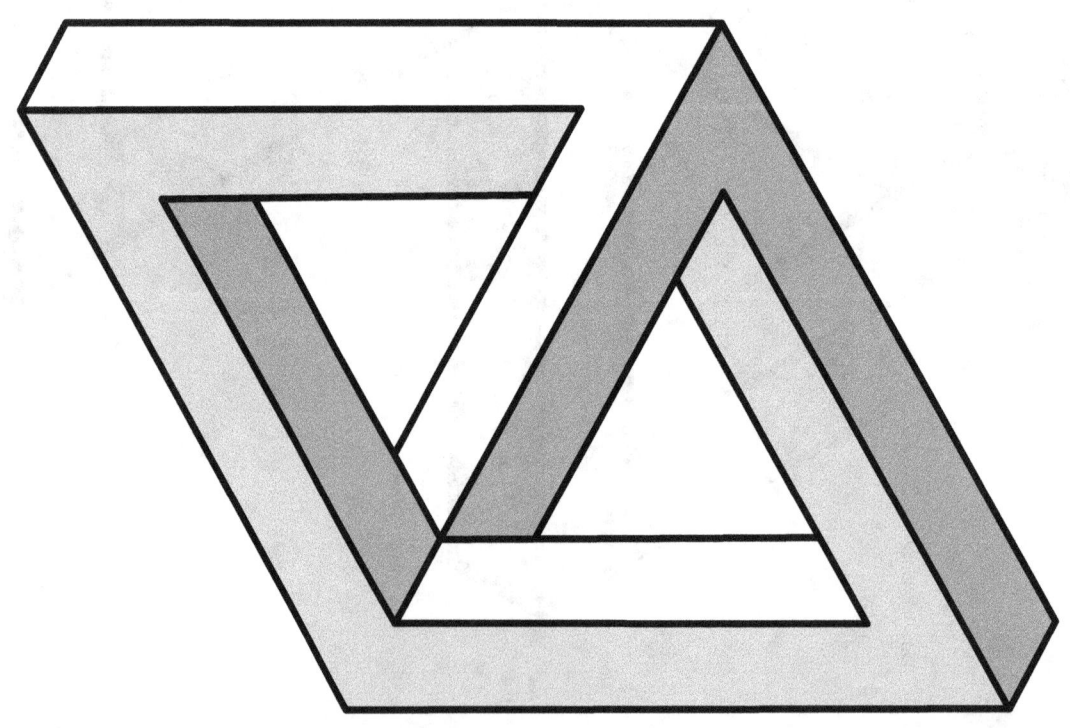

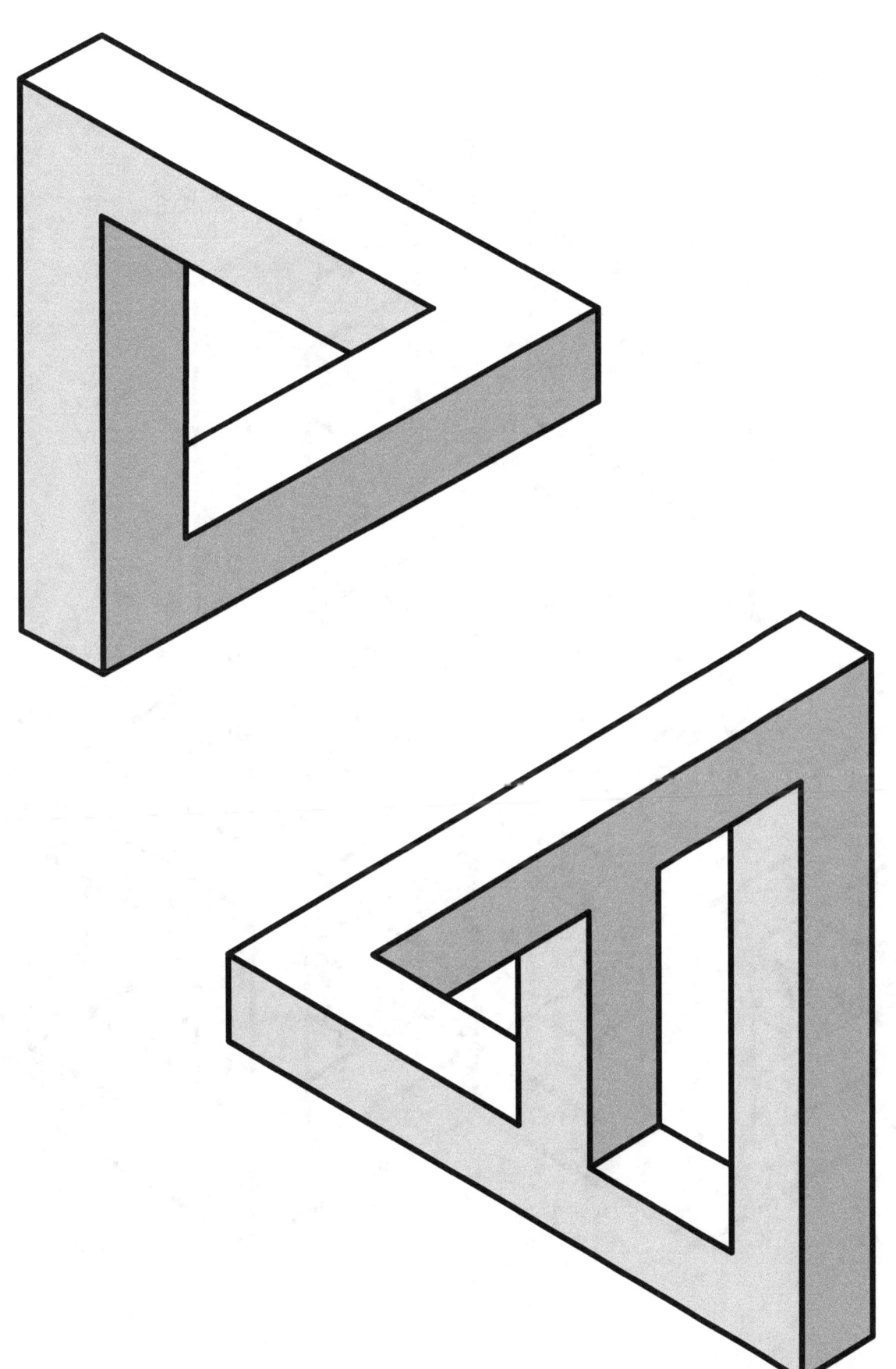

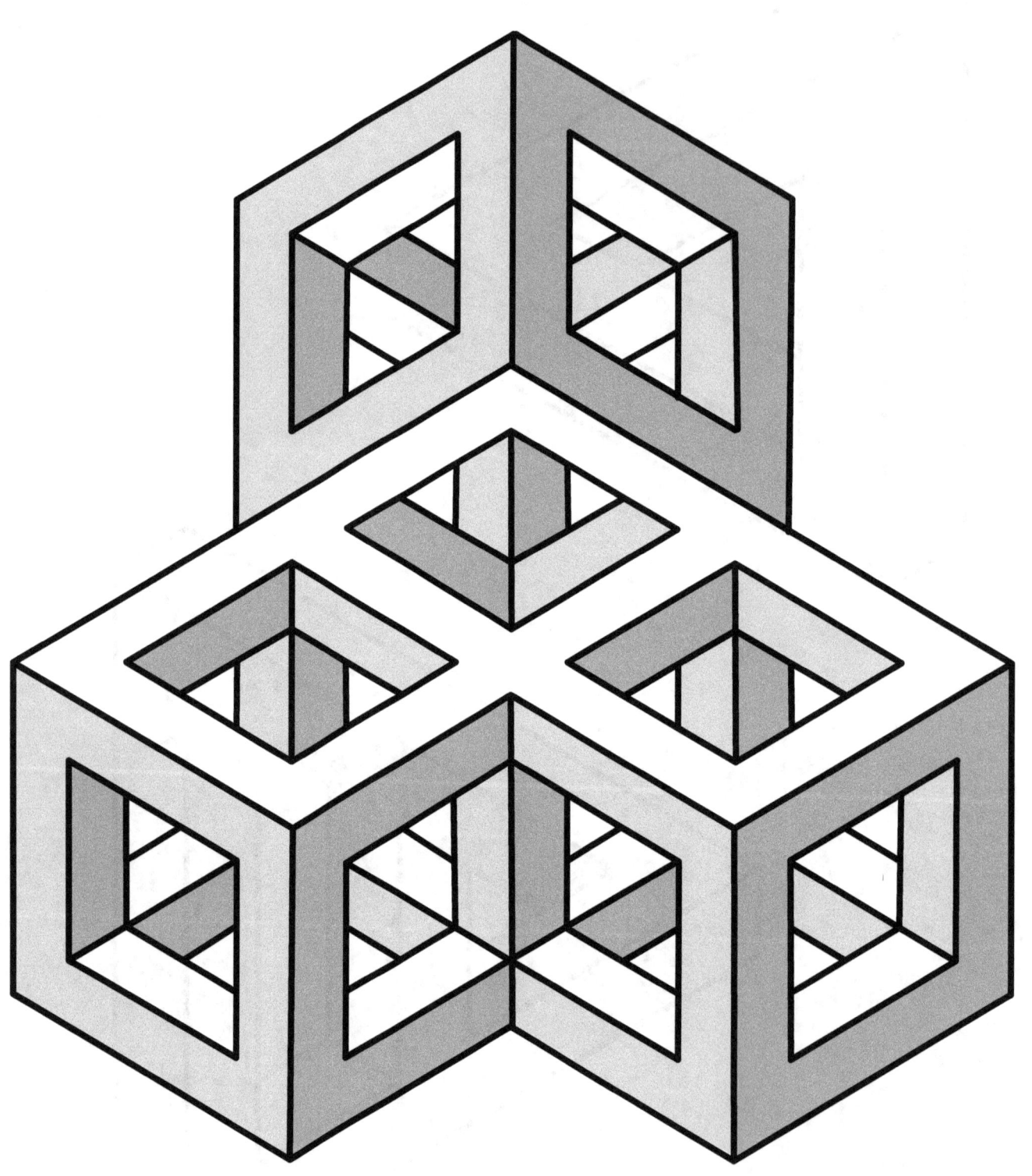

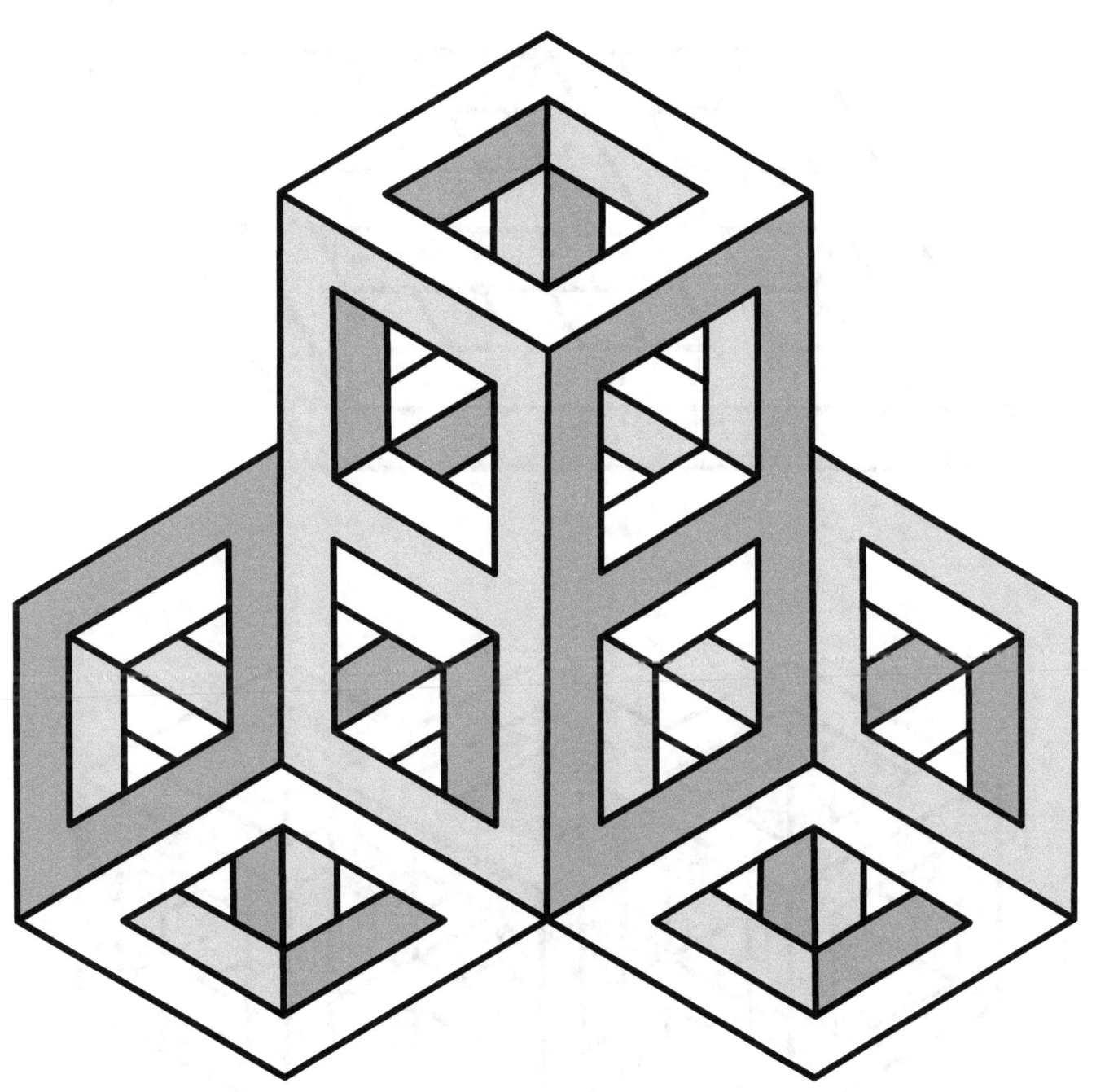

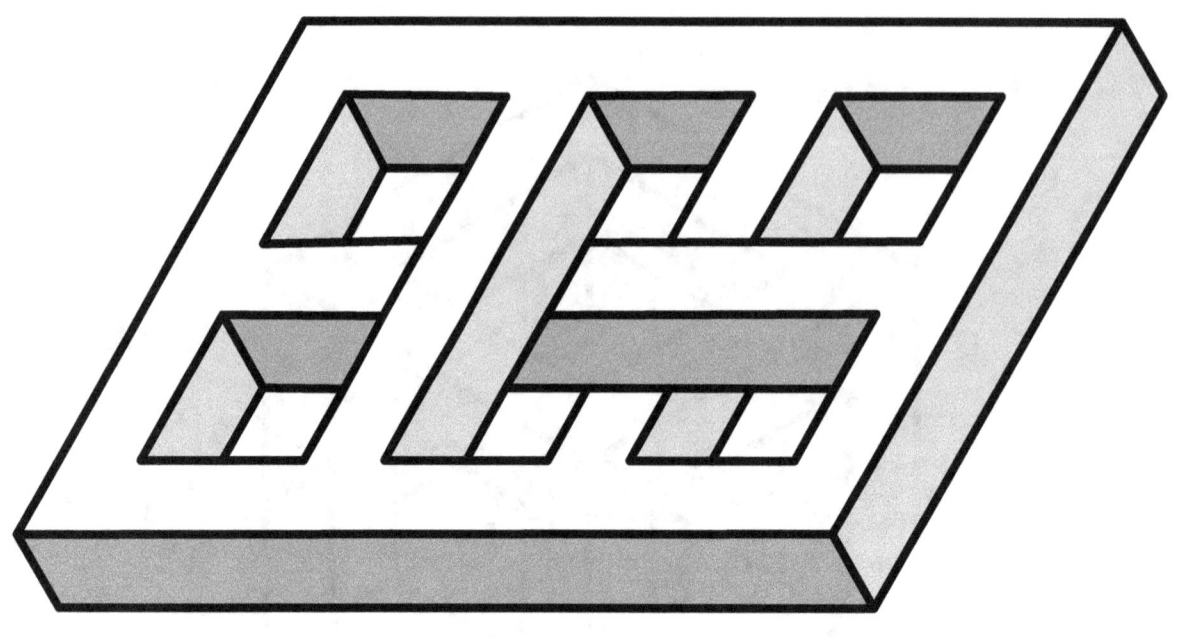

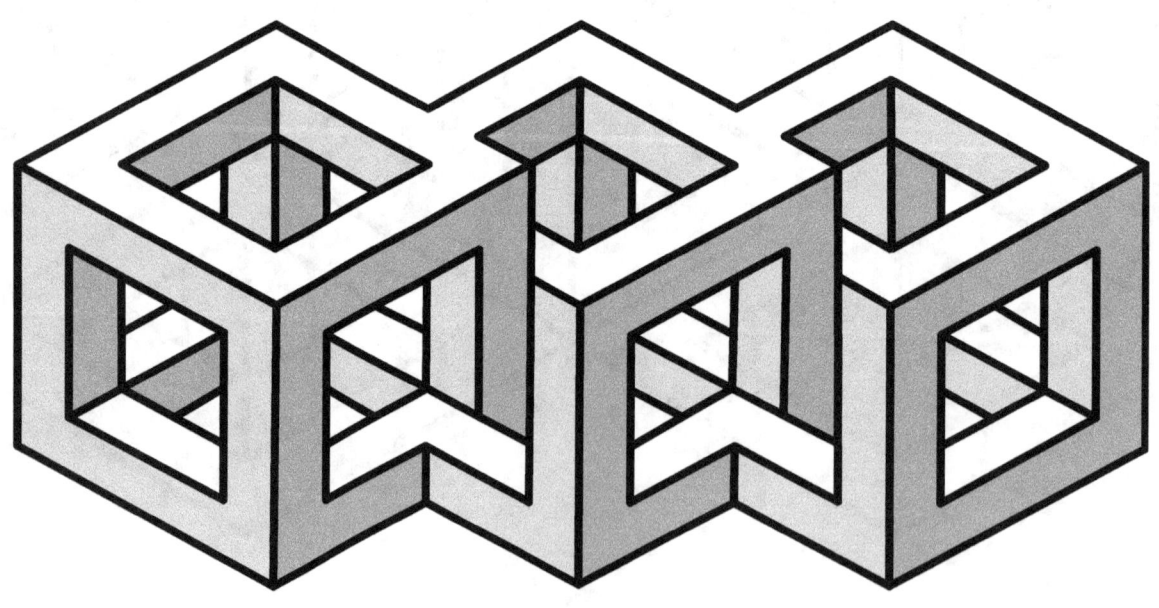

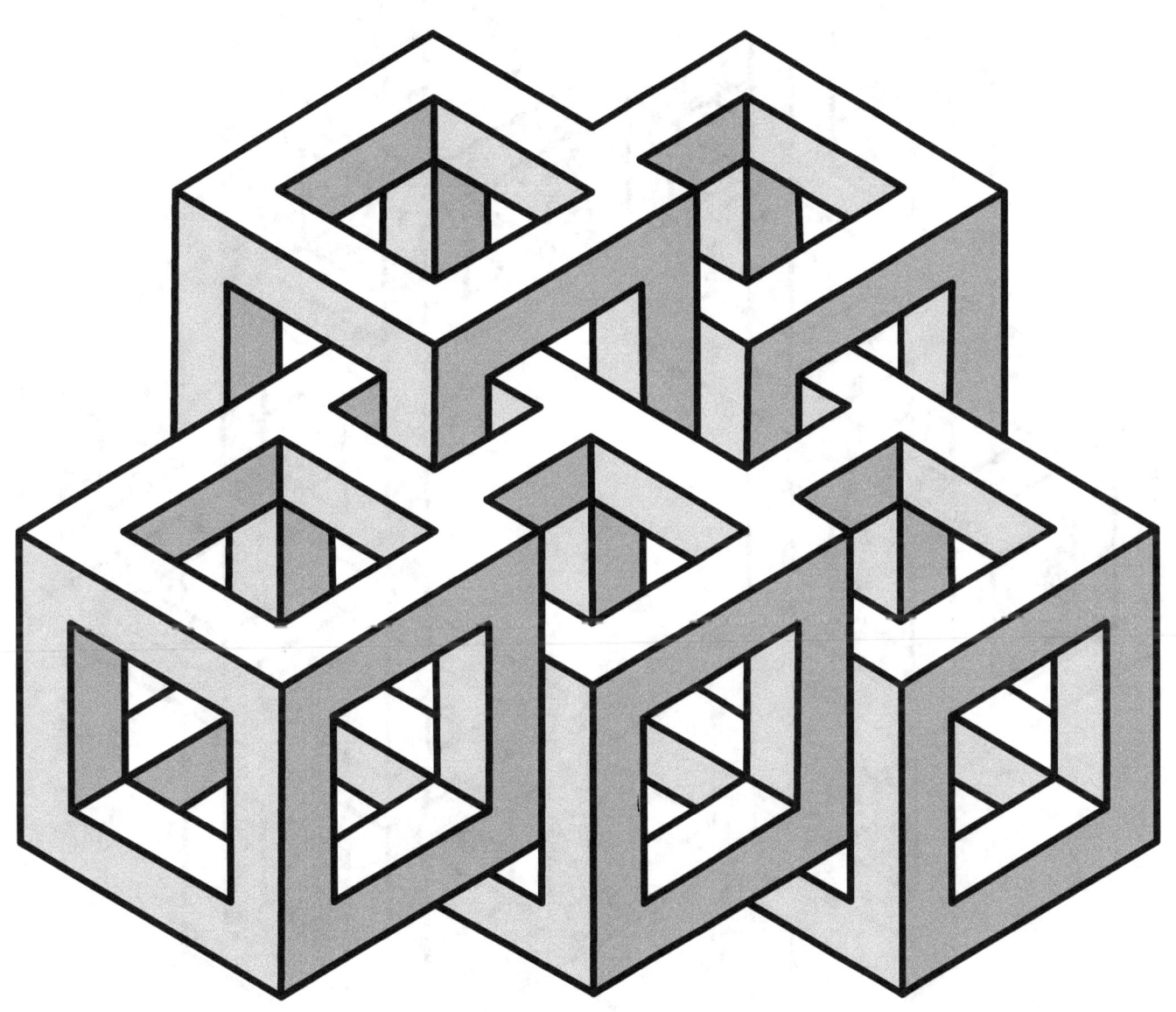

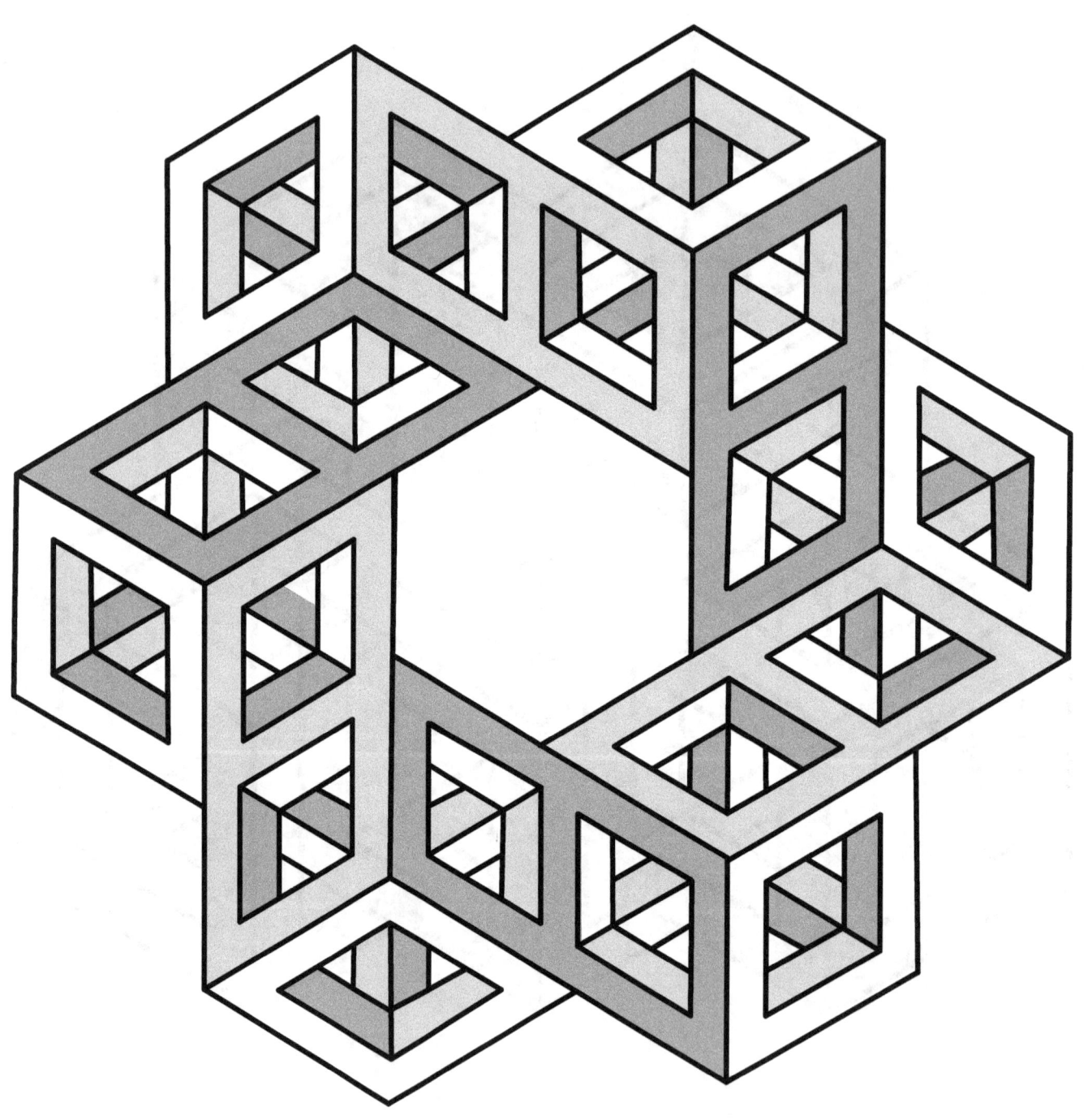

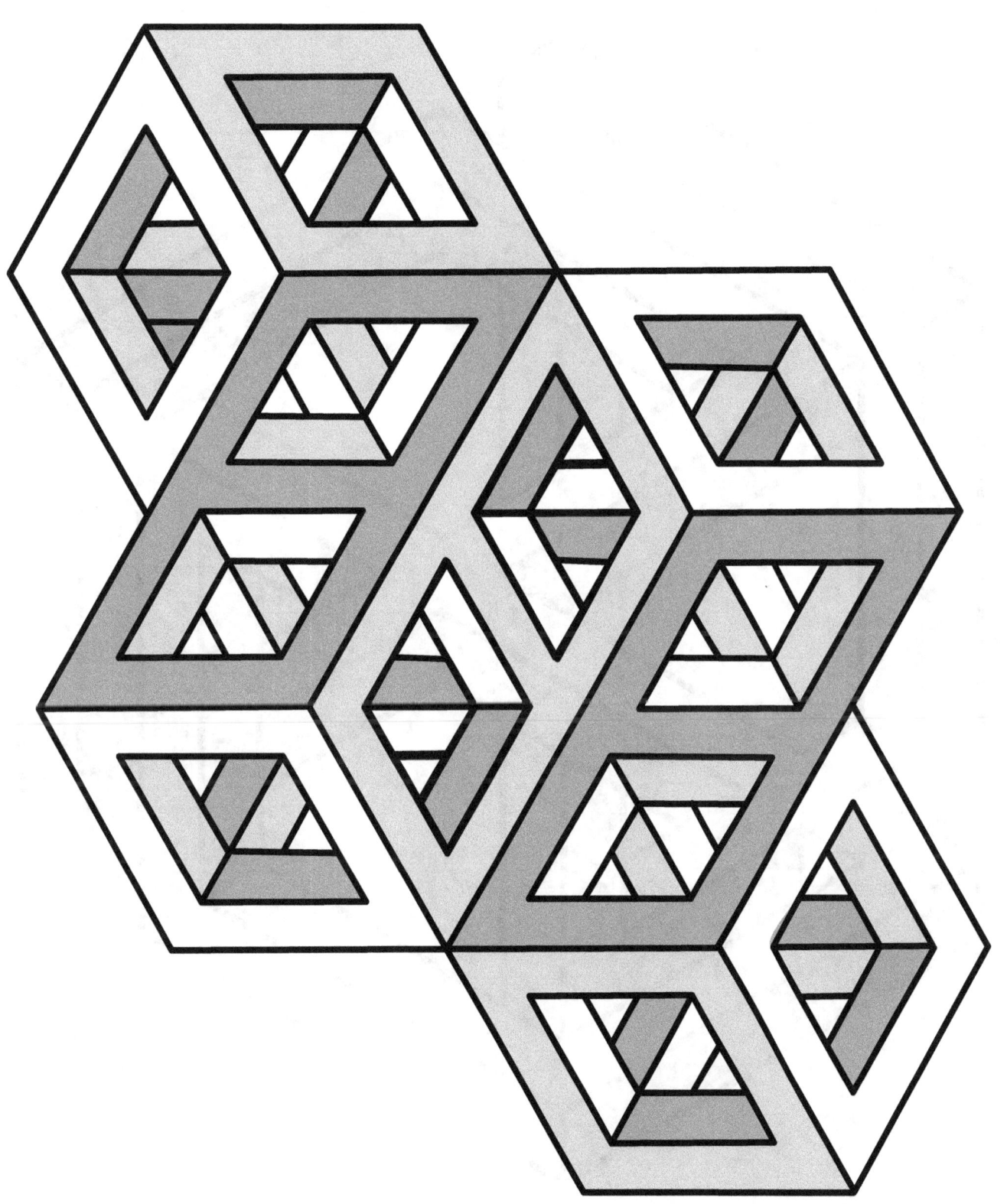

95

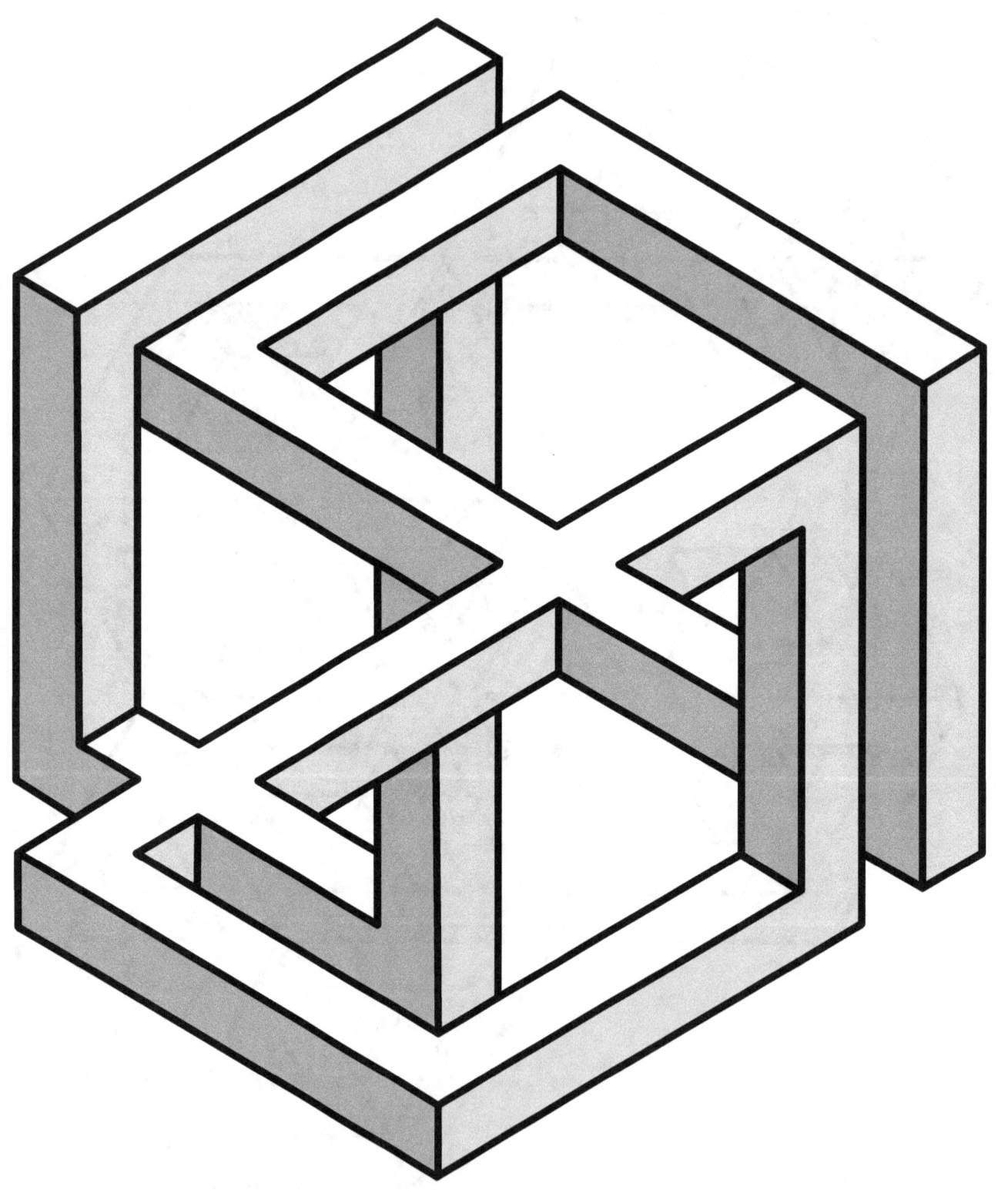

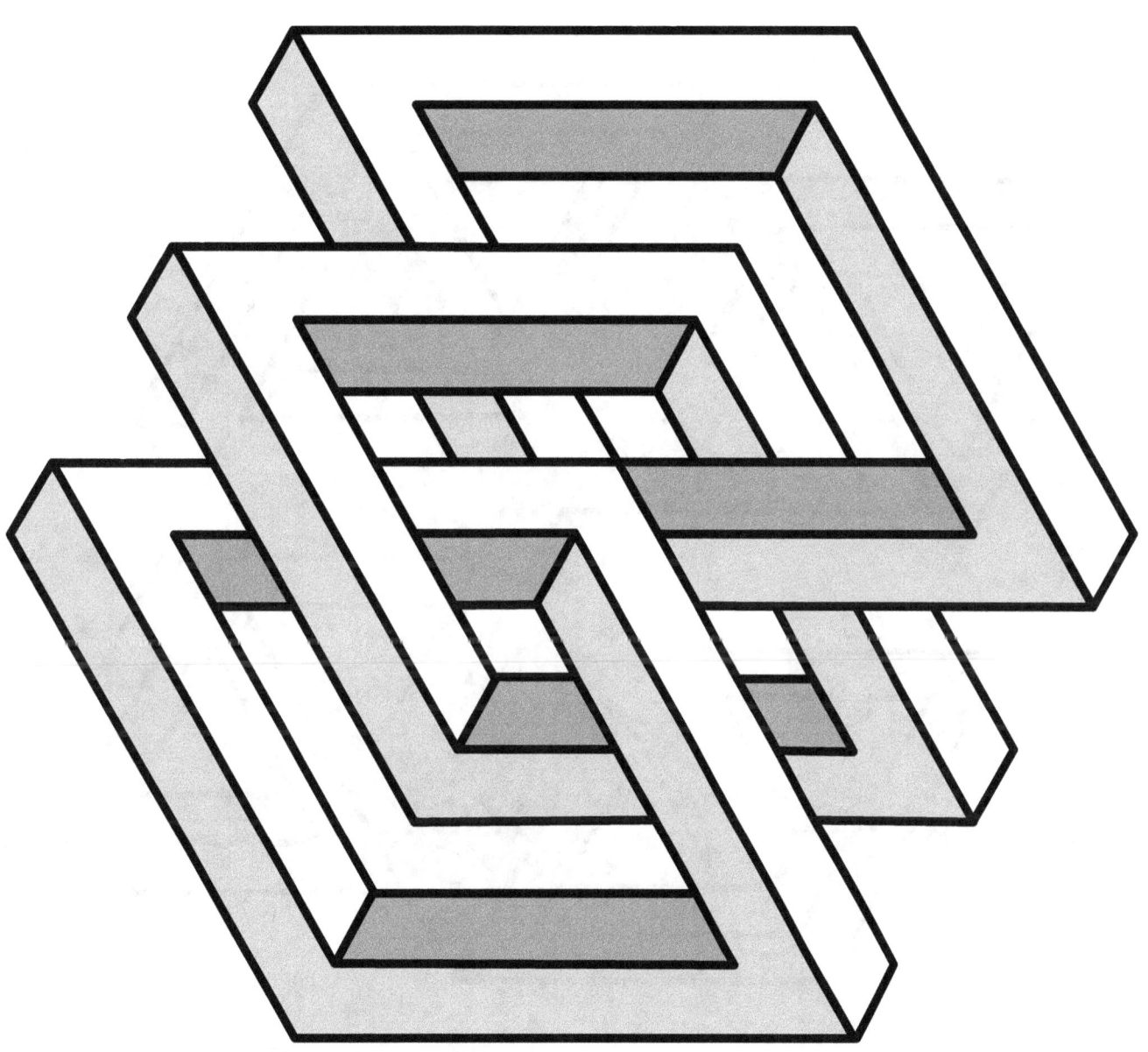

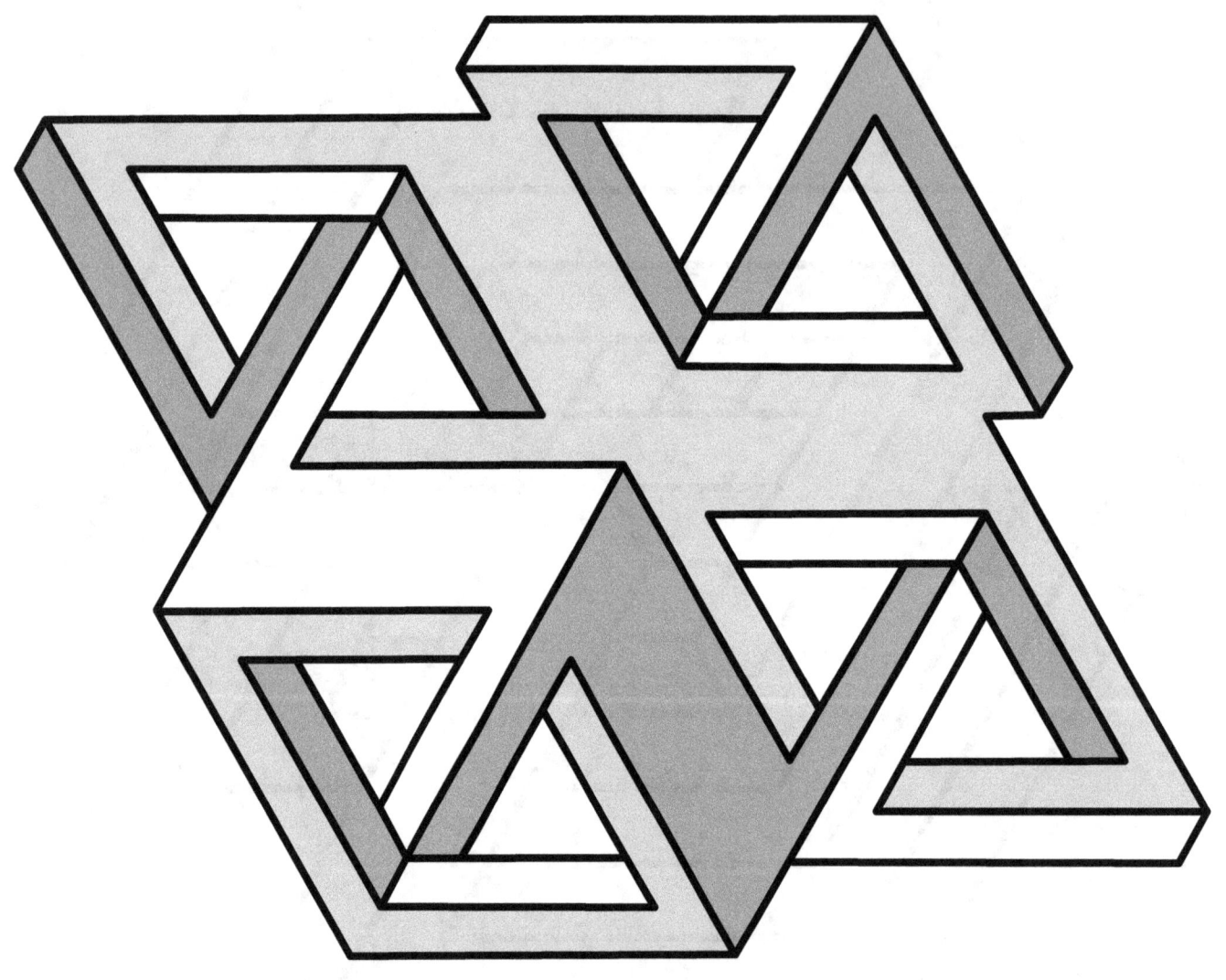

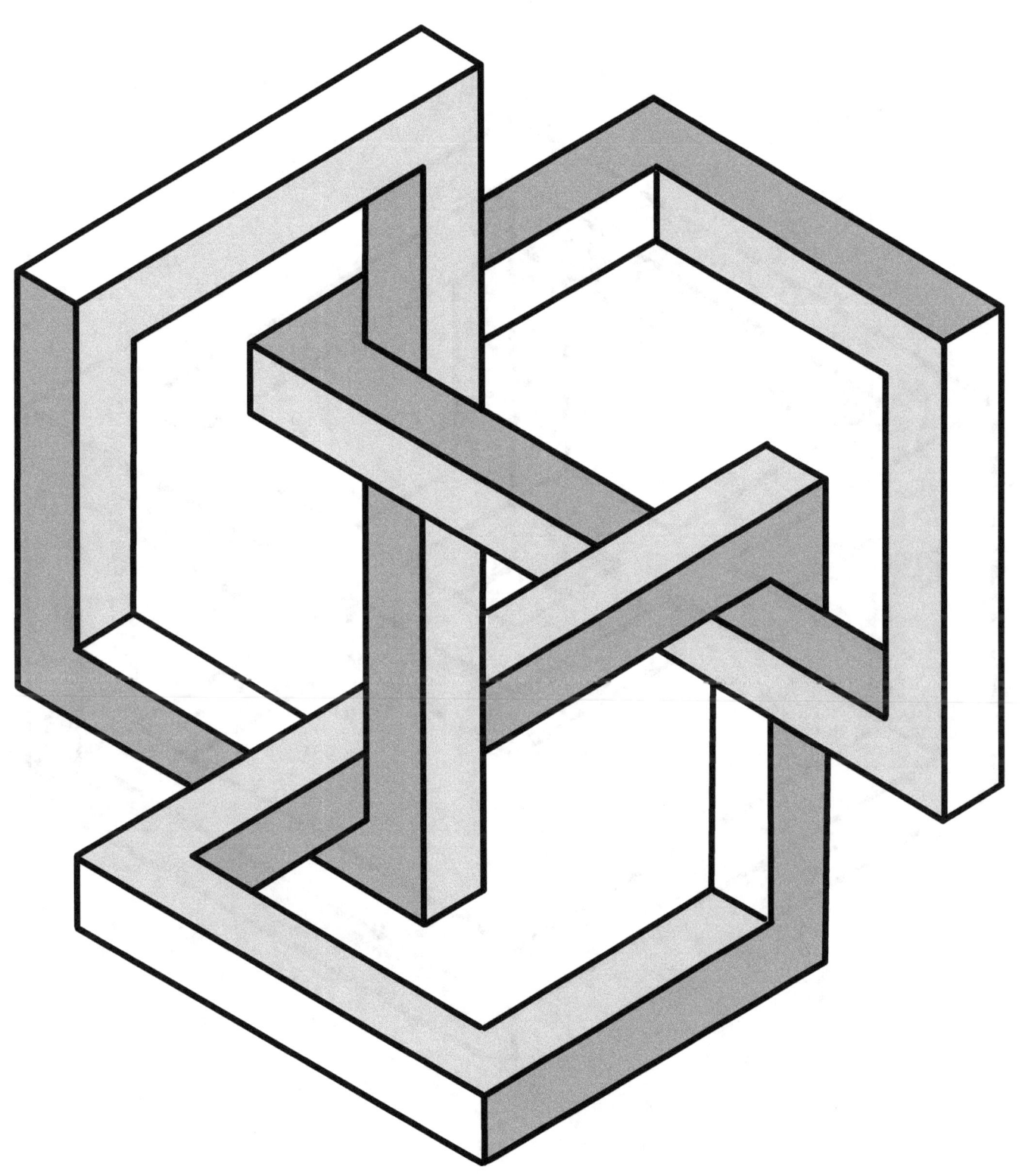

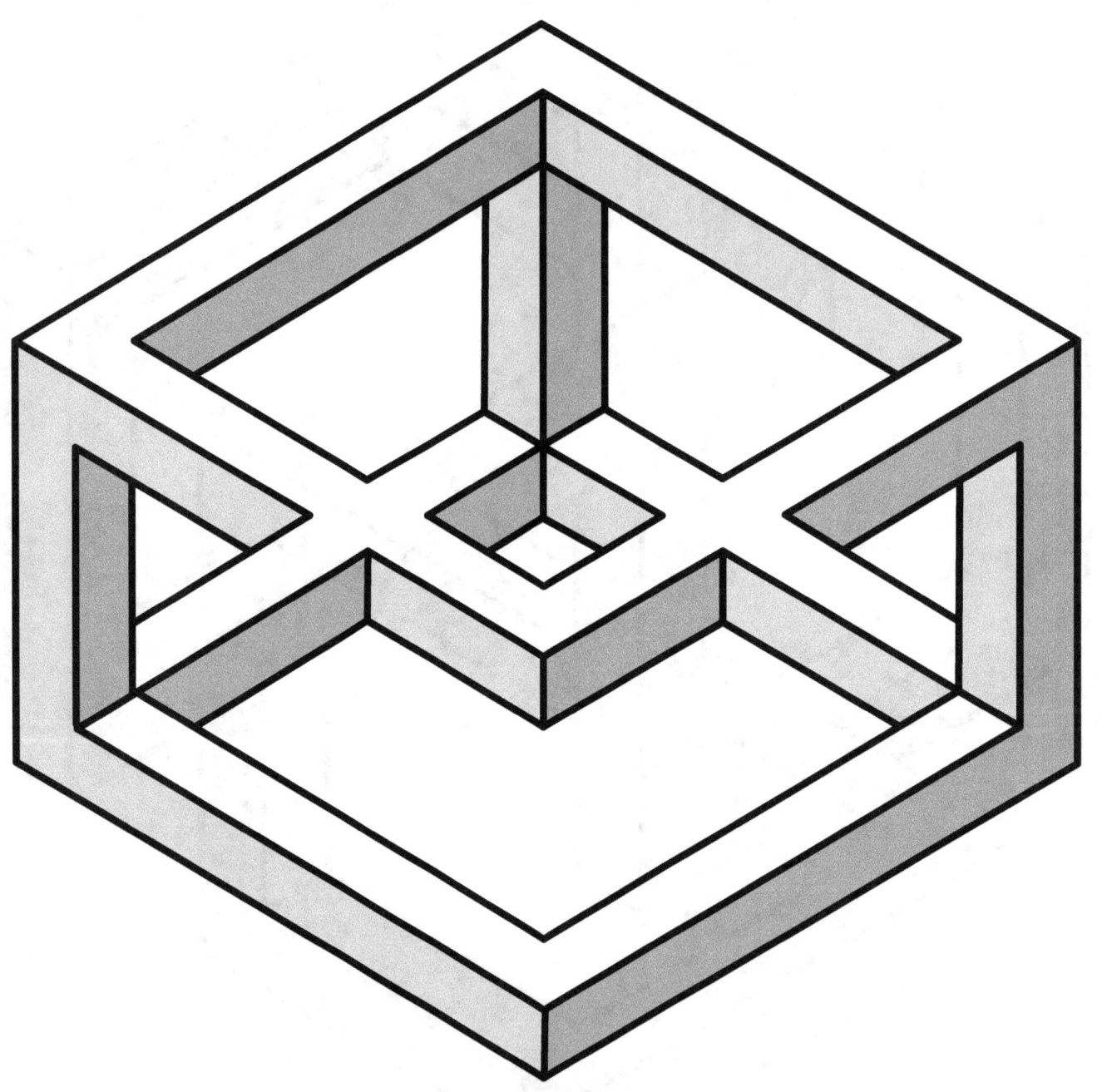

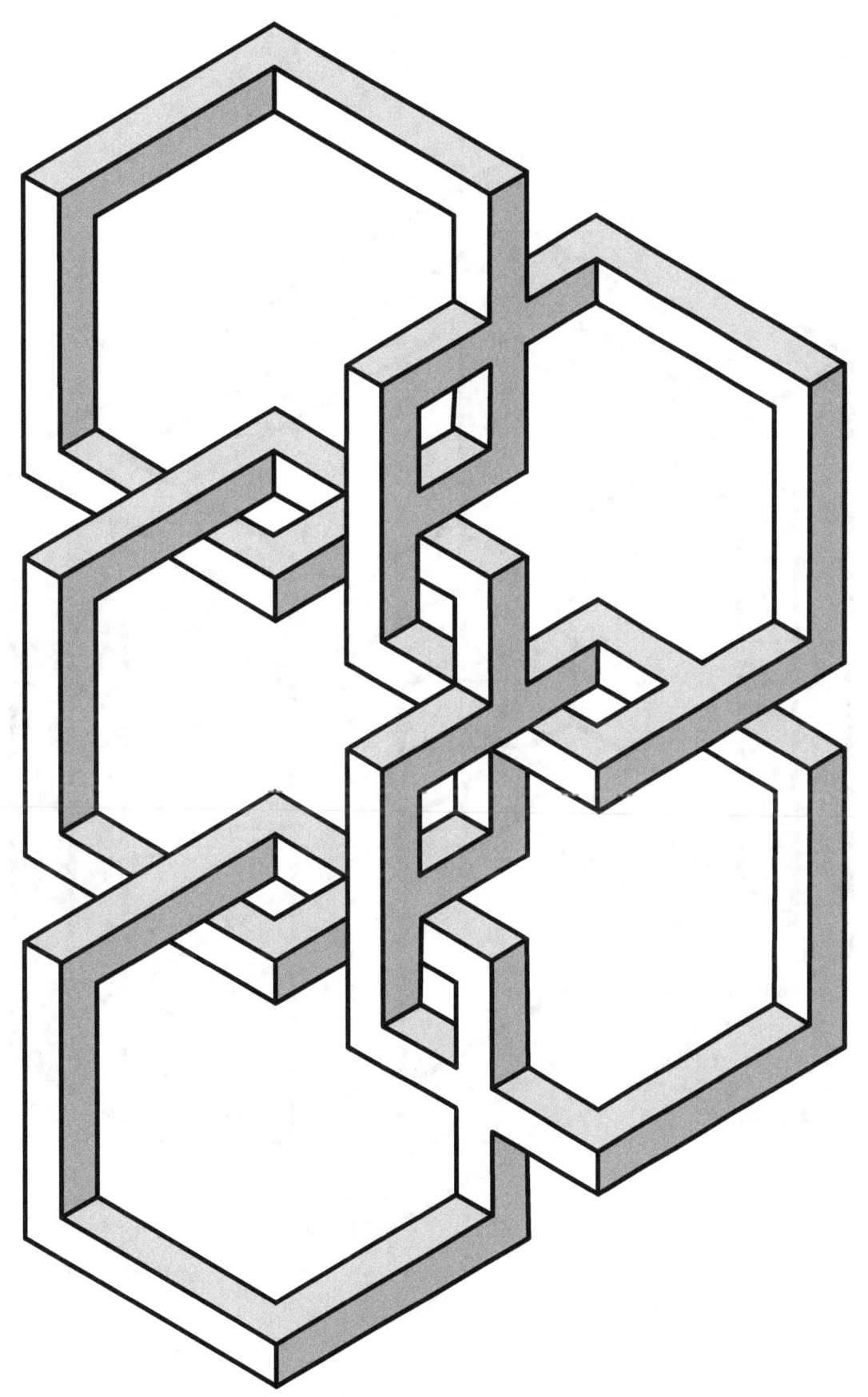

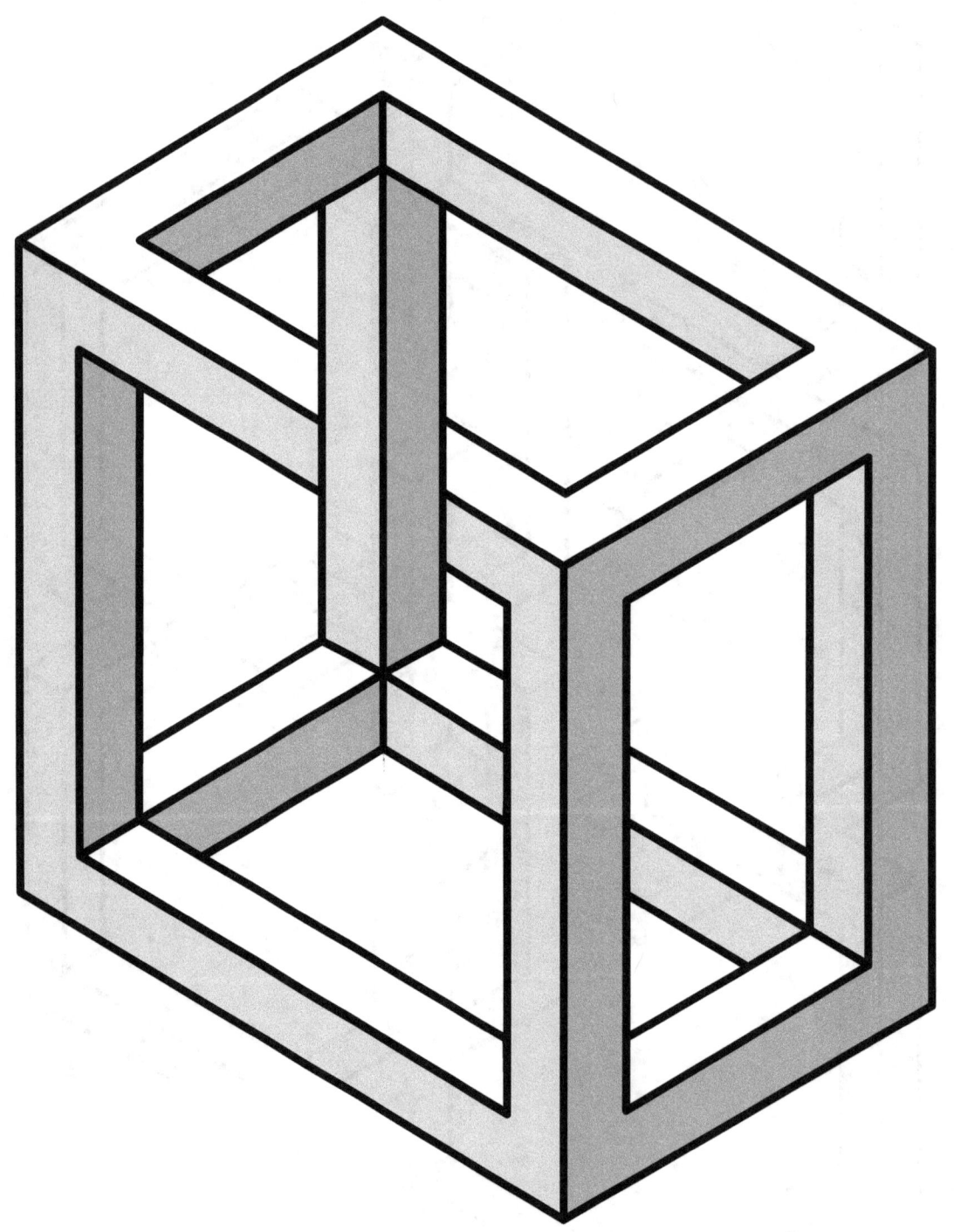

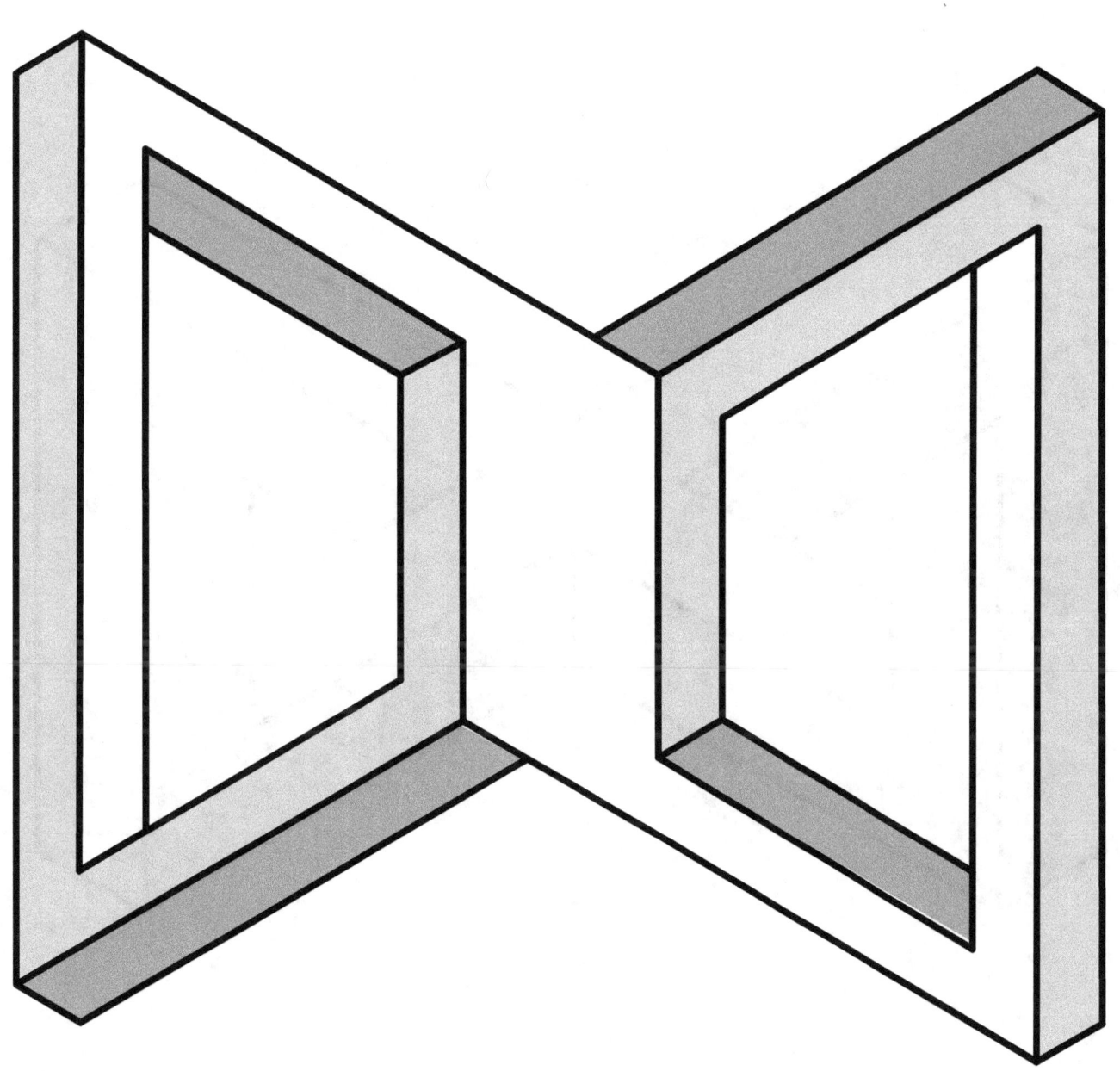

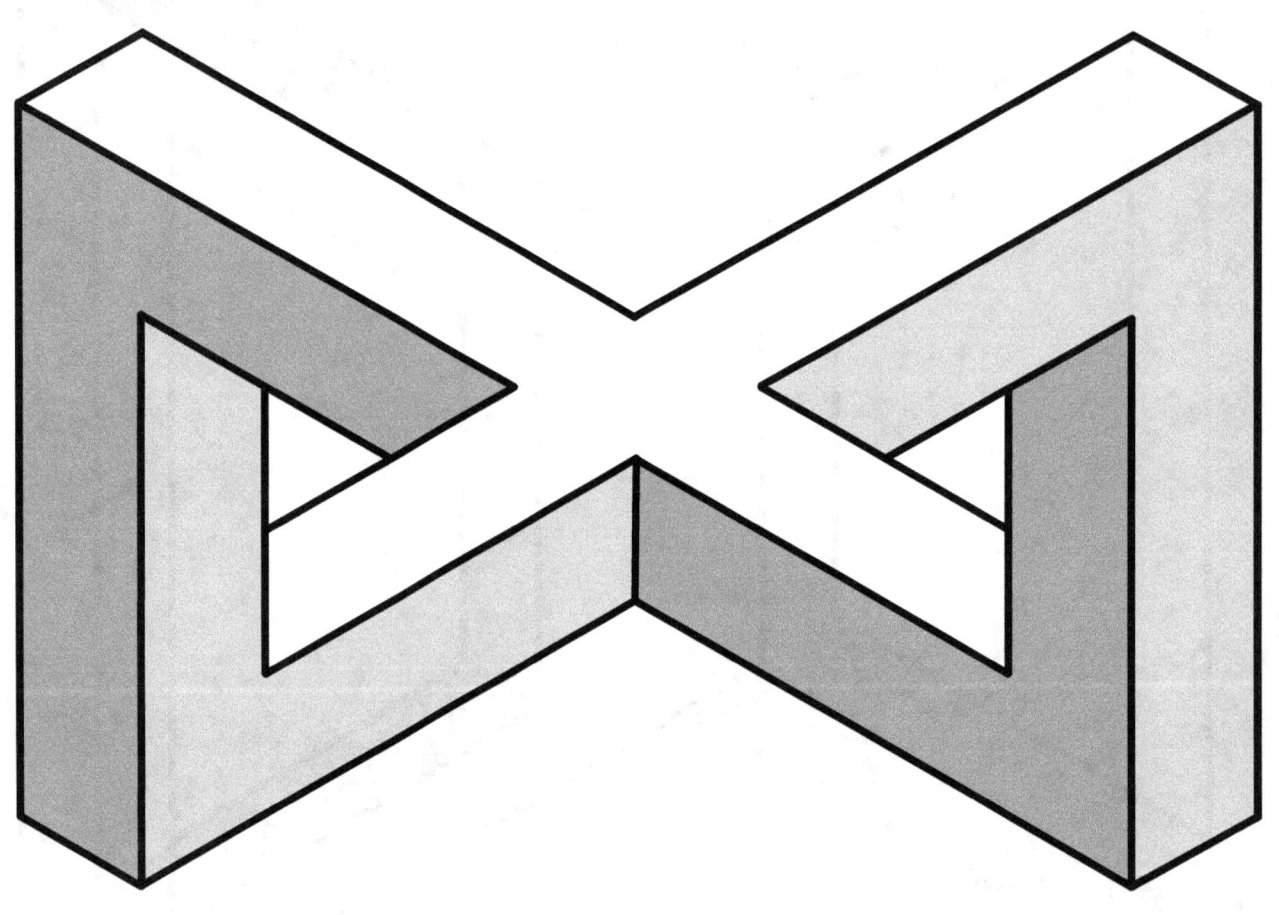

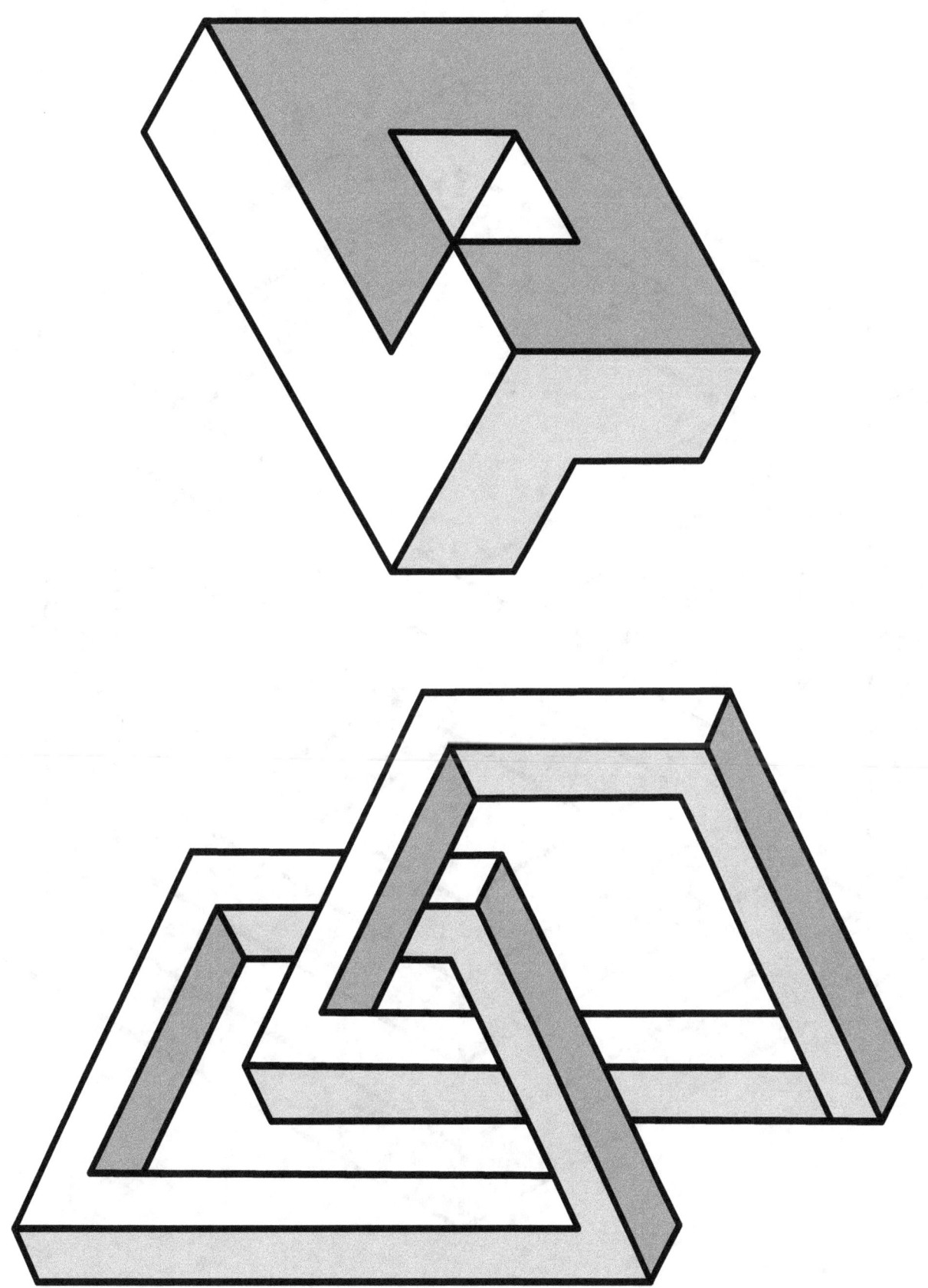

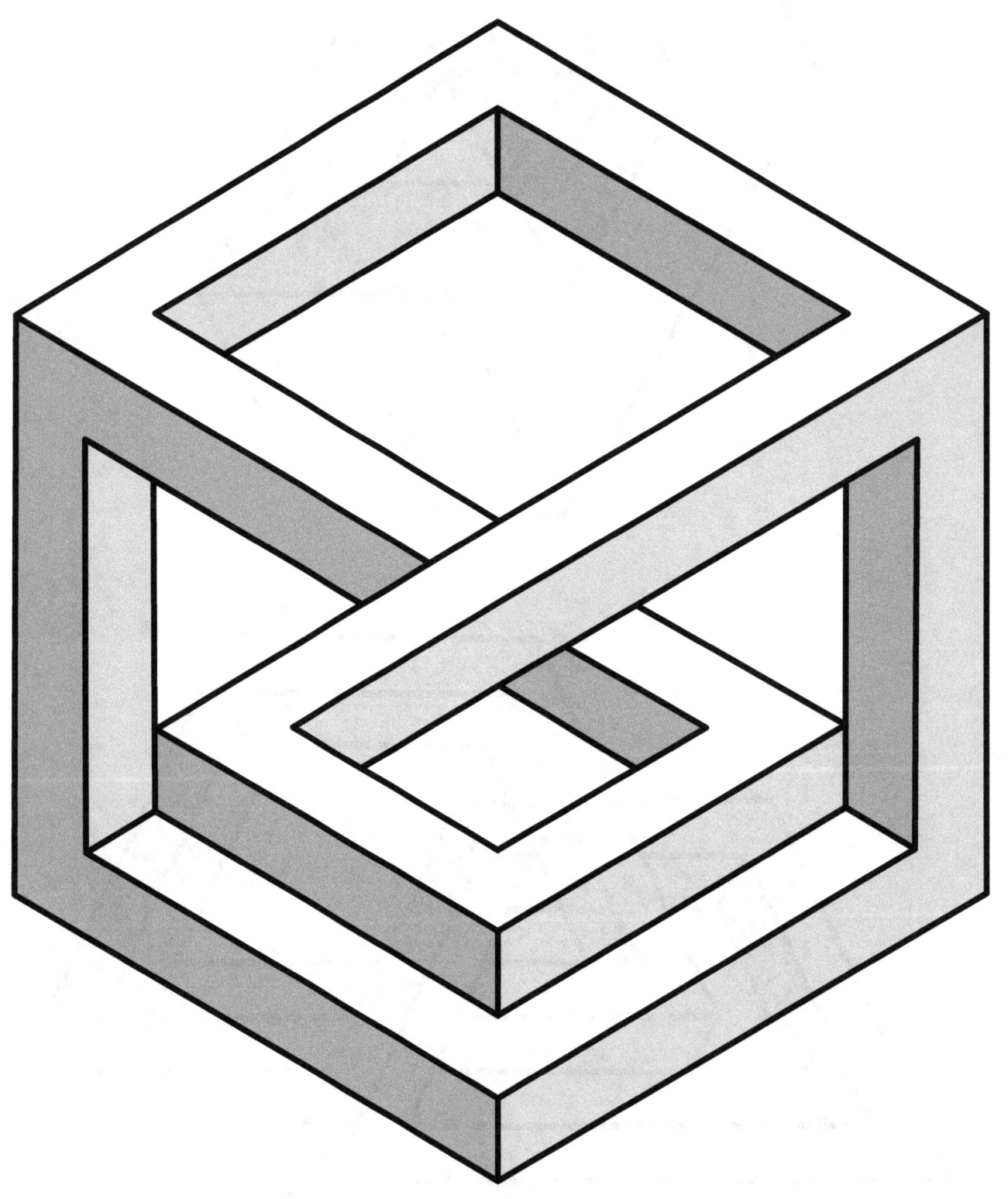

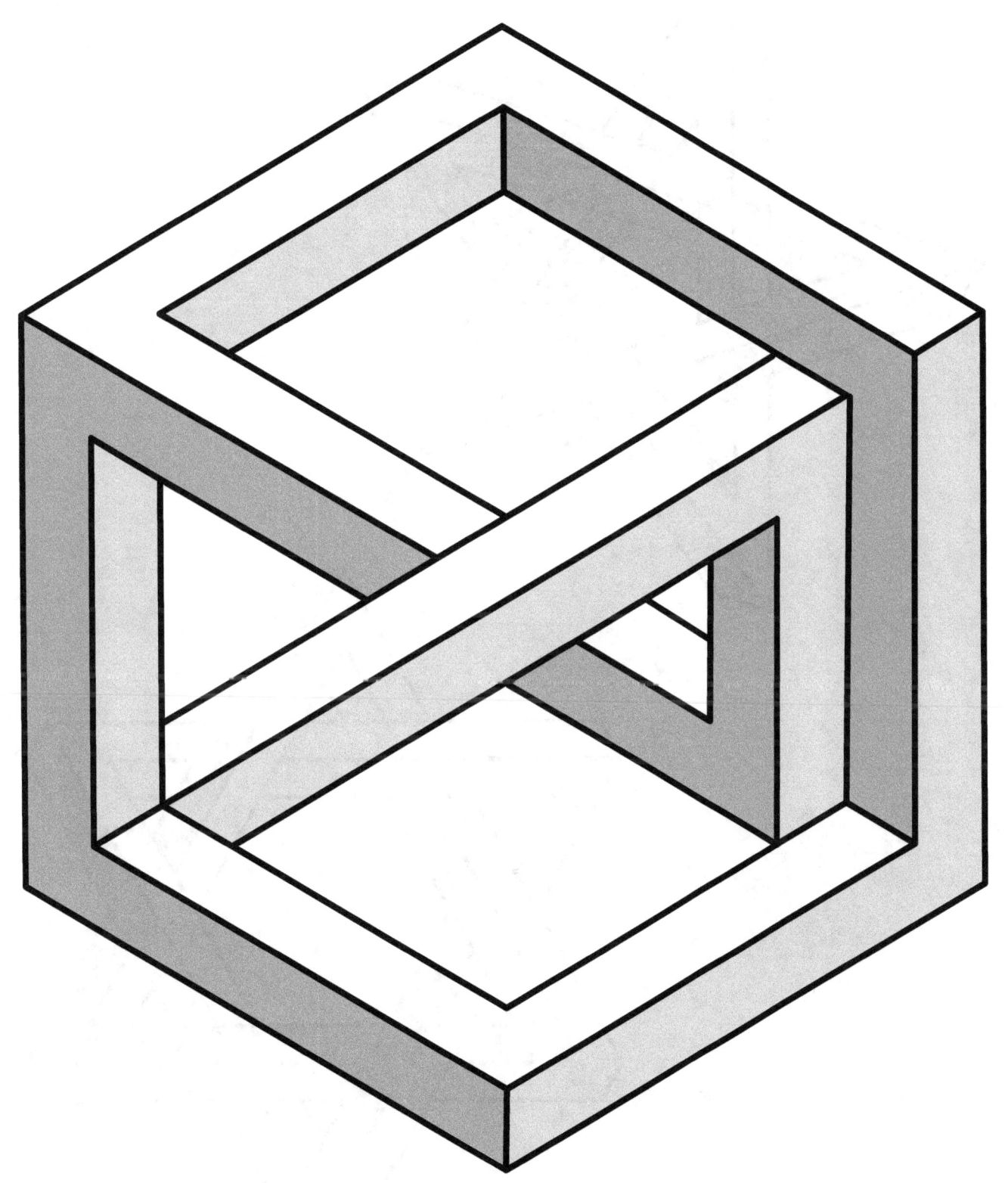

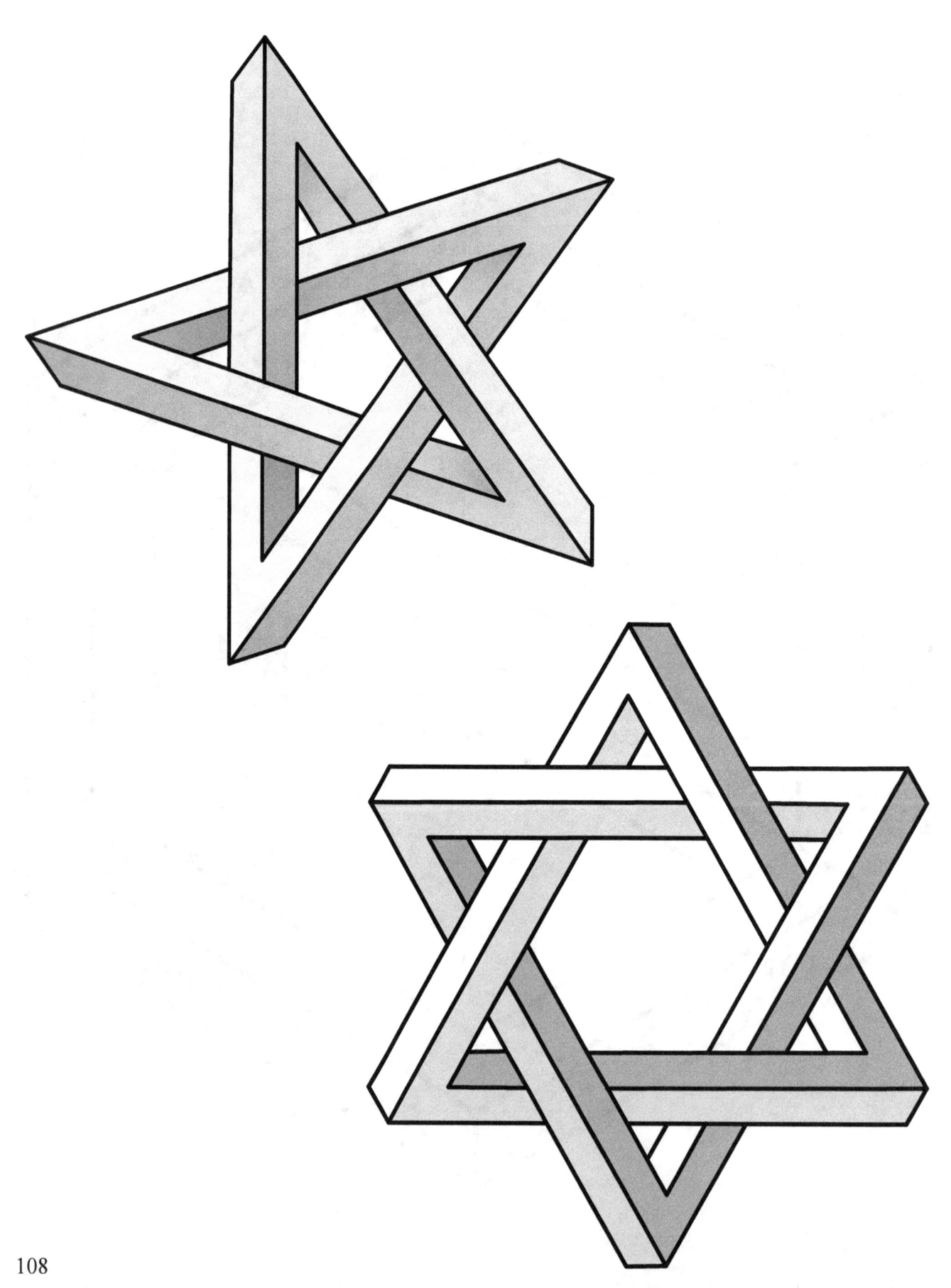

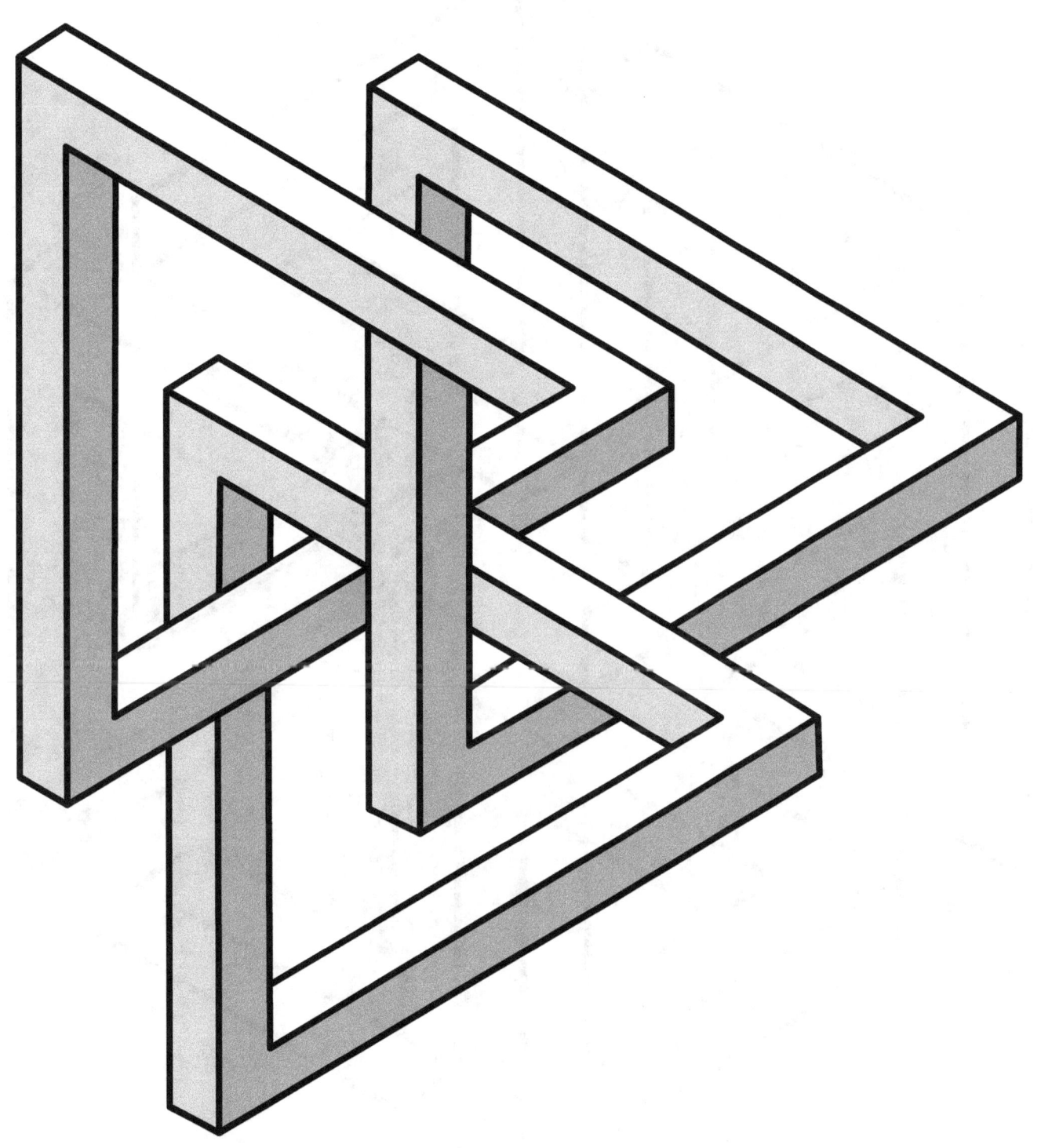

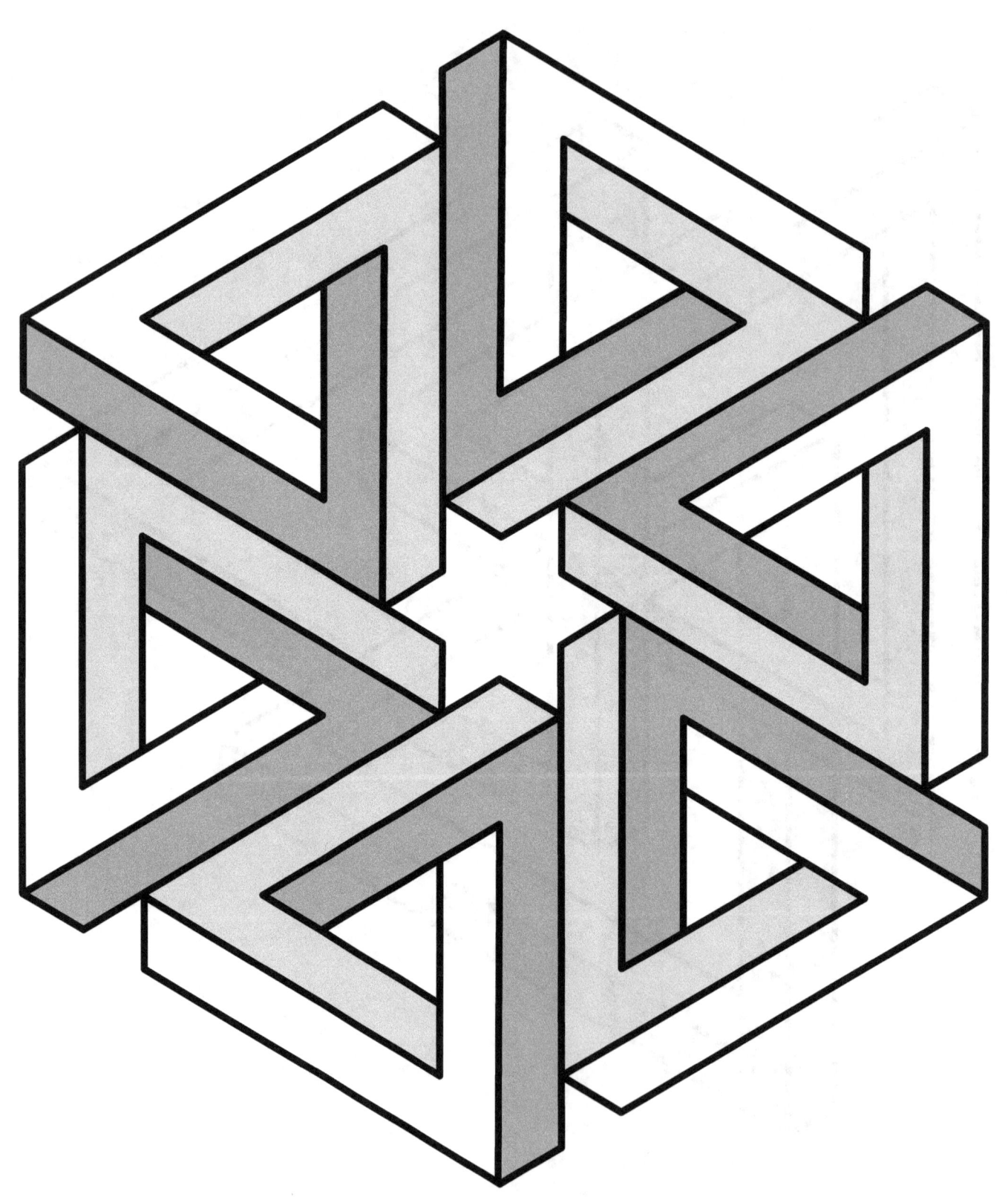

Patterns

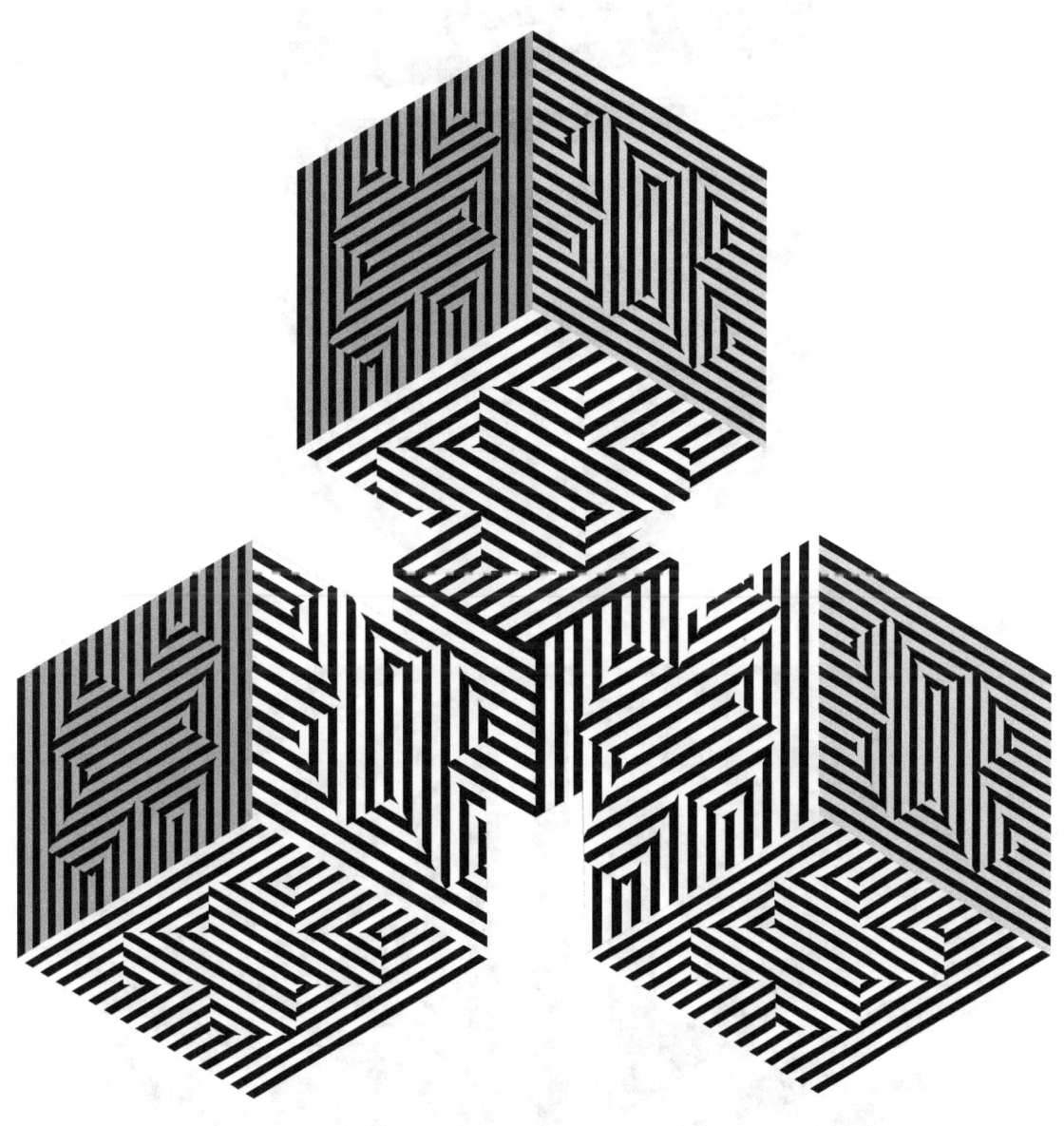

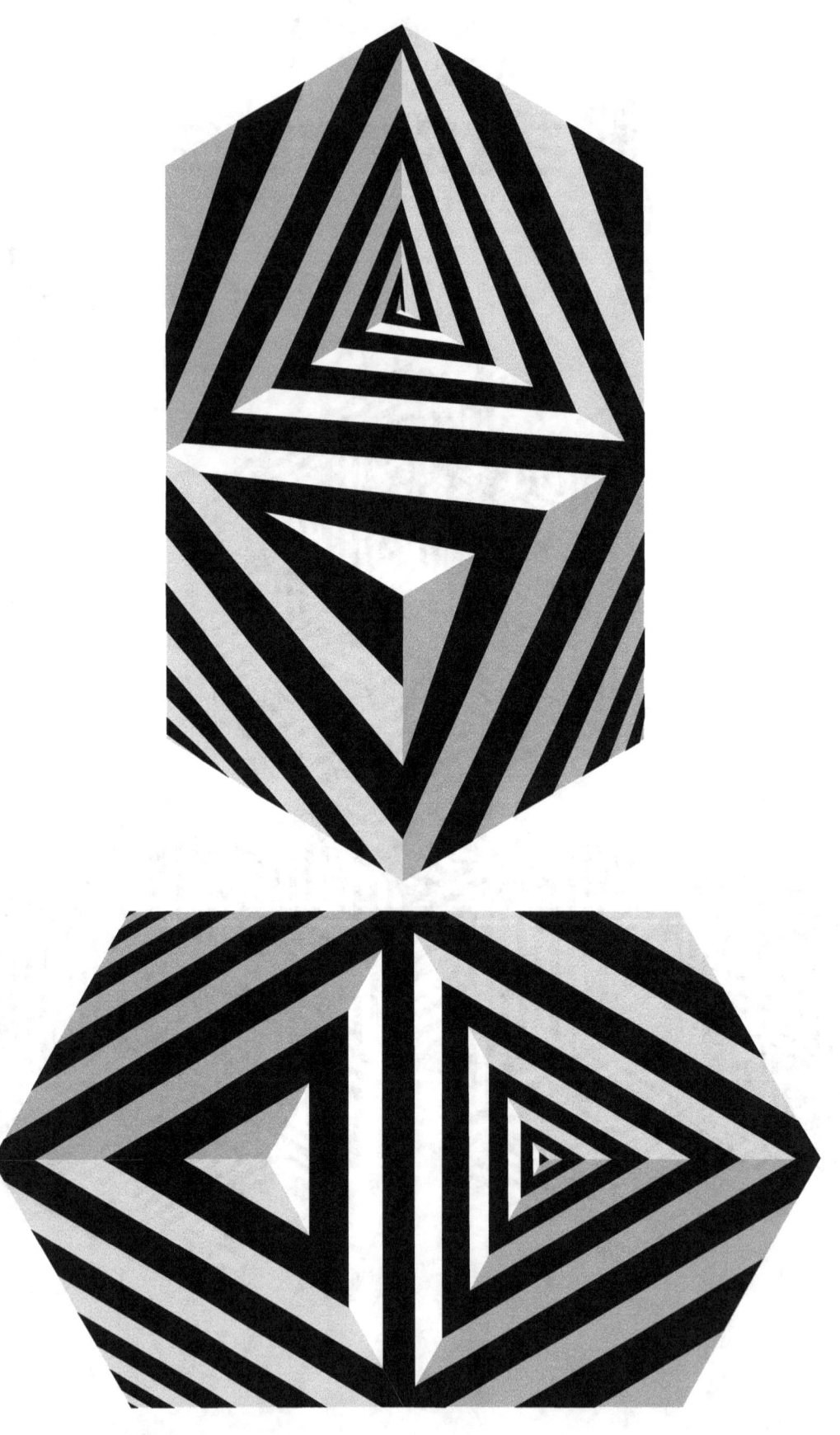

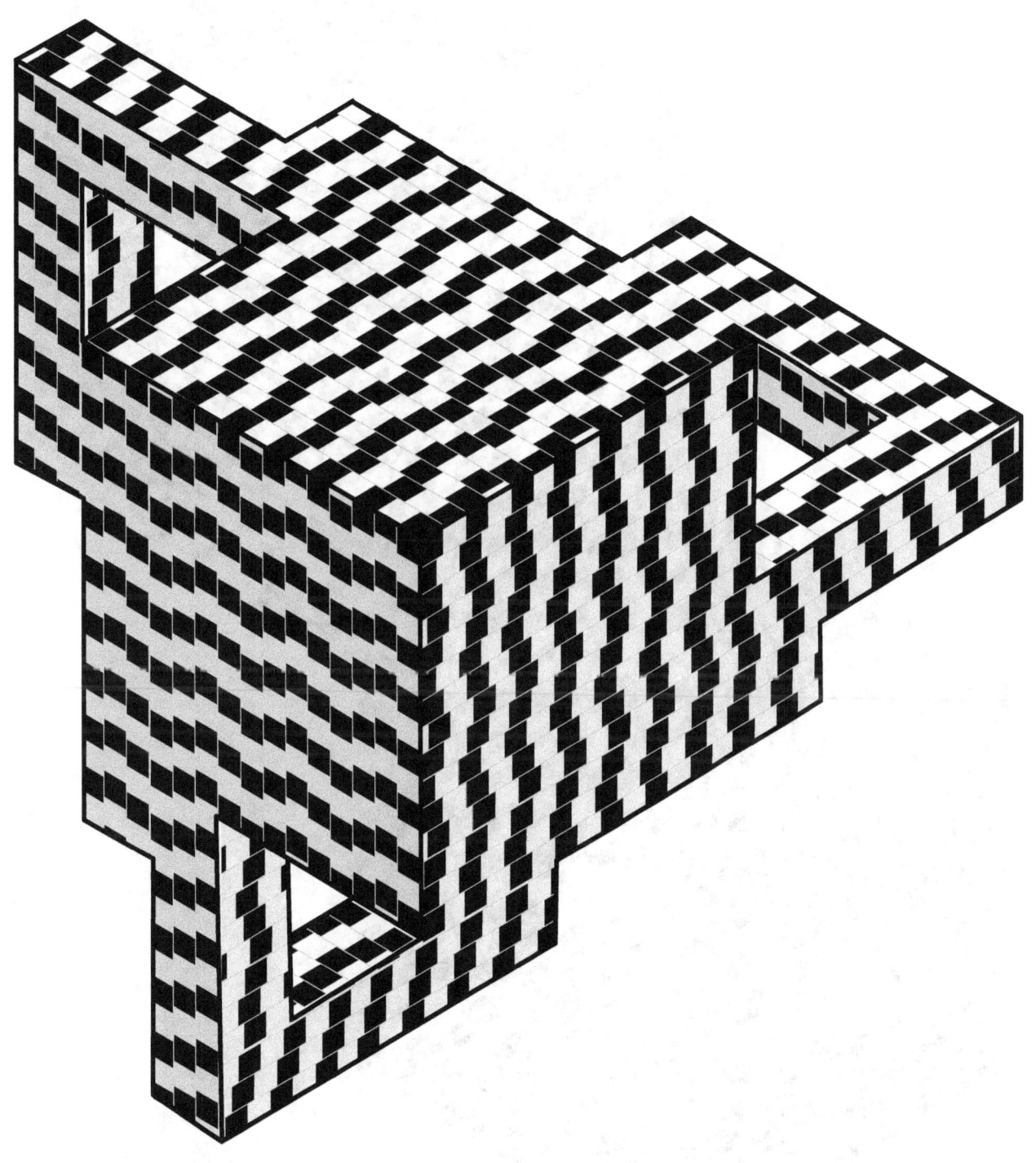

113

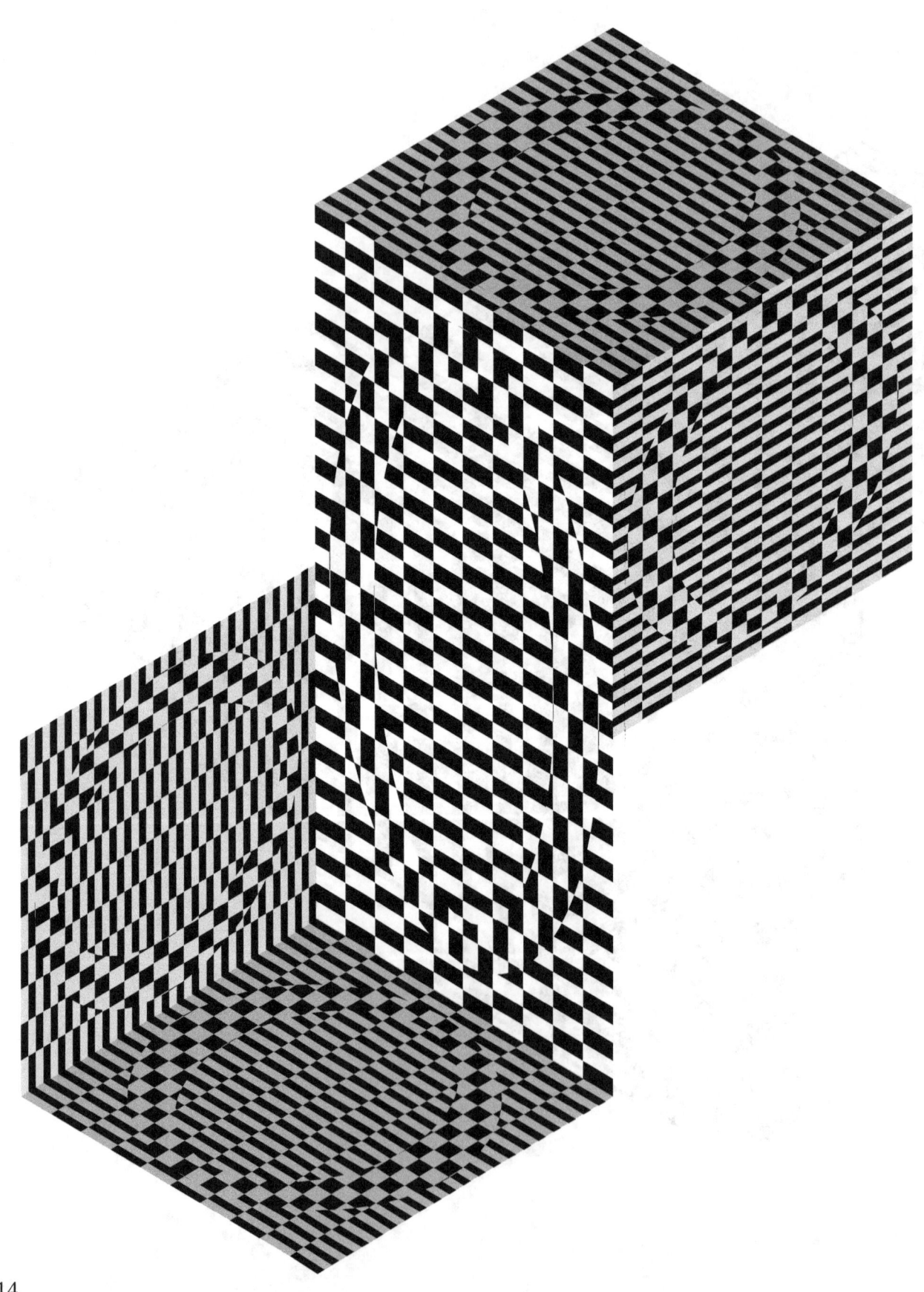

114

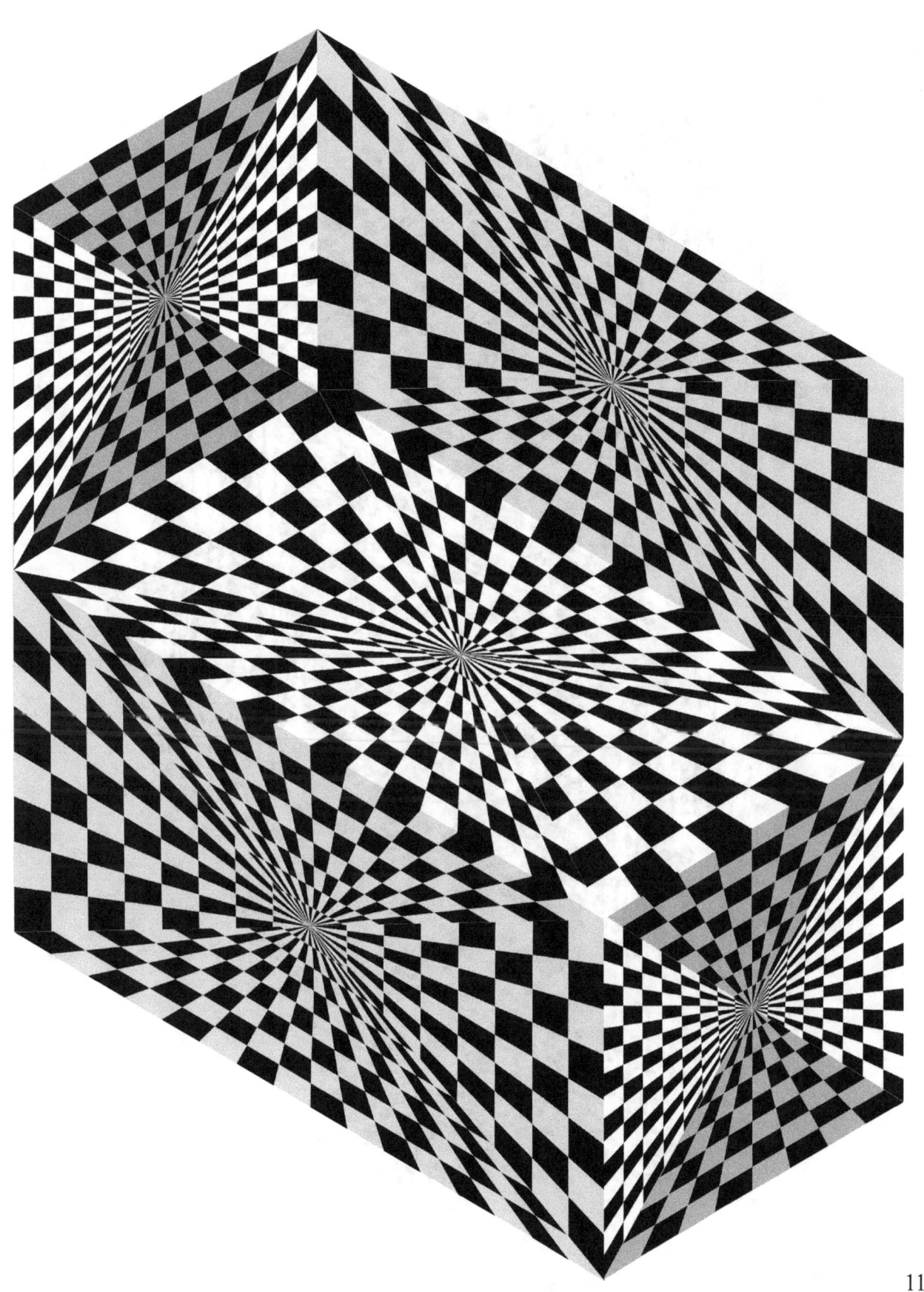

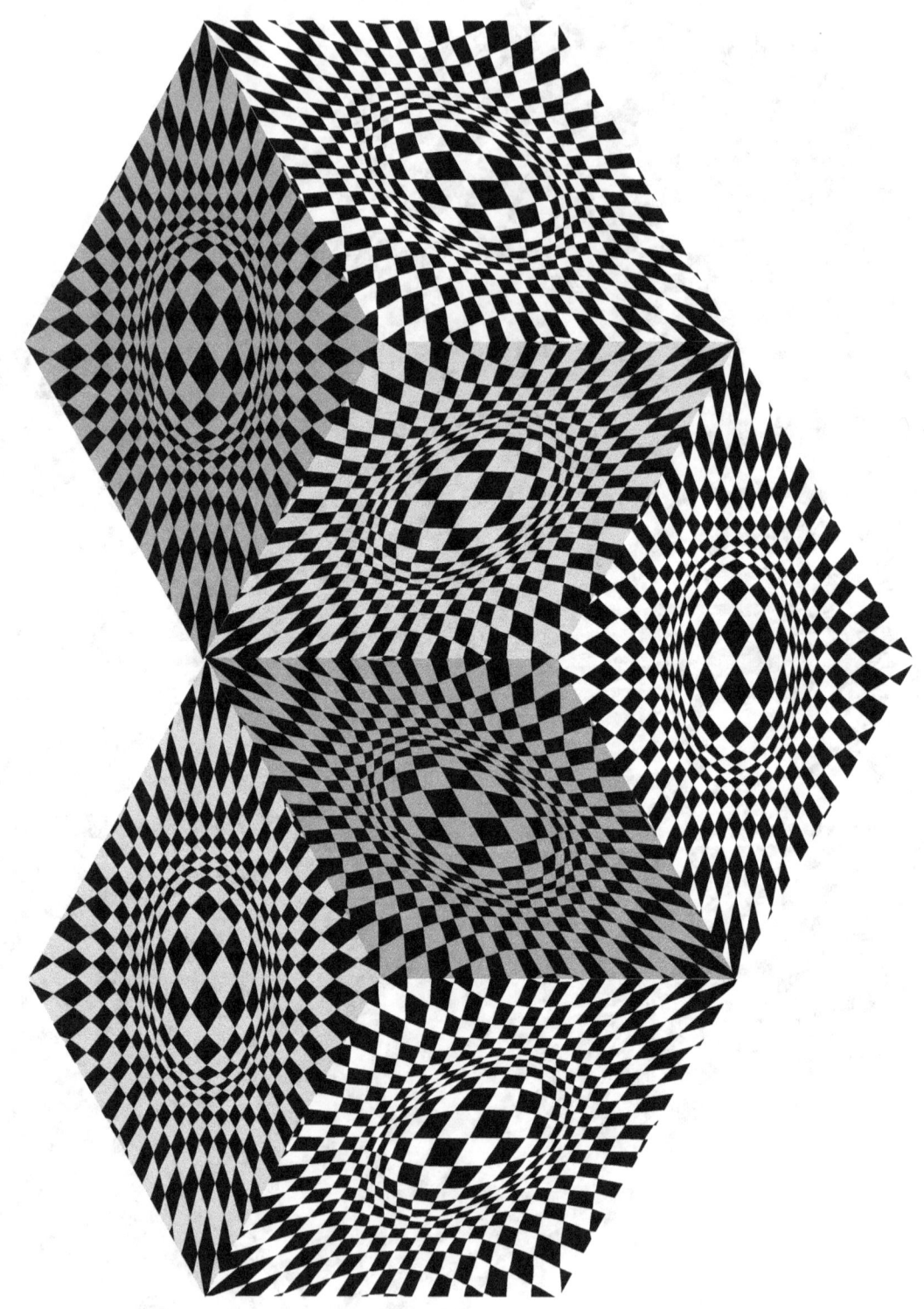

116

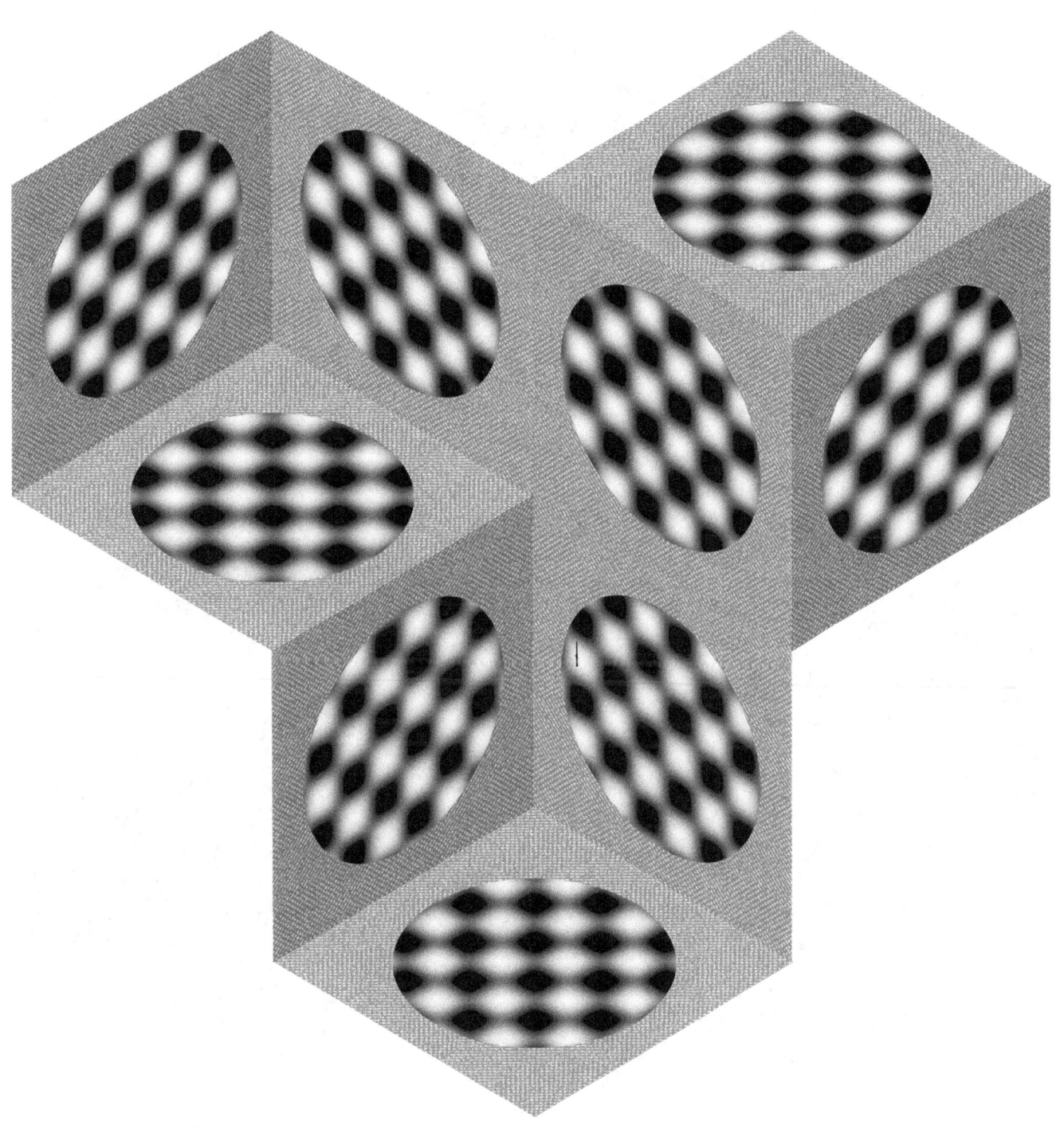

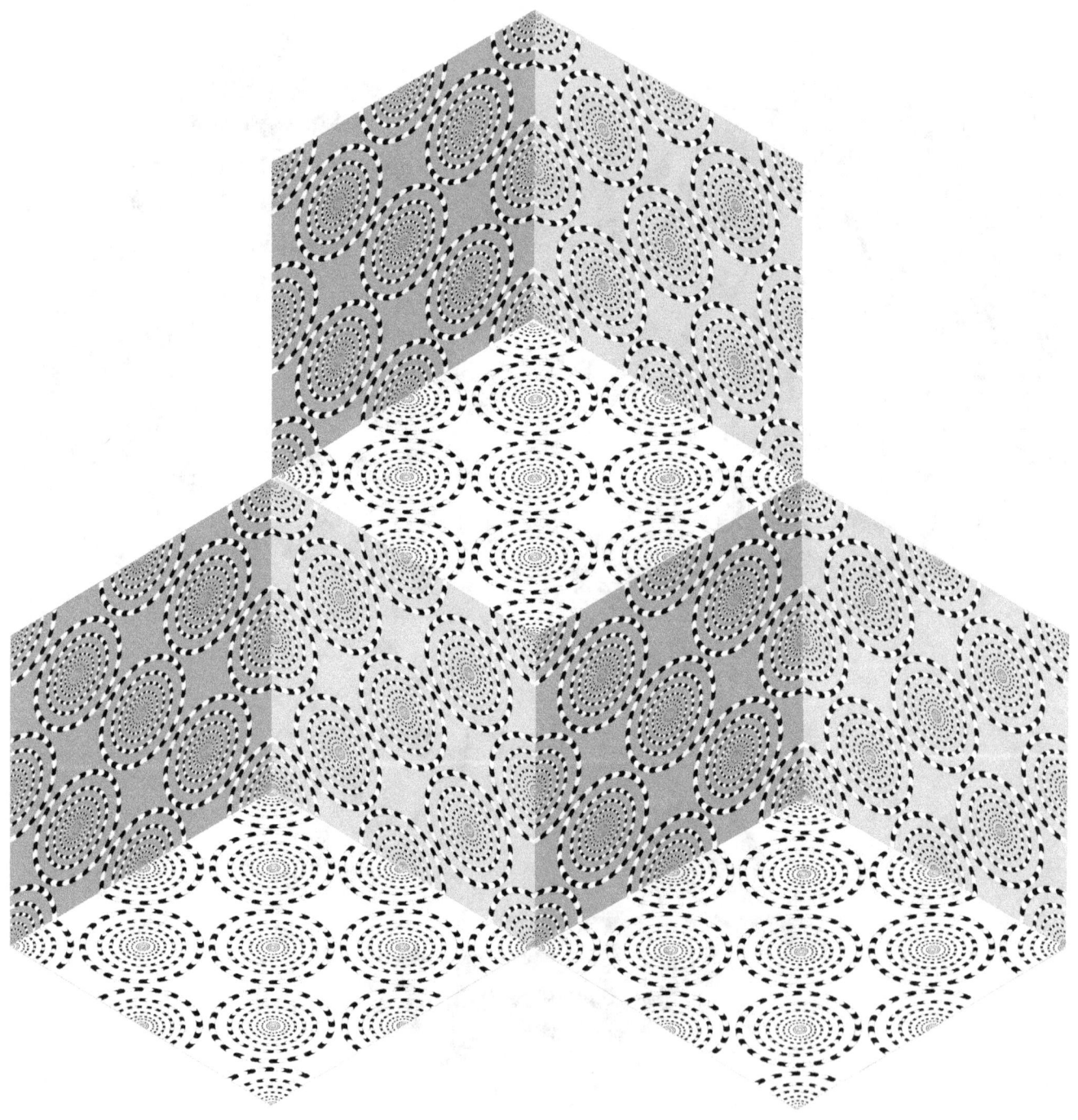

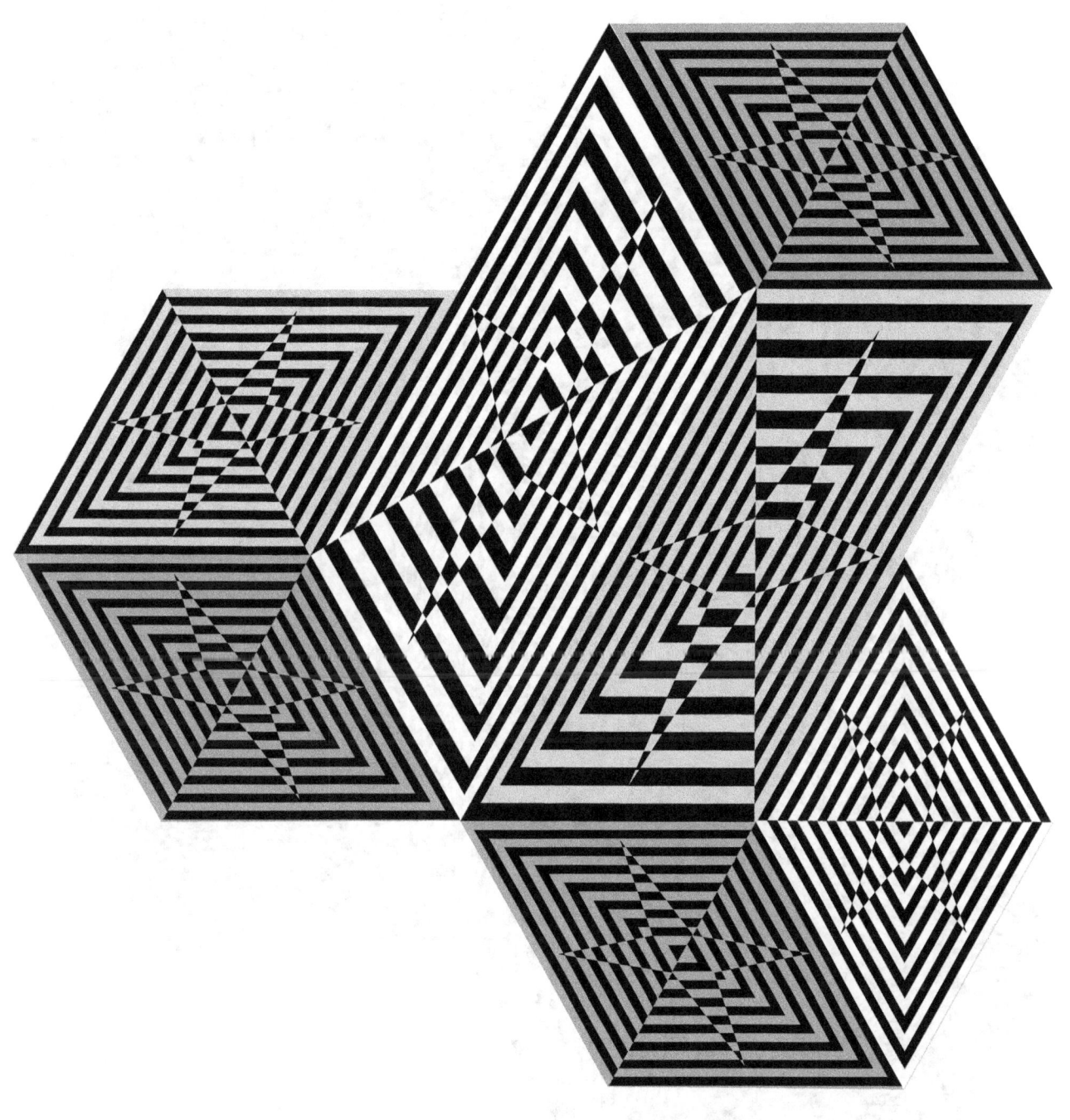

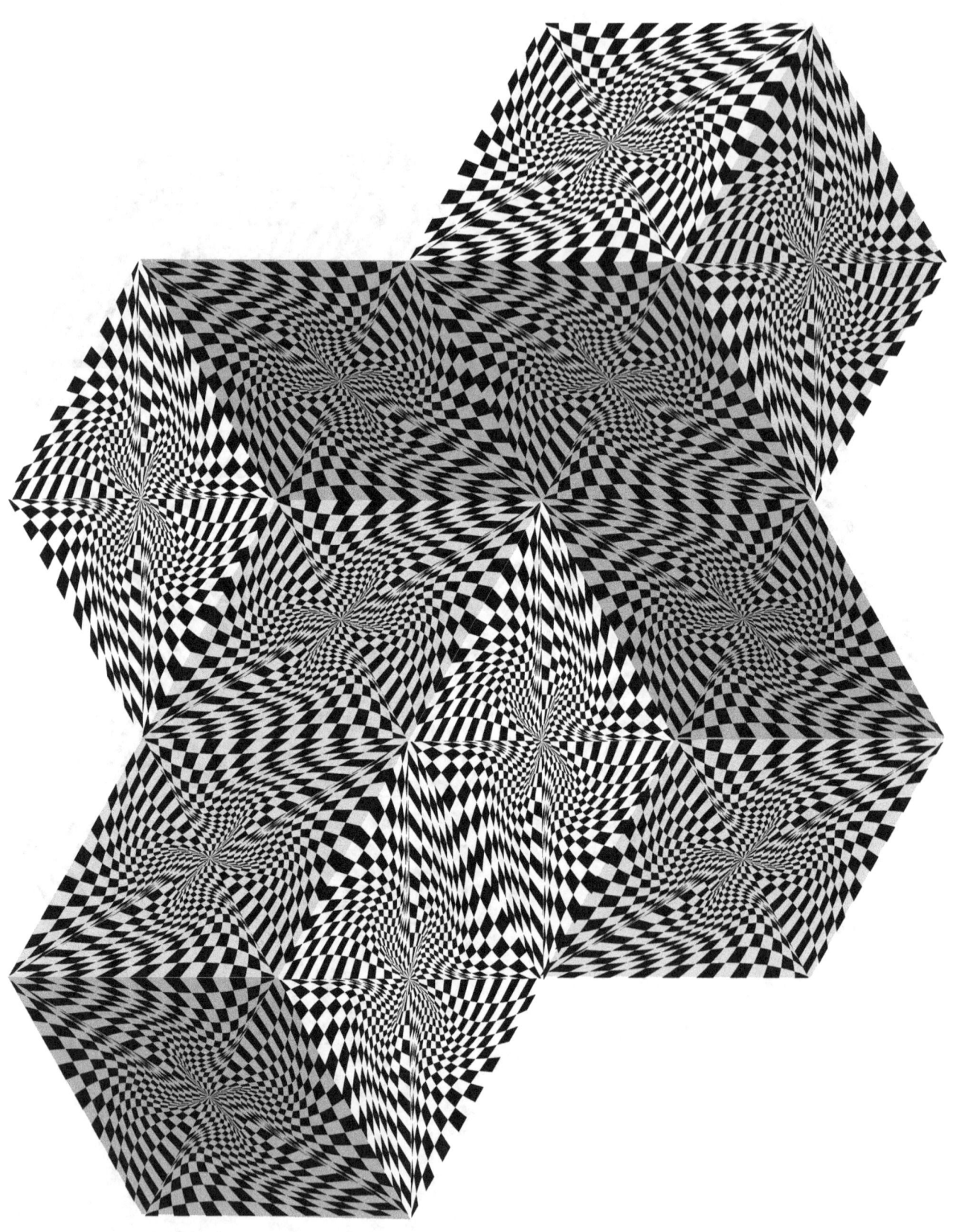

Structures

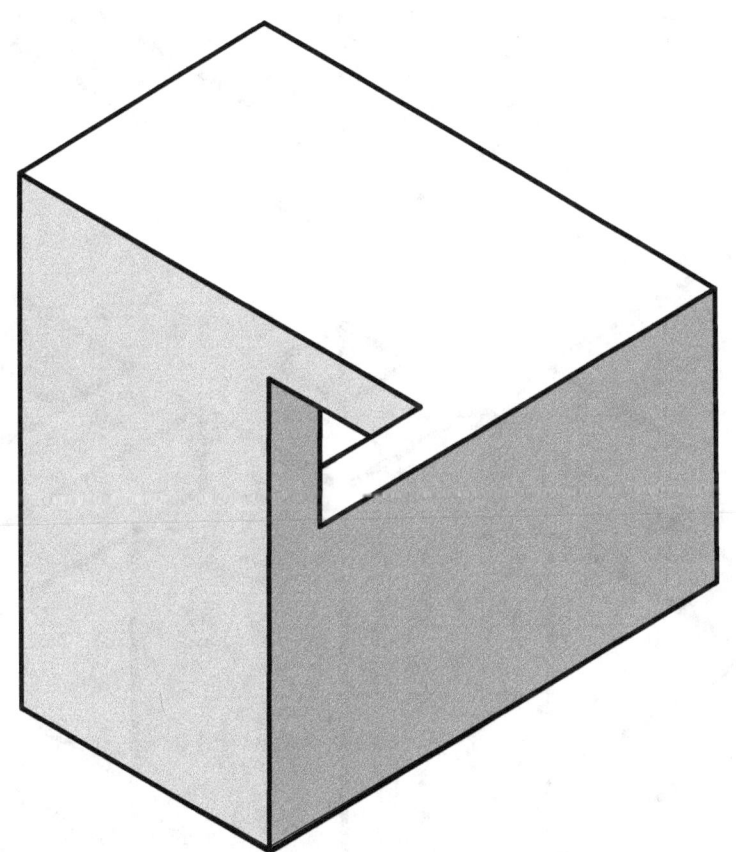

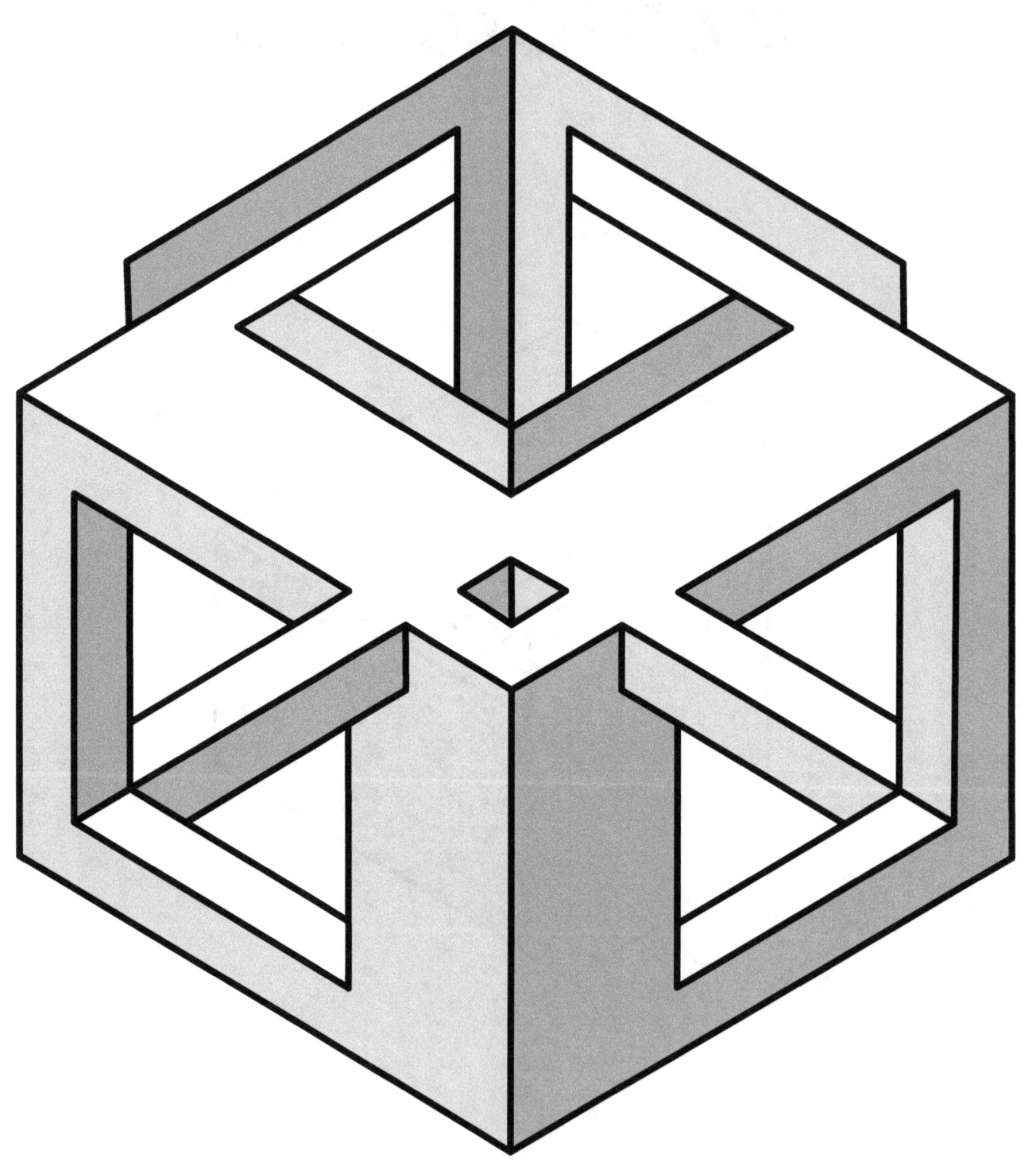

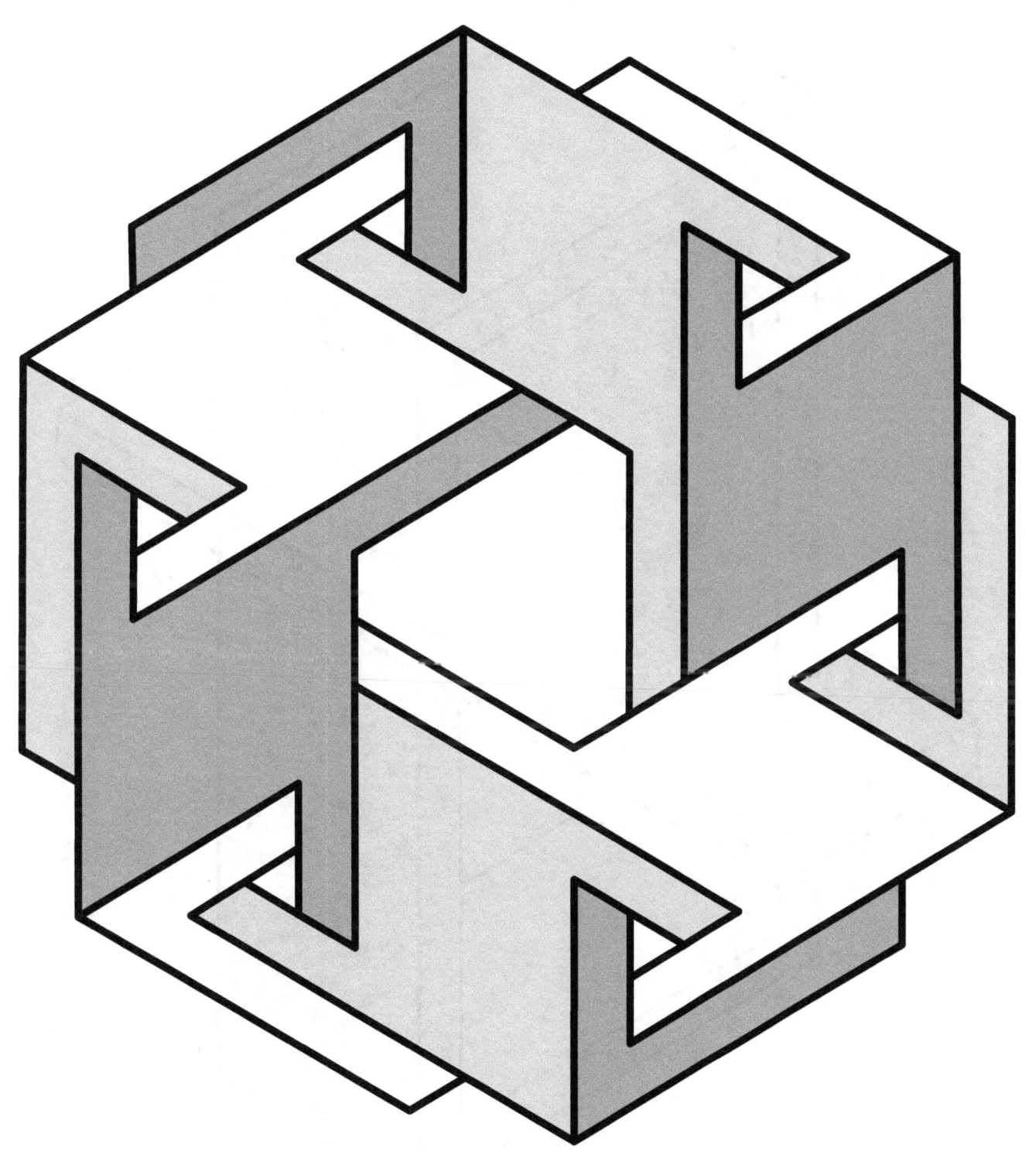

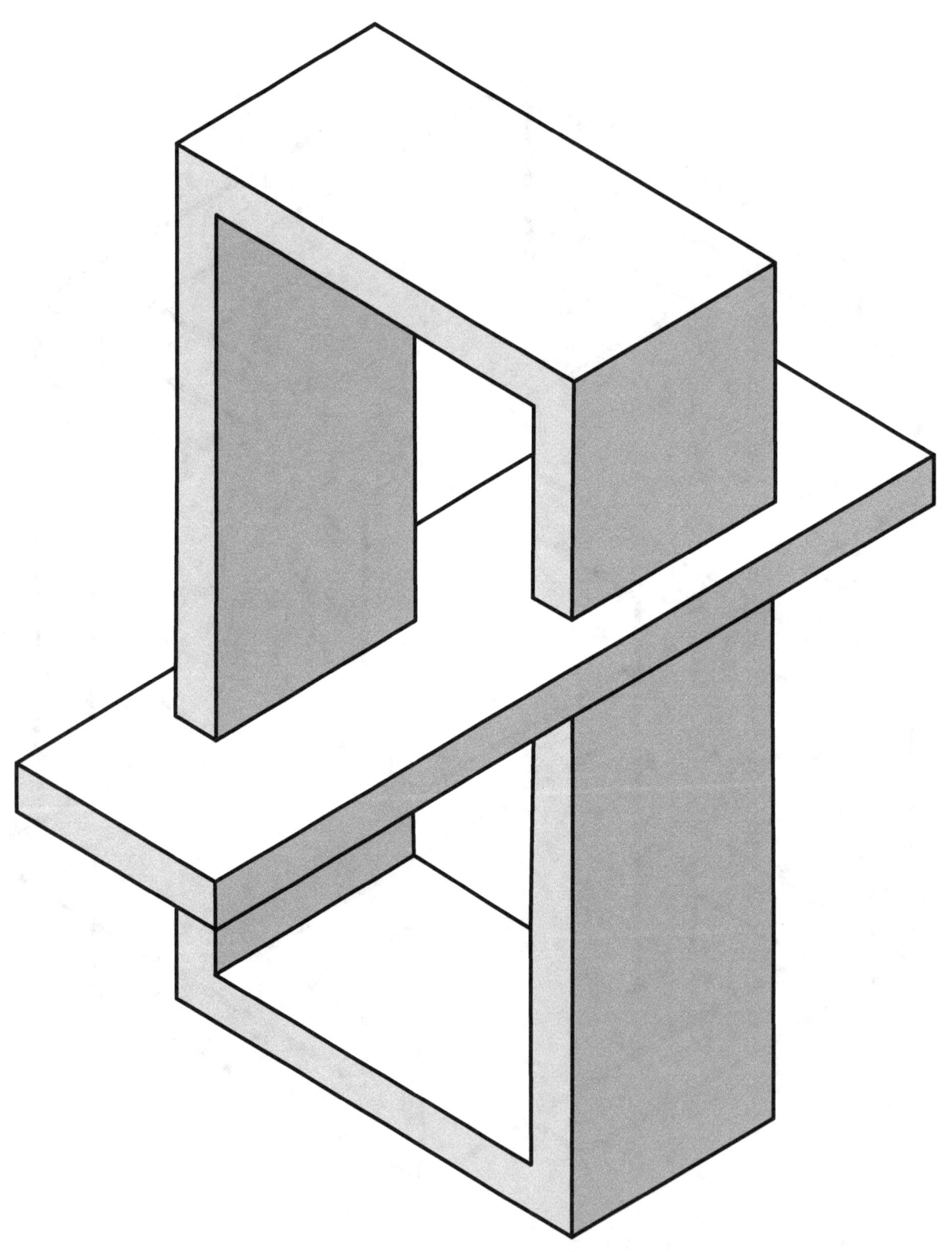

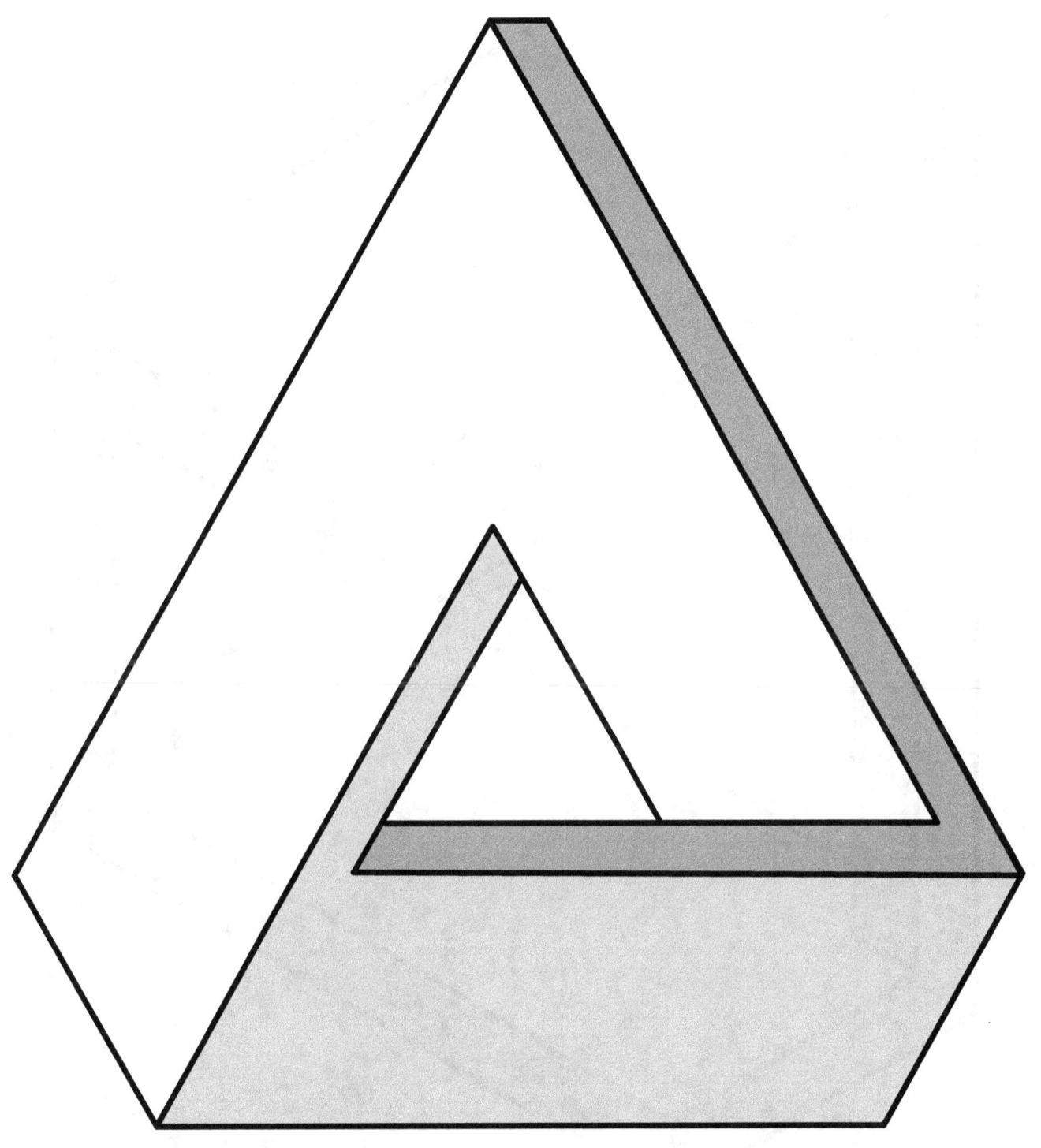

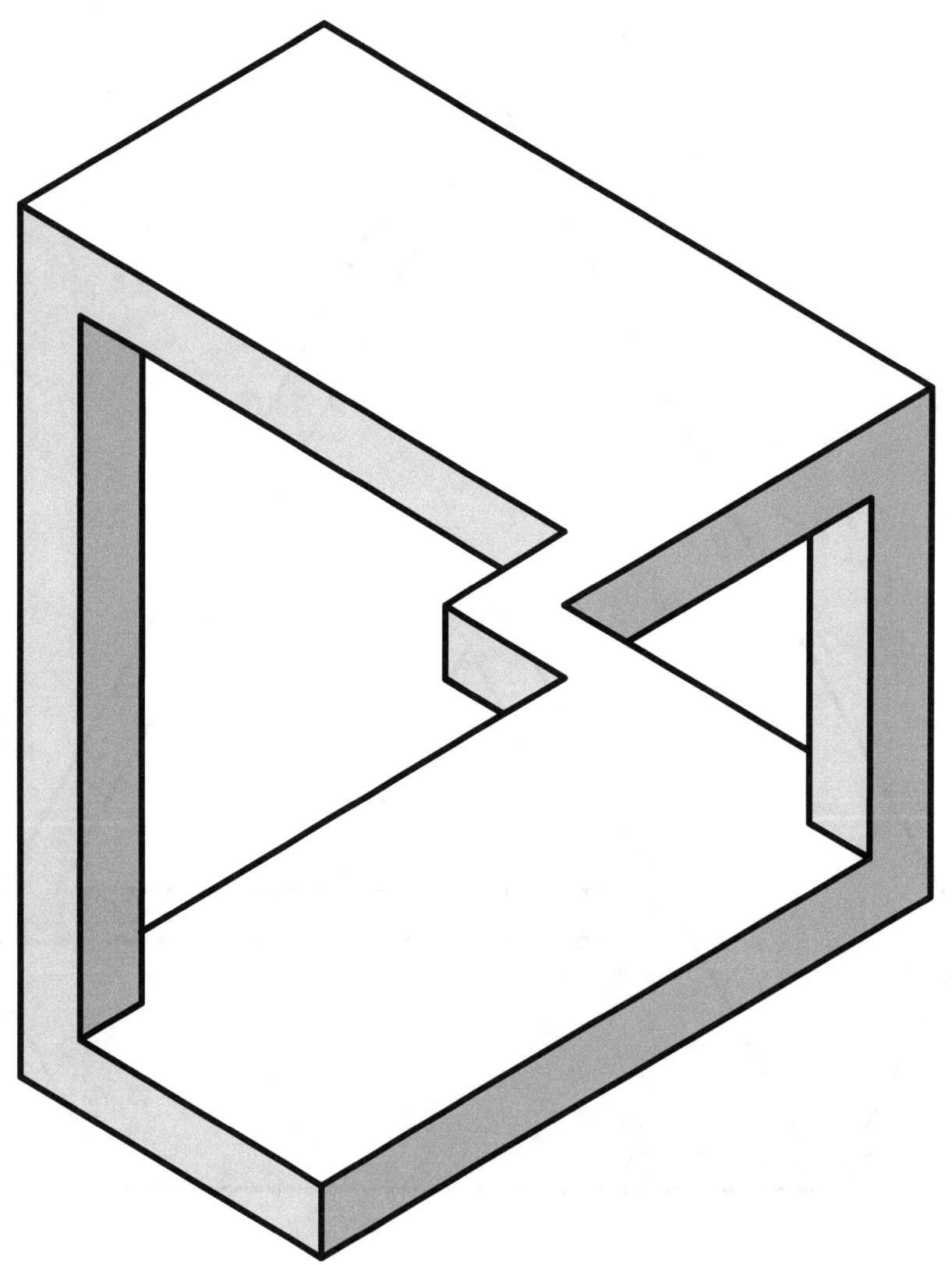

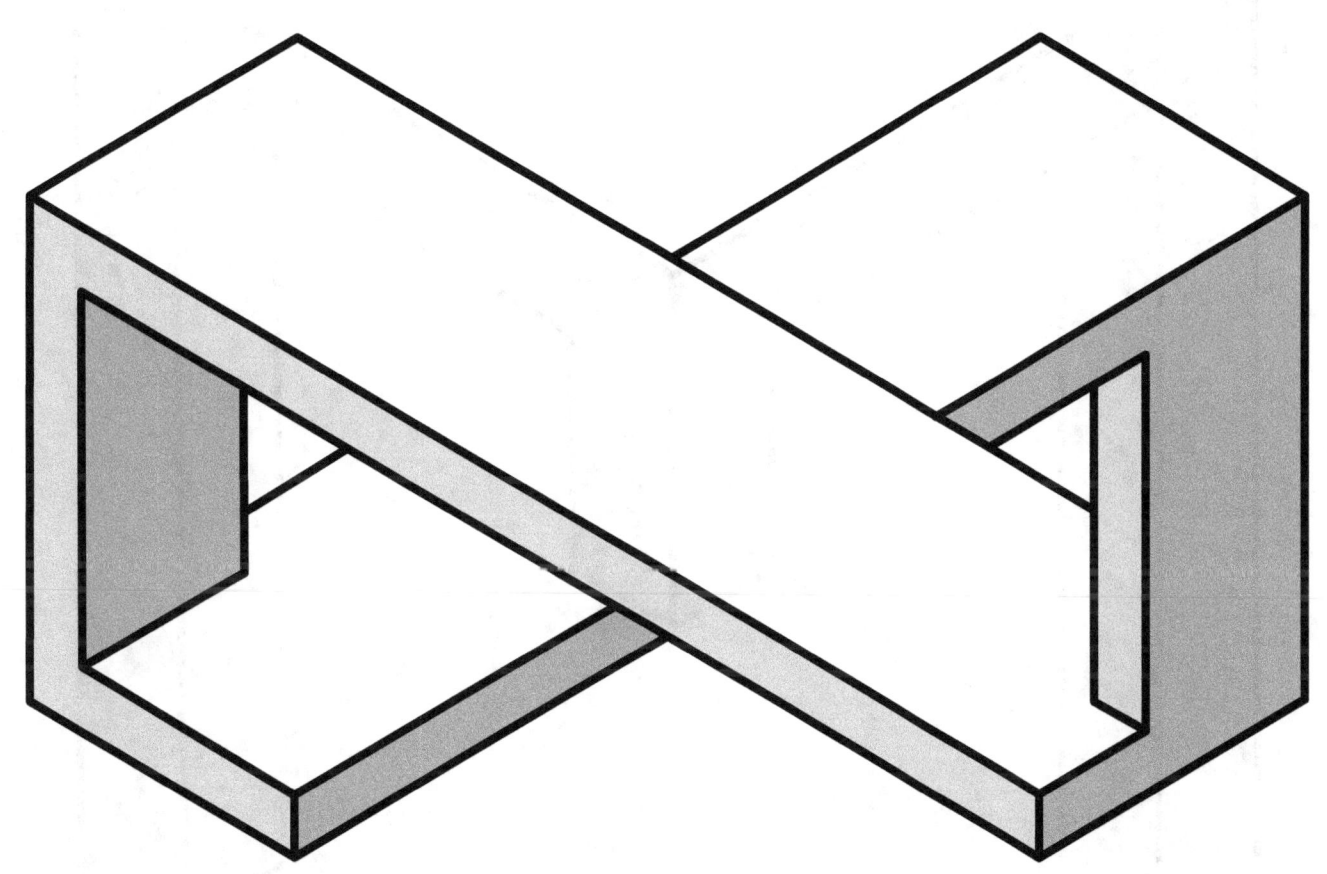

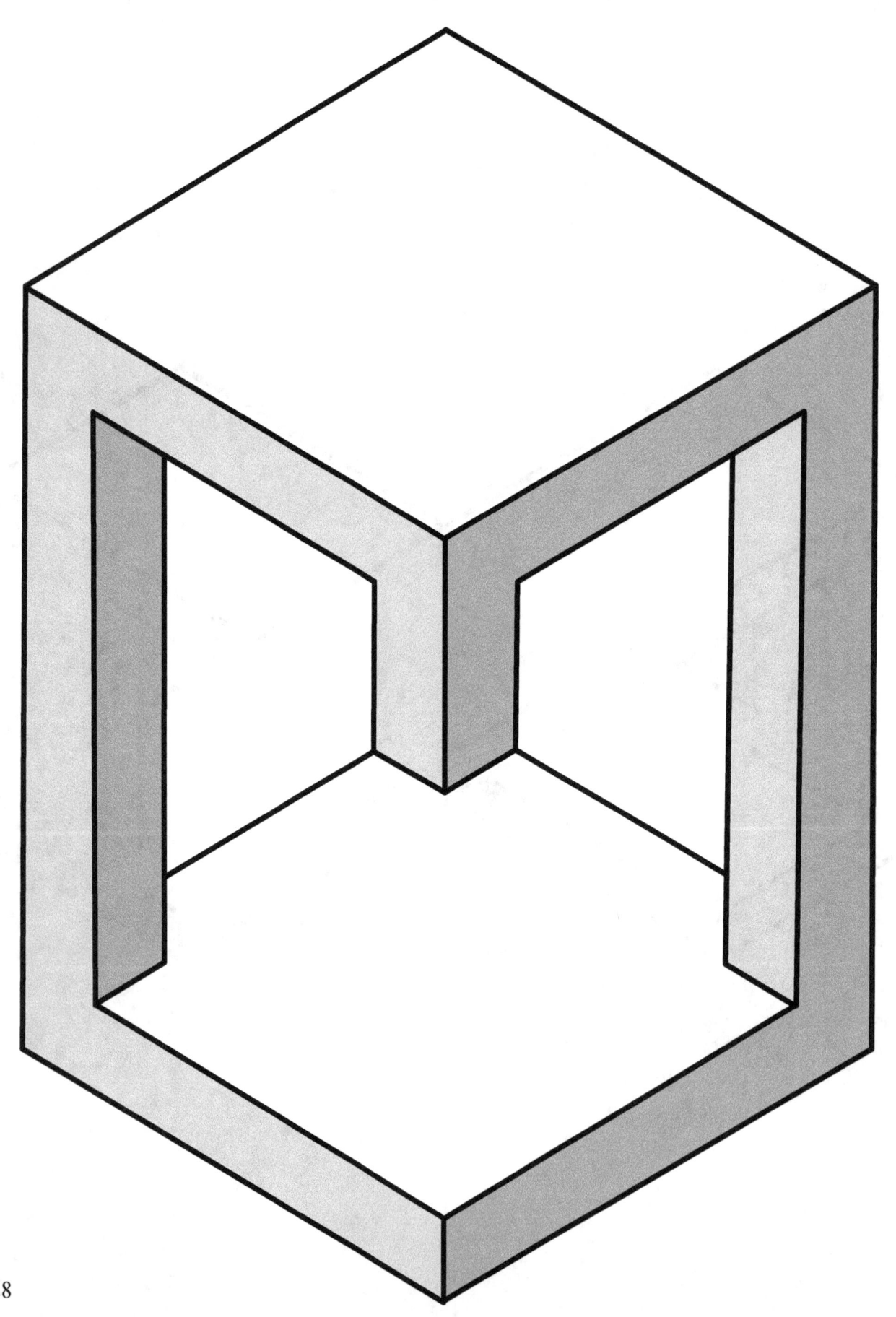

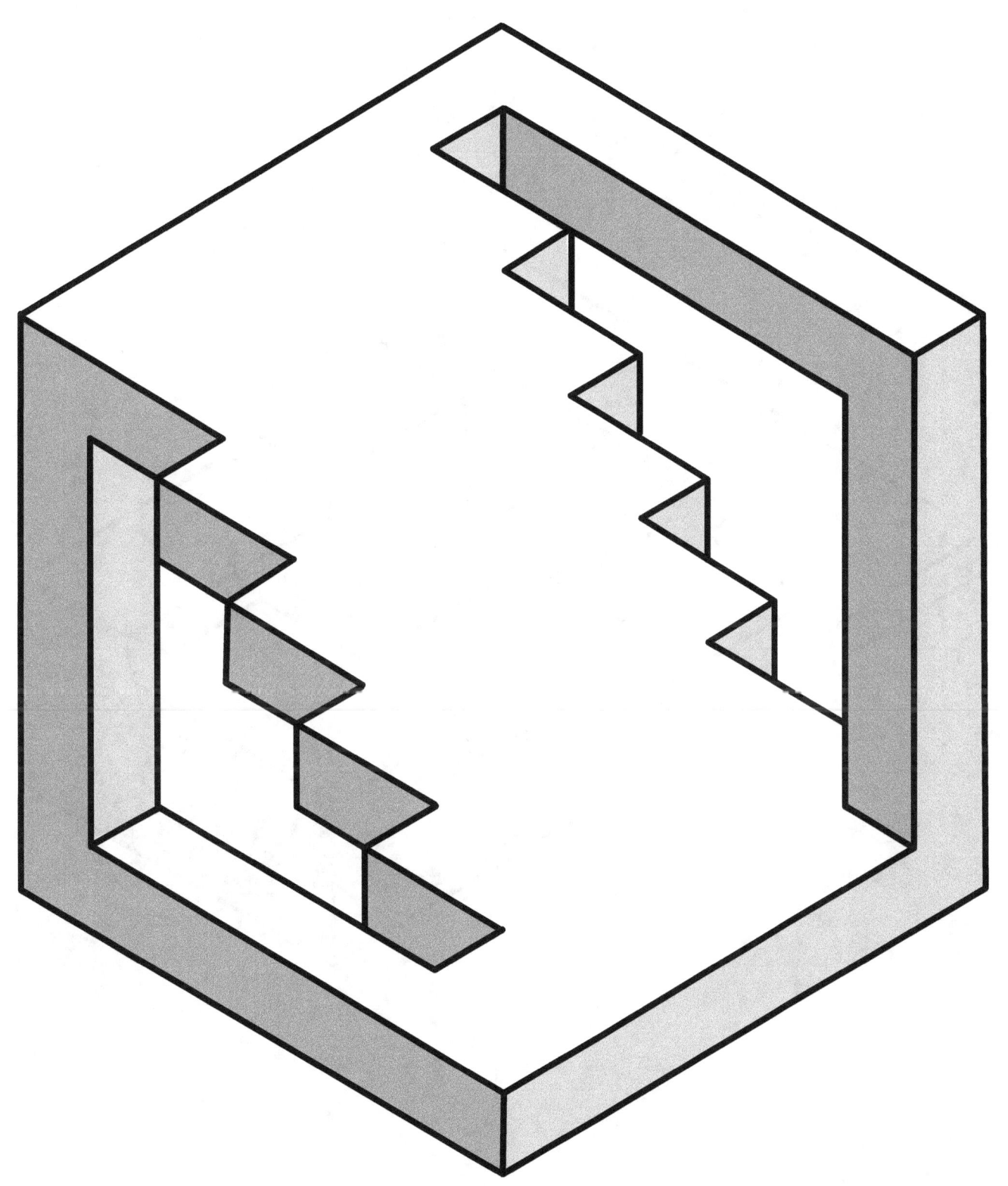

129

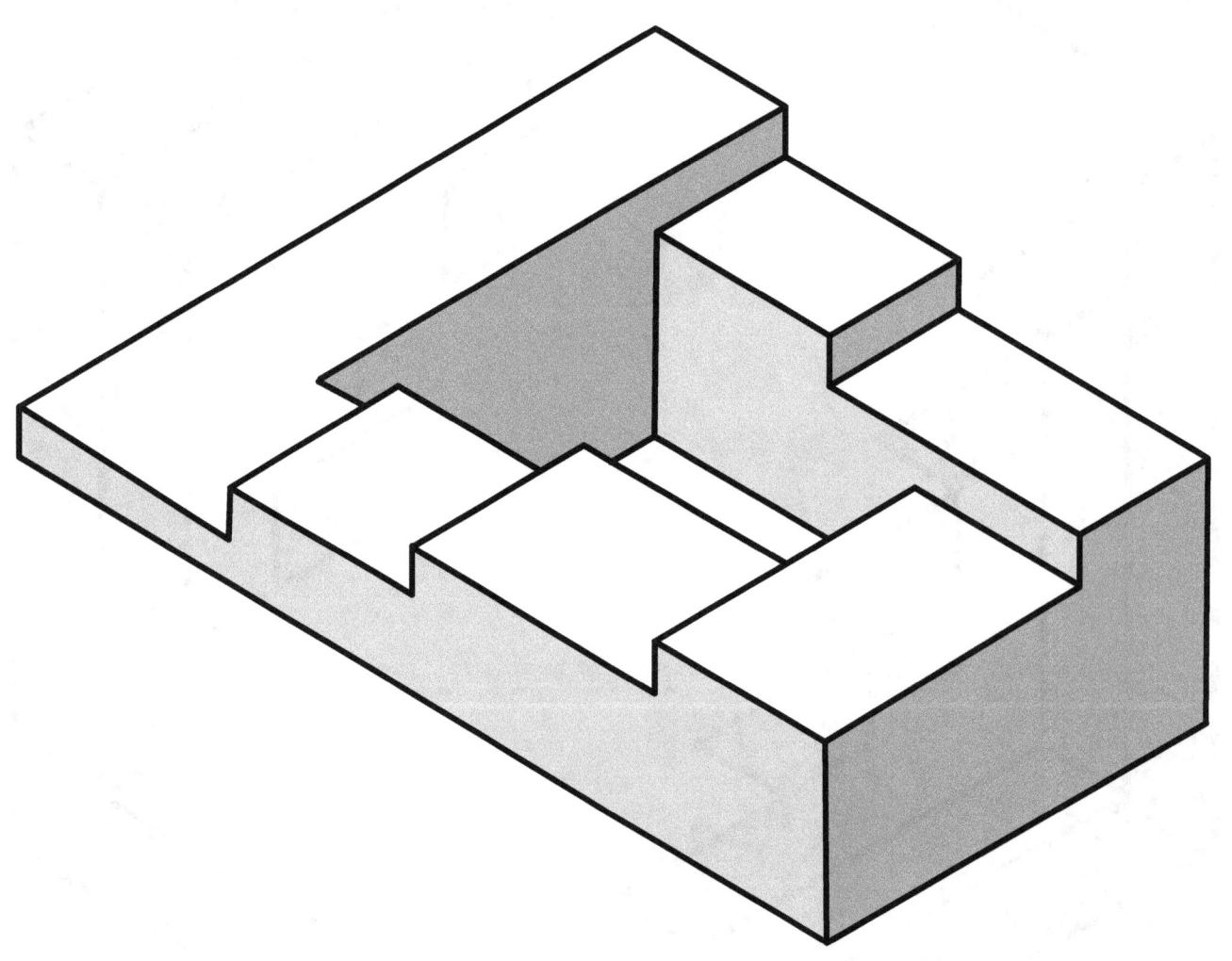

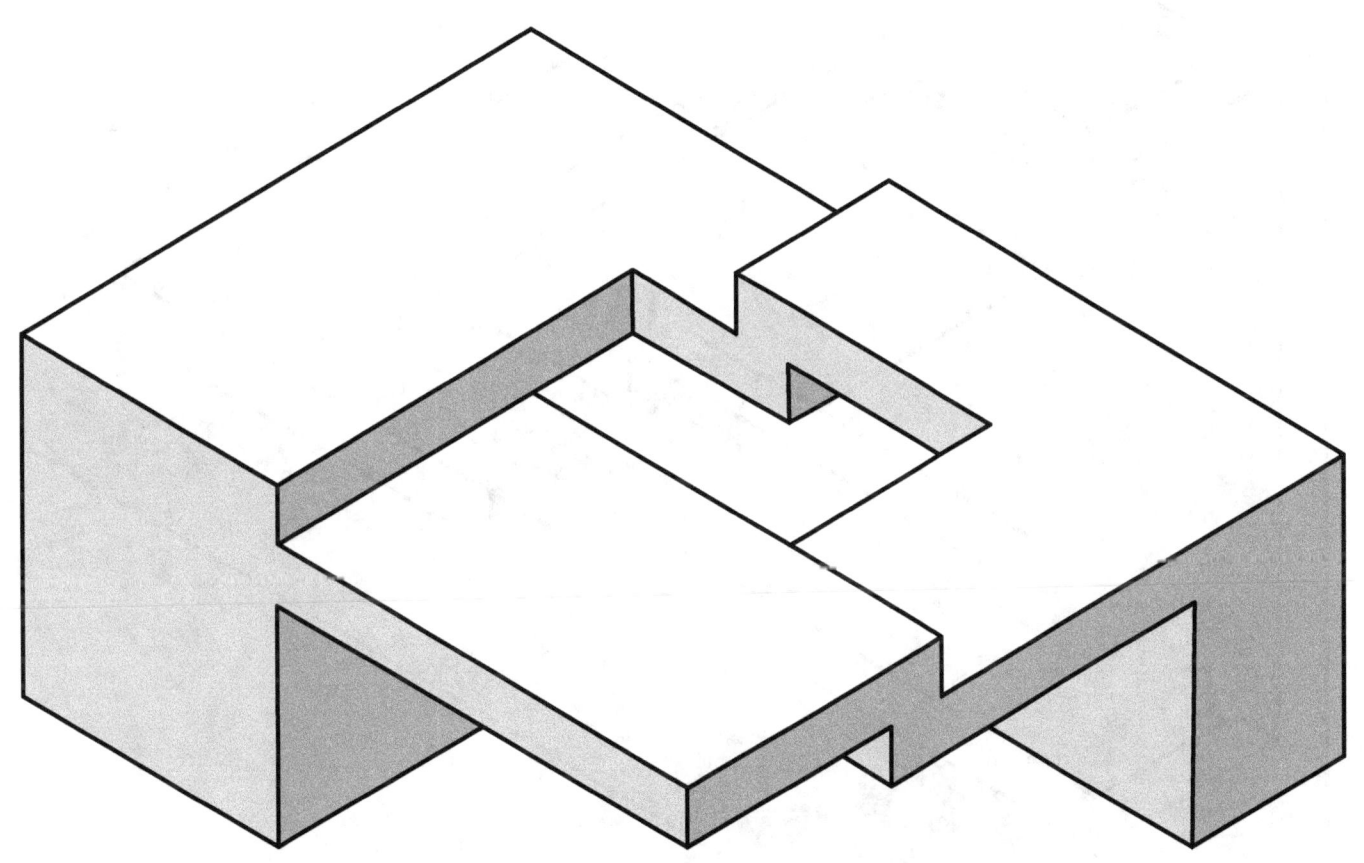

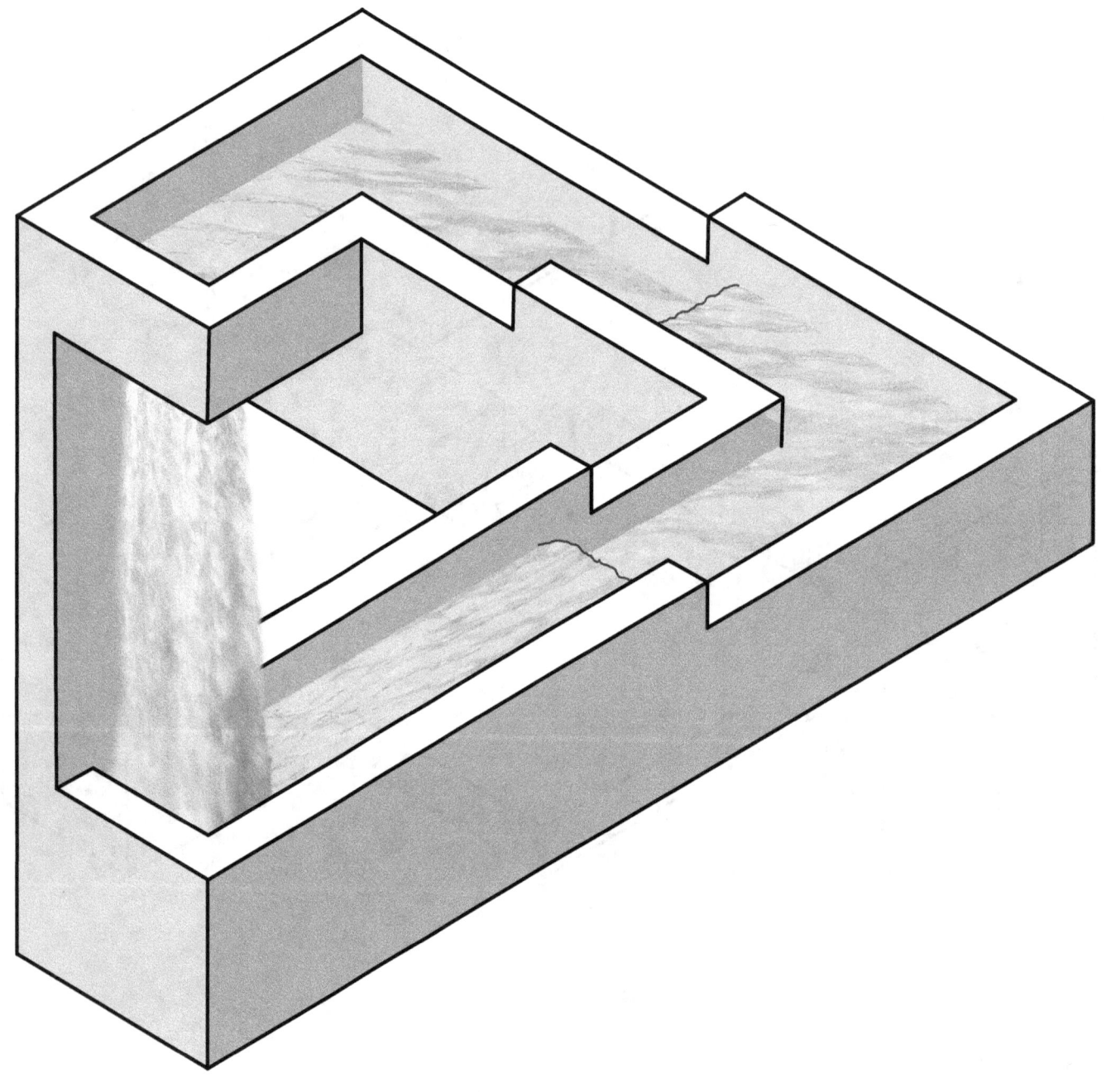

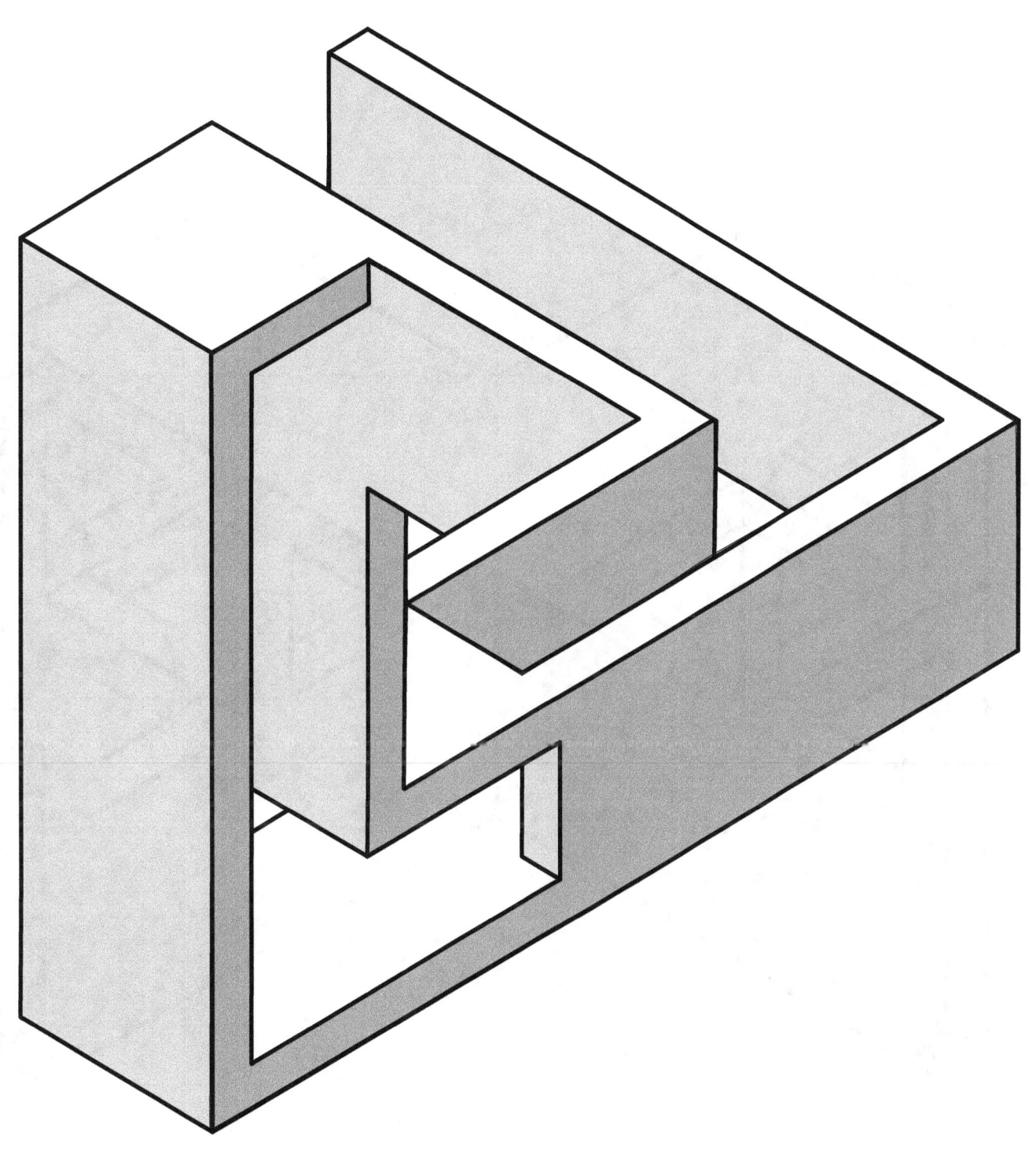

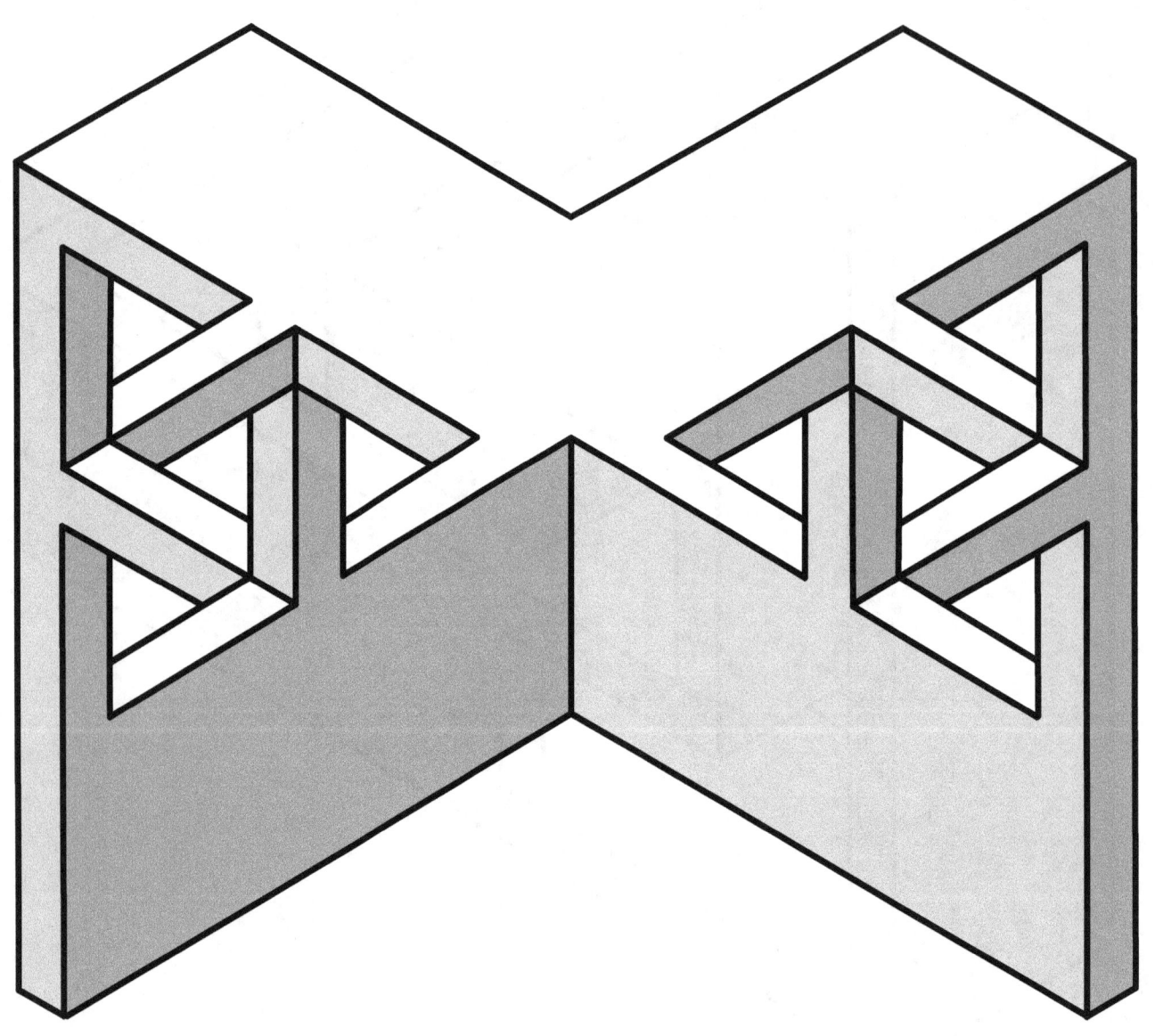

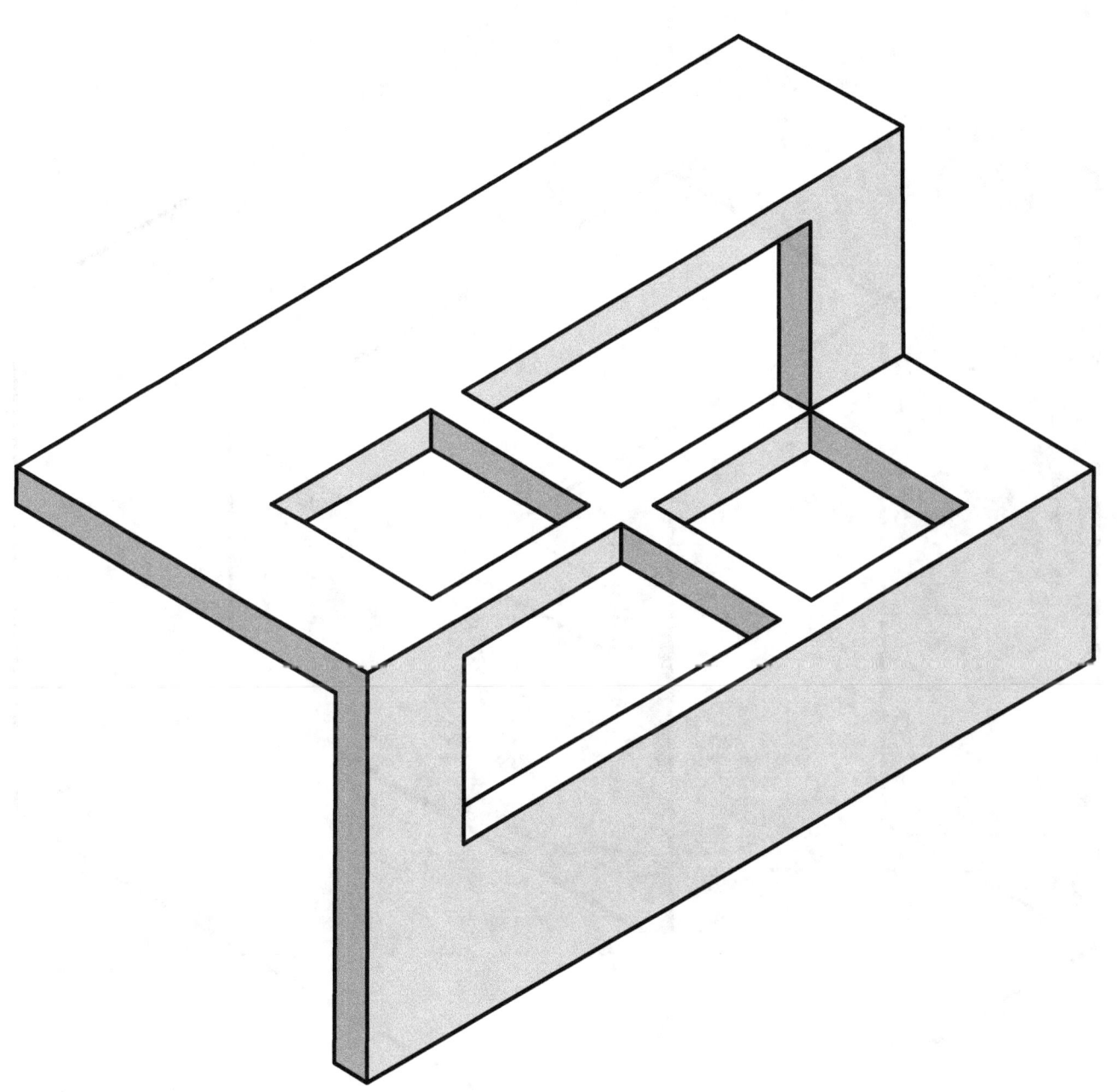

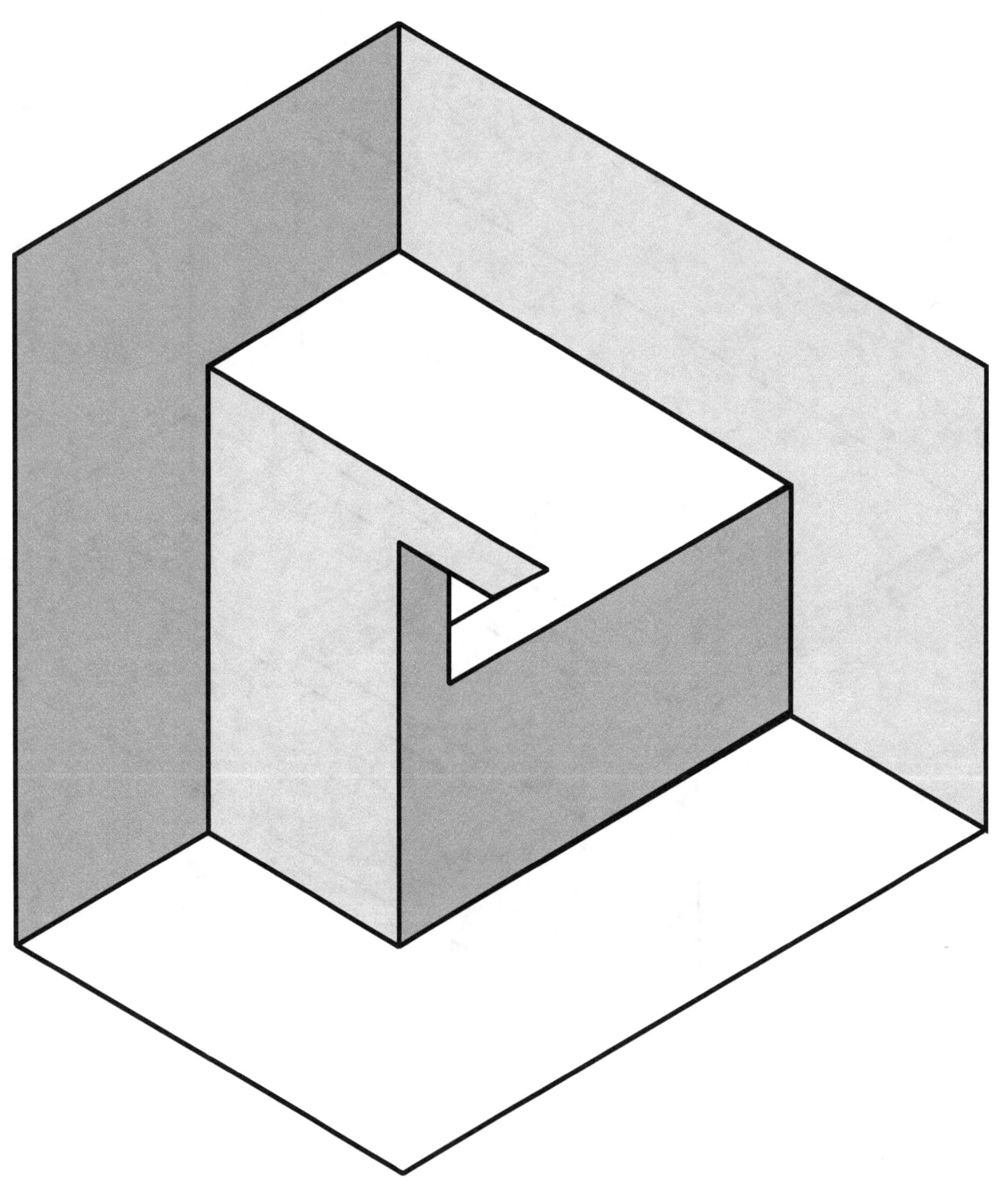

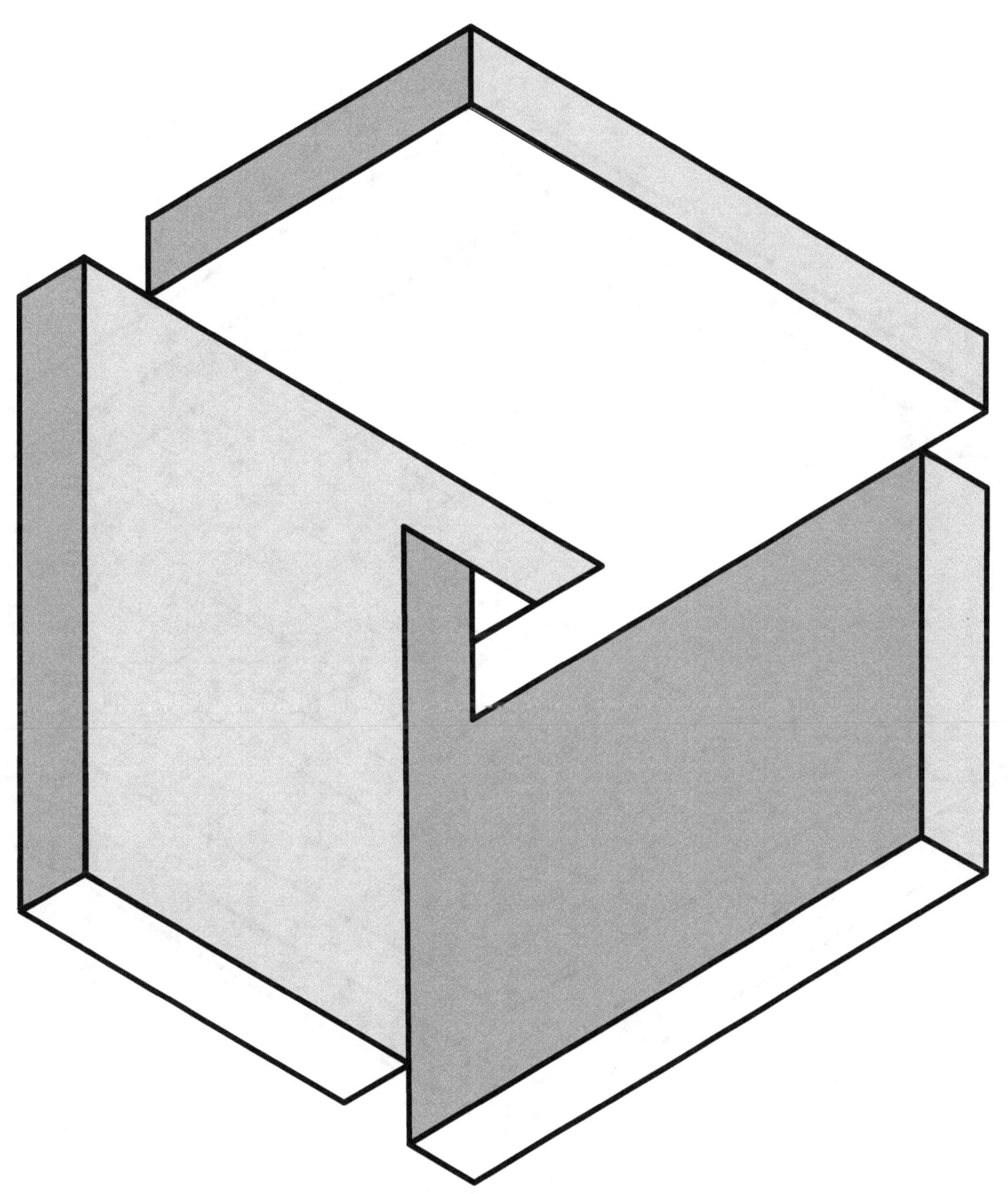

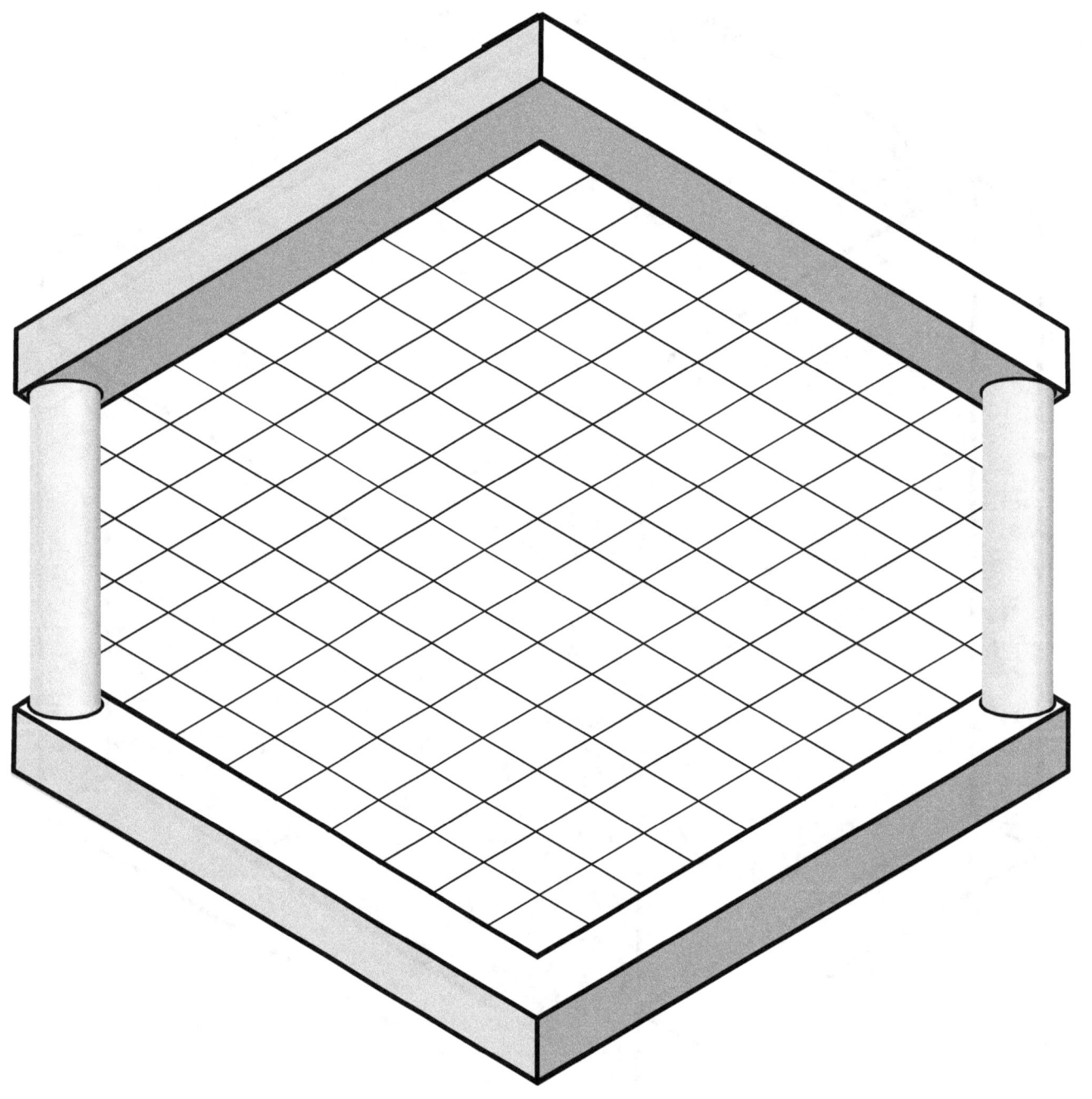

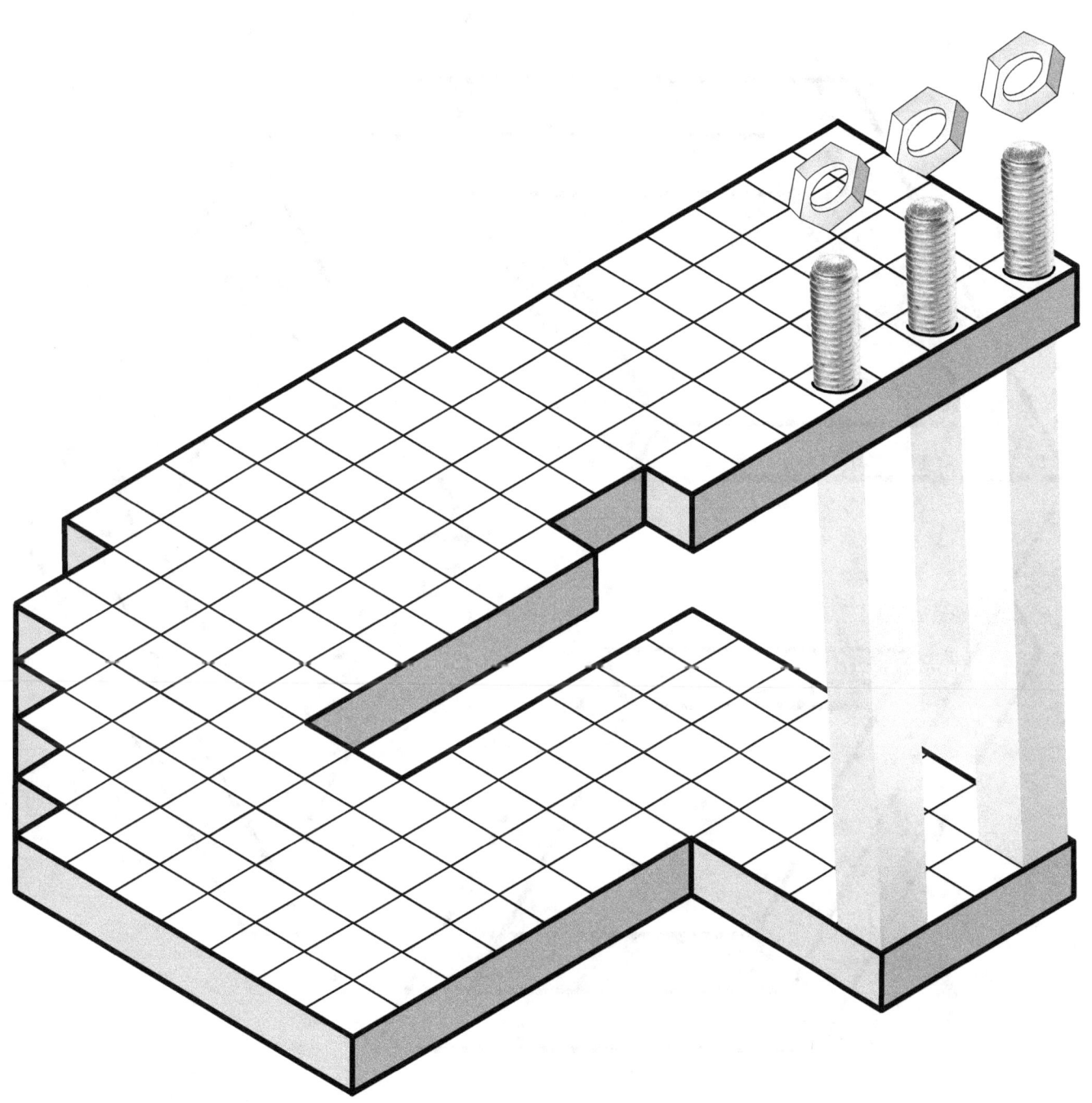

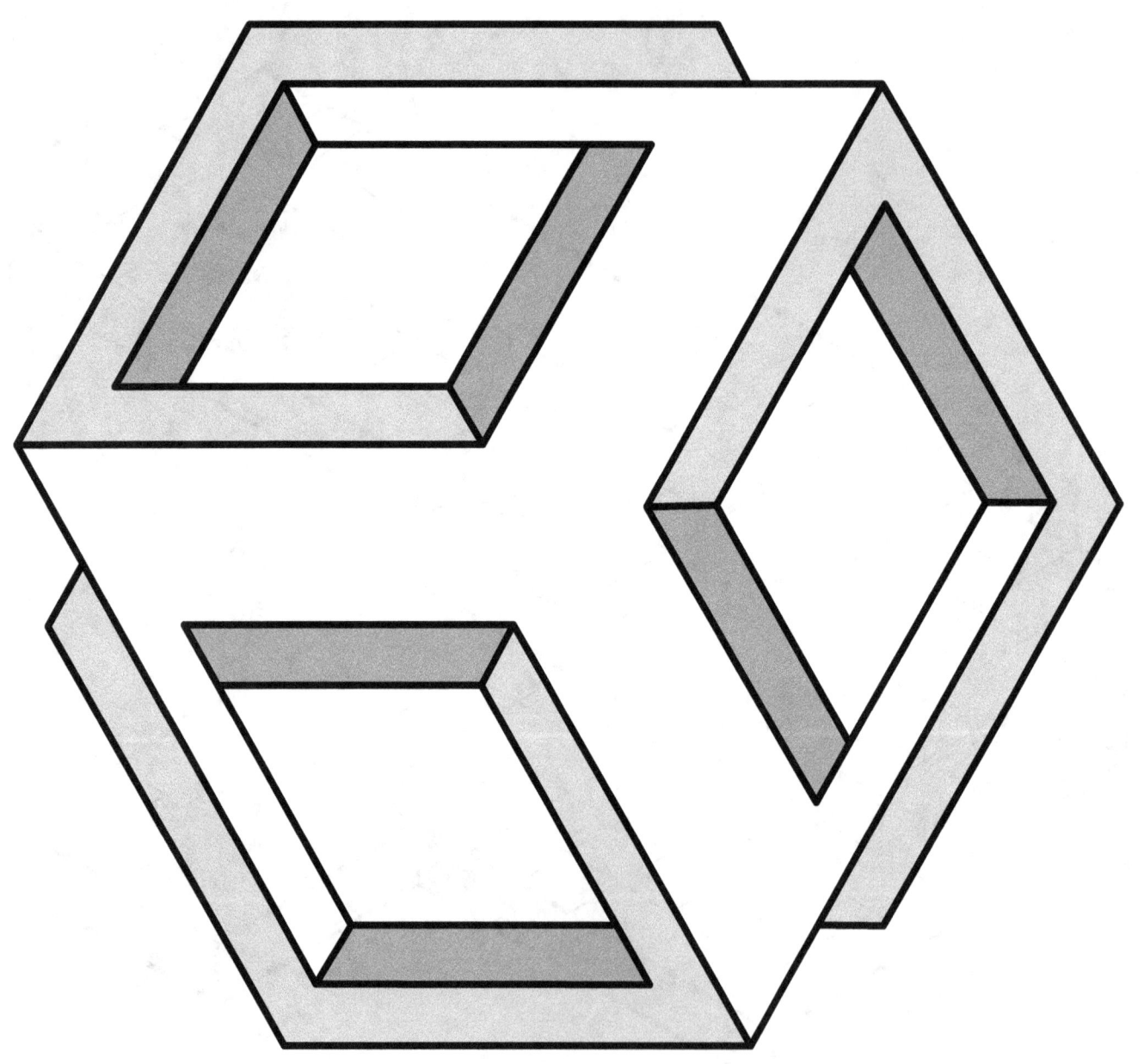

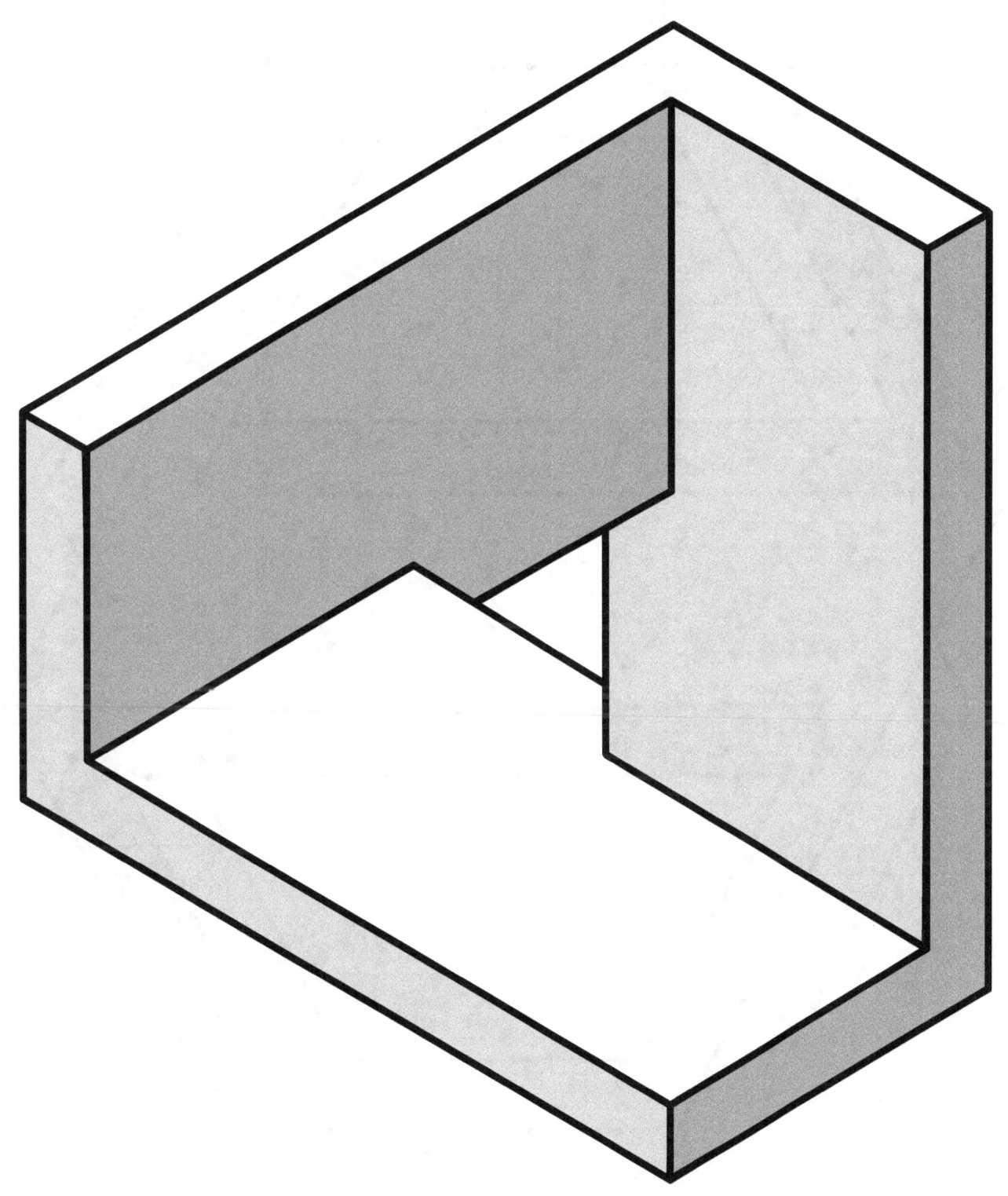

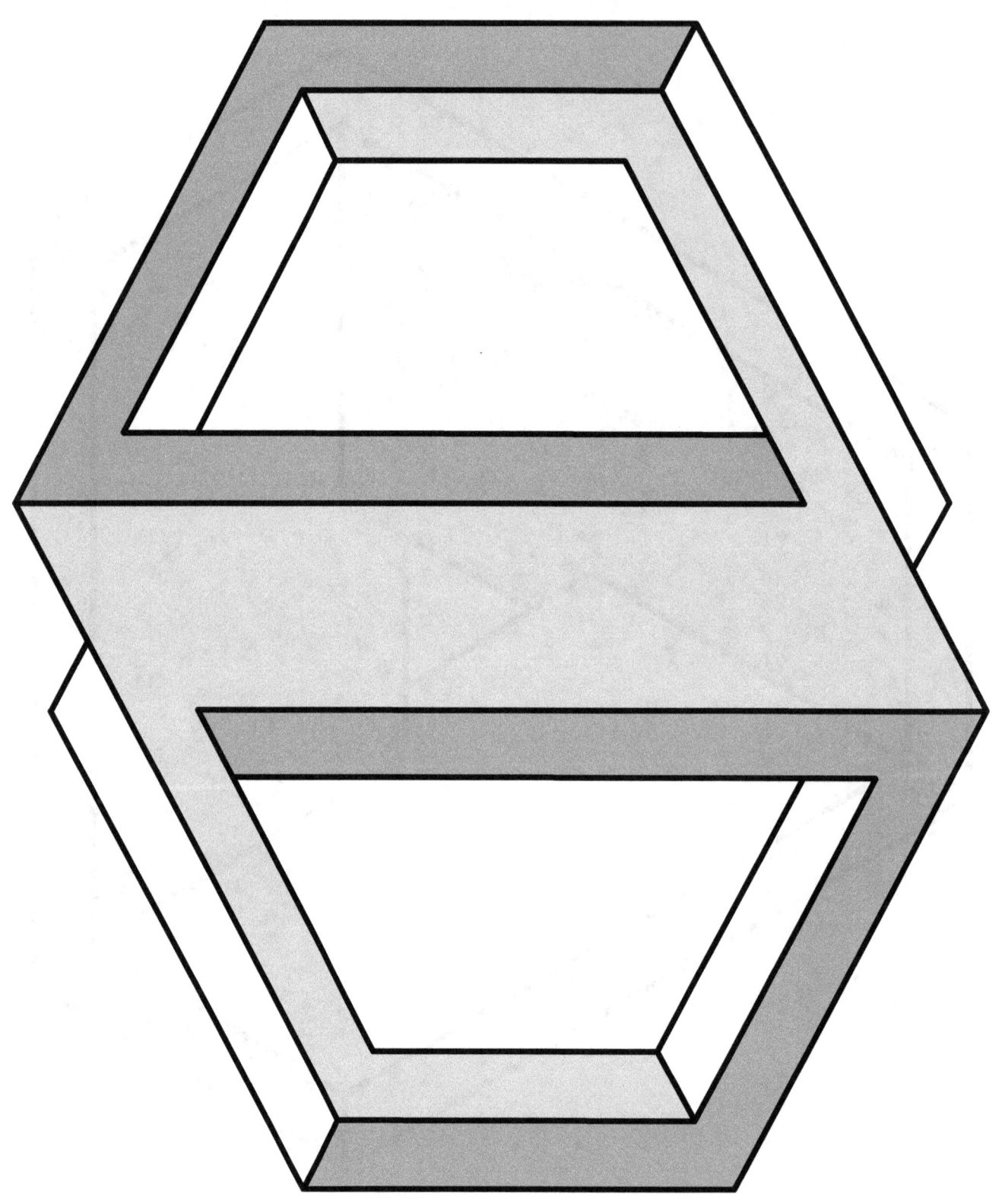

www.ingramcontent.com/pod-product-compliance
Lightning Source LLC
Chambersburg PA
CBHW080915170526
45158CB00008B/2119